Empirical Analysis of Entrepreneurship and Economic Growth

INTERNATIONAL STUDIES IN ENTREPRENEURSHIP

Series Editors:
Zoltan J. Acs
University of Baltimore
Baltimore, Maryland USA

David B. Audretsch
Max-Planck-Institute for Research into Economic Systems
Jena, Germany

Empirical Analysis of Entrepreneurship and Economic Growth

by

André van Stel
Erasmus University Rotterdam, The Netherlands,
Max Planck Institute of Economics, Jena, Germany, and
EIM Business and Policy Research, Zoetermeer, The Netherlands

 Springer

Library of Congress Control Number: 2005933707
ISBN-10: 0-387-27963-6   e-ISBN 0-387-29419-8
ISBN-13: 978-0387-27963-3

Printed on acid-free paper.

Printed in the United States of America.

9 8 7 6 5 4 3 2 1

springeronline.com

TABLE OF CONTENTS

FOREWORD

Employment in OECD countries is under pressure from global competition of low-cost countries in Asia and Eastern Europe. Many policy makers in Western countries believe that 'entrepreneurship' offers a way out and are inclined to promote entrepreneurship policies. However, remarkably little is known about the exact nature of the relationship between entrepreneurship and economic growth, let alone about the influence of policy measures. In part this has to do with the elusive nature of entrepreneurship; people have different ideas about what actually constitutes entrepreneurship. The lack of research is also due to the limited availability of data bases concerning numbers of entrepreneurs, particularly at the country level. As a result, to date almost no scientific evidence on the relationship between entrepreneurship and economic growth is available. This book starts to dig a way out of the darkness by presenting a selection of sophisticated studies, using different concepts of entrepreneurship and using different scientific models. For this purpose the author has collected several unique cross-country and cross-regional data bases on numbers of entrepreneurs. In short, the book is strongly recommended for all those who are interested in empirical evidence on the relation between entrepreneurship and economic growth. The reader will discover that economic reality is more nuanced than the simple intuition that 'more entrepreneurship is good for the economy'.

Roy Thurik
Professor of Economics and Entrepreneurship at Erasmus University Rotterdam, EIM Business and Policy Research in Zoetermeer and the Max Planck Institute of Economics in Jena.

Chapter 1

INTRODUCTION

The importance of entrepreneurship for achieving economic growth in contemporary economies is widely recognized, both by policy makers and economists. It is deeply embedded in the current European policy approach that the creativity and independence of entrepreneurs contribute to higher levels of economic activity. Indeed, according to the European Commission (2003, p. 9), "The challenge for the European Union is to identify the key factors for building a climate in which entrepreneurial initiative and business activities can thrive. Policy measures should seek to boost the Union's levels of entrepreneurship, adopting the most appropriate approach for producing more entrepreneurs and for getting more firms to grow." Audretsch (2003, p. 5) states that "Entrepreneurship has become the engine of economic and social development throughout the world."

The relation between entrepreneurship and economic growth is embedded in several strands of the economic literature. A first strand of literature involves the general understanding of the role of entrepreneurship in the modern economy. Seminal contributions were made by Schumpeter (1934), Knight (1921) and Kirzner (1973). These economists stress different aspects of the role of the entrepreneur. While Schumpeter stresses the innovating aspect, Knight stresses the risk assuming aspect. Kirzner, finally, stresses the role of the entrepreneur in leading markets to equilibrium. Acs (1992) discusses the contribution of small firms in modern economies. He claims that small firms play an important role in the economy as they are agents of change by their entrepreneurial activity, as they are a source of considerable innovative activity, as they stimulate industry evolution and as they create an important share of the newly generated jobs. The role of small firms and entrepreneurship in stimulating economic growth is complex, because various intermediate variables are at play. Examples of such variables are entry and exit of firms (competition), innovation and variety of supply. Economists have started to build theoretical frameworks which try to capture the role of the intermediate variables. An example of such a framework is provided by Thurik et al. (2002).

A second strand of literature involves the mathematical modelling of economic growth. Although entrepreneurship played no role in the neoclassical growth model –which assumes that technological progress is exogenous– it does play a role in some of the more recent endogenous growth models. For instance, Aghion and Howitt (1992) introduce a model where firms invest resources in research to achieve a new product that makes the previous product obsolete. Firms are motivated by the prospect of monopoly rents once the innovation is patented. Economic growth and technological progress at the macro level are then endogenously determined by competition among firms (entrepreneurs) that generate innovations.

A third strand involves the empirical modelling and measurement of the relation between entrepreneurship and economic growth. This book makes a contribution to this third strand of literature. The consequences of entrepreneurship, in terms of economic performance, have generated an extensive empirical literature (Carree and Thurik, 2003). However, this literature has generally been restricted to two units of observation – that of the establishment or firm, and that of the region. Between these two units of observation, studies at the regional level are in the minority. Noticeably absent are studies linking the impact of entrepreneurship on economic performance for the unit of observation of the country (Carree and Thurik, 2003, p. 437).[1] We aim at extending the literature on the impact of entrepreneurship on economic growth at the country and the regional level.

The nature of this book is empirical. In seven out of the eight chapters in this book (apart from this introductory chapter and the concluding chapter), economic models are introduced and confronted with empirical data. Each chapter is separately readable and deals with a different aspect of the link between entrepreneurship and economic growth. The common denominator, however, is that the relationships are investigated at either the country level (Chapters 2, 3, 4, 7 and 8) or the regional level (Chapters 5 and 6). Chapter 9 of this book is devoted to EIM's COMPENDIA data base (COMParative ENtrepreneurship Data for International Analysis), which attempts to harmonize data on business ownership across 23 OECD countries, from 1972 onwards. The construction of harmonized cross-country data bases on numbers of entrepreneurs is important as the limited availability of comparable cross-country data is actually one of the reasons why research at the country level has been lacking in empirical entrepreneurship literature. The COMPENDIA data base is also used for the analysis in Chapter 2.

Besides the focus on countries and regions, this book contributes to the literature in at least four ways. First, while most studies model a linear relationship between entrepreneurship and economic growth, this

---

[1] This is also apparent from the absence of entrepreneurship as an explanatory variable in the empirical growth literature. See Table 1 in Bleaney and Nishiyama (2002).

book introduces the notion of an 'optimal' industry structure, operationalized either in terms of the number of business owners or in terms of the small-firm share in value-of-shipments. The concept of an optimal level implies that the number of entrepreneurs in an economy can either be too low or too high. We provide empirical evidence for the existence of an 'optimal' industry structure. Second, it is investigated whether the impact of entrepreneurship on economic growth varies with the development level of an economy, with the sector of economic activity, and with the quantity and quality of entrepreneurial supply. Empirical evidence is provided showing that the impact is dependent upon all these three aspects. Third, we pay extensive attention to statistical measurement issues concerning entrepreneurship. The relative absence of studies at the national level linking entrepreneurship to economic growth is in part due to severe constraints in measuring entrepreneurship in a cross-national context (Carree and Thurik, 2003). Apart from constructing the COMPENDIA data base (see Chapter 9), massive efforts have been conducted to construct harmonized data bases on business ownership at the country-sector level (used in Chapter 3) and on startup rates at the regional level (used in Chapter 6). We claim that this careful attention to the data greatly improves the reliability of empirical analyses. Fourth and finally, when talking about cross-country data sets on entrepreneurship, the world's biggest research program in this area, the Global Entrepreneurship Monitor (GEM), may not be left unmentioned (see Reynolds et al., 2000, 2002). This book provides one of the first attempts to empirically link entrepreneurial activity to economic growth in the framework of an economic model, making use of the main entrepreneurial activity measure of the GEM data base, the Total Entrepreneurial Activity rate (TEA).

The organization of this introductory chapter is as follows. In Section 1.1 we describe the increased importance of entrepreneurship and small businesses since the last quarter of the previous century. Also the main causes of this development are briefly discussed. In Section 1.2 we provide a theoretical framework explaining how entrepreneurship may lead to economic growth at the country or regional level. The next sections pay attention to the measurement of entrepreneurship and economic performance (Section 1.3) and the various units of analysis (Section 1.4) that are covered in this book.

1.1 The Increased Importance of Entrepreneurship

The role of entrepreneurship in the economy has changed dramatically over the last half century. During the post-World War II era, the importance of entrepreneurship and small businesses seemed to be fading away (Audretsch, 2003). Giant corporations were seen as the most powerful engine of economic and technological progress in the early post-war period. Large firms were thought to have a competitive advantage over small and new ones, due to scale economies in the production of new economic and technological knowledge (Schumpeter, 1950). Indeed, the share of small firms in most Western economies was decreasing constantly during this period. However, from the 1970s onwards things have changed. There is ample evidence that the share of small businesses in manufacturing in Western economies has started to rise (Acs and Audretsch, 1993; Thurik, 1999). Also, Acs et al. (1994) report that a majority of OECD-countries experienced an increase in the self-employment rate during the 1970s and 1980s. Further evidence of a recent increase in self-employment in many OECD countries appears from EIM's data set COMPENDIA. For instance, for the United Kingdom, the number of non-agricultural self-employed (including the incorporated self-employed) as a fraction of total labour force increased from 7.8% in 1972 to 10.5% in 2000, and in the United States this fraction increased from 8.0% to 10.0% in the same period (see Van Stel, 2003).

There are several reasons for the revival of small business and self-employment in Western economies. Notably, in many sectors, new technologies have reduced the necessity of scale economies to arrive at competitive advantages (Meijaard, 2001). Developments like globalization, the ICT-revolution and the increased role of knowledge in the production process have led to increased dynamics and uncertainty in the world economy from the 1970s onwards (Thurik et al., 2002). In turn, these developments have created room for (groups of) small firms to act as agents of change (Audretsch and Thurik, 2000, 2004). The larger role in technological development for small and new firms is referred to by Audretsch and Thurik (2001) as a regime switch from the 'managed' to the 'entrepreneurial' economy. In particular, Audretsch and Thurik argue that the model of the managed economy is the political, social and economic response to an economy dictated by the forces of large-scale production, reflecting the predominance of the production factors of capital and (unskilled) labor as the sources of competitive advantage. By contrast, the model of the entrepreneurial economy is the political, social and economic response to an economy dictated not just by the dominance of the production factor of knowledge – which Romer (1990, 1994) and Lucas (1988) identified as replacing the more traditional factors as the source of competitive advantage – but also by a very different, but complementary, factor they had overlooked: entrepreneurship capital, or the capacity to engage in and generate entrepreneurial activity. See also Audretsch and Thurik (2004). The revival of entrepreneurship is discussed in more detail in Chapters 2 and 4 of this book.

1.2 The Effect of Entrepreneurship on Economic Performance [2]

The big importance of entrepreneurship for economic growth in modern 'entrepreneurial' economies is related to the increased importance of knowledge in the economic process. In the old, 'managed' economies, land, labour and capital were the main factors of production. However, globalization and the telecommunications and computer revolutions have drastically reduced the cost of shifting not just capital but also information out of the high-cost locations of Europe and into lower-cost locations around the world. This means that economic activity in high-cost locations is no longer compatible with routinized tasks. Rather, globalization has shifted the comparative advantage of high-cost locations to knowledge-based activities, and in particular search activities, which cannot be costlessly transferred around the globe. Knowledge as an input into economic activity is inherently different from land, labour and capital. It is characterized by high uncertainty, high asymmetries across people and is costly to transact (Thurik and Wennekers, 2004).[3]

In entrepreneurial economies principal-agent problems in evaluating the expected value of new ideas will emerge more often than in managed economies. It is the uncertainty inherent in new economic knowledge, combined with asymmetries between the agent possessing the new knowledge and the decision making bureaucracy of the incumbent organization with respect to its expected value that potentially leads to a gap between the valuation of that knowledge (Acs and Audretsch, 2003, p. 71). This gap may stimulate the agent possessing the new knowledge to start a new firm, in an attempt to appropriate the new knowledge.[4] However, given the uncertainty of the new knowledge it is not a priori clear whether the economic value of the new knowledge is actually high or low. Only after observing their performance in the industry do the new firms become aware of the actual economic value of their idea (passive learning).

At the aggregate level of industries, countries and regions the many individual attempts of economic agents trying to commercialize their new knowledge compose a mosaic of new experiments. In

---

[2] This section is based on Thurik and Wennekers (2004) and Carree and Thurik (2003).

[3] Knowledge, as opposed to information, is often highly specific in nature and therefore difficult to transmit through formal means of communication. Face-to-face contacts are important for the diffusion of knowledge (Audretsch and Thurik, 1999).

[4] In this way, entrepreneurship serves as a conduit for knowledge spillovers. The knowledge spills over from the source (i.e. the agent holding the knowledge) to a new firm in which it is commercialized (Audretsch and Keilbach, 2004). Chapter 5 of this book focuses on a different aspect of knowledge spillovers: do knowledge spillovers occur predominately between, or rather within industries?

evolutionary terms this can be termed 'variety'. A process of competition between these various new ideas and initiatives takes place continuously leading to the selection of the most viable firms and industries.[5] Variety, competition, selection and also imitation expand and transform the productive potential of a regional or national economy. This occurs by replacement or displacement of obsolete firms, by higher productivity and by expansions of new niches and industries. Furthermore, there are also important feedback mechanisms. Competition and selection amidst variety undoubtedly enable individuals (and firms) to learn from both their own and other's successes and failures. These learning processes enable individuals to increase their skills and adapt their attitudes (active learning). The outcome of these so-called spillovers will be new entrepreneurial actions, creating a recurrent chain of linkages (Carree and Thurik, 2003). The resultant of this chain of dynamic processes is economic growth.

1.3 Measuring Entrepreneurship and Economic Performance

When investigating entrepreneurship, an important question is what we understand by 'entrepreneurship'. There is little consensus about what actually constitutes entrepreneurship (Audretsch, 2003, p. 2). This is related to the fact that it is an ill-defined, at best multi-dimensional concept (Wennekers and Thurik, 1999). It may be argued that it covers at least three dimensions: (dealing with) risk and uncertainty, the perception of profit opportunities, and innovation and change (Hébert and Link, 1989). Also, definitions of entrepreneurship typically vary between the economic and management perspectives (Audretsch, 2003). An interesting combination of these perspectives is reflected by the definition chosen in the *Green Paper Entrepreneurship in Europe* (European Commission, 2003): "Entrepreneurship is the mindset and process to create and develop economic activity by blending risk-taking, creativity and/or innovation with sound management, within a new or an existing organisation". For a discussion on various views on entrepreneurship we refer to Hébert and Link (1989) and Wennekers and Thurik (1999).

Measuring Entrepreneurship

---

[5] Jovanovic (1982) labels this process as noisy selection. The efficient firms grow and survive whereas the inefficient firms decline and fail. This selection process is characterized by high levels of business dynamics (entry and exit of firms) in markets. The effect of these dynamics on industry growth is investigated empirically in Chapter 8 of this book.

Entrepreneurship has to be operationalized for empirical analysis. To this end we use entrepreneurship as a broad concept. We use several measures of entrepreneurship. Each measure represents a different aspect of entrepreneurship. In this book four such aspects are distinguished. First, we can think of entrepreneurship as owning and managing an incumbent business. This aspect of entrepreneurship translates into measures like the number of self-employed or business owners (used in Chapters 2, 3 and 9) and the number of firms (used in Chapter 5). Second, entrepreneurship may refer to the extent in which markets are penetrated by new entrants. This can be measured by the number of new-firm startups (used in Chapters 6 and 8). Third, entrepreneurship may refer to the process of starting a new business, including activities required in the pre-startup phase. This may be called entrepreneurial activity (used in Chapter 7). Finally, one can think of entrepreneurship as the share of small firms in total value-of-shipments of an economy (used in Chapter 4).

Countries or regions may rank very differently on these different aspects of entrepreneurship. This is illustrated by Figure 1.1. In this figure entrepreneurial activity rates and business ownership rates are displayed for the G7-countries. Entrepreneurial activity is highest in the United States, reflecting the dynamic character of the US economy. Relatively many individuals are in the process of starting a *new* business or are the owner/manager of a *young* business (younger than 3.5 years). However, as regards *incumbent* businesses, the United States has an average value, and for instance Italy has a much higher business ownership rate. While there are relatively many new businesses in the United States (high entry rate), there is also a relatively high exit rate, as many of the new firms do not survive. Also, many incumbents are forced out of the market by the new entrants (see also Chapter 8). This makes that the number of business owners remains more or less constant. However, through the high levels of entry and exit, the business population is continuously changing and, arguably, improving. In contrast, while Italy has a high business ownership rate, the low entrepreneurial activity rate indicates that there is not much development in the composition of the business population. These different aspects of entrepreneurship may have different implications for economic performance, as is investigated in several of the chapters in this book.

Figure 1.1. Entrepreneurial activity and business ownership in G7-countries, 2002 [1]

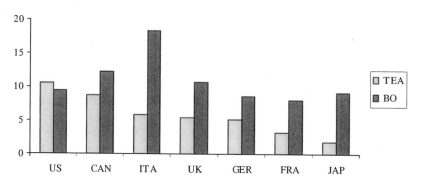

[1] TEA is the Total Entrepreneurial Activity rate (source: GEM) which measures the sum of nascent entrepreneurs and young businesses as a percentage of adult population. BO is the business ownership rate (source: COMPENDIA) which measures the number of non-agricultural business owners (of unincorporated as well as incorporated businesses) as a percentage of total labour force.

Of course, there is always a discrepancy between the theoretical concept of entrepreneurship (whatever concept is chosen) and the empirical operationalisation. For instance, as regards measuring the number of business owners, one has to realise that business ownership (self-employment) and 'Schumpeterian' entrepreneurship are related but not synonymous concepts (Wennekers and Thurik, 1999). Entrepreneurship in a 'Schumpeterian sense' refers to the activity of introducing 'new combinations' of productive means in the market place. Business ownership (self-employment) means owning and managing a business, or otherwise working on one's own account. Thus, on the one hand Schumpeterian entrepreneurs are a small fraction of the business owners, while on the other hand some entrepreneurs (so-called intrapreneurs) do not work on their own account. Also, a disadvantage of using business ownership as a proxy for entrepreneurship is that it treats all businesses as the same, both high-tech and low-tech, and the businesses are not weighted for impact (Audretsch, 2003). Nevertheless, a major advantage of the business ownership measure is that it is measured and can be compared across countries and over time.

Measuring Economic Performance

In studies investigating the relation between entrepreneurship and economic performance, various performance measures have been used, dependent on the unit of analysis. At the *individual* level, individual earnings generated from a self-owned firm has been the most typical performance measure. At the unit of observation of the *enterprise* and *establishment*, the most commonly used performance measures include employment growth, survival, profitability, exports, foreign direct investment, innovation and productivity. At the spatial unit of observation such as the *country* or *region*, which is the unit of observation used in this book, employment growth has been the main performance measure (Audretsch, 2003). While the current book also uses employment growth in two of the chapters (6 and 8), two other performance measures are used as well, these are growth of per capita income (Chapter 2), and growth of (sectoral) GDP (Chapters 3, 4, 5 and 7). Note that in all chapters of this book, economic performance is measured in terms of some measure of *growth*.

1.4 Units of Analysis Used in this Book

The relationship between entrepreneurship and economic performance can be measured for different units of observation, most typically the individual level, the firm level and the spatial level such as country or region. As mentioned, this book uses the spatial level as unit of observation. However, this is only one dimension along which entrepreneurship and economic performance can be measured. In particular, several chapters in this book do not only distinguish between different countries or regions, but also between different sectors and/or different time periods. Sectors are collections of industries, like manufacturing or services. Concerning the time dimension, several of the chapters use data over a long period of time, which enables to investigate the dynamics involved in the relationship. Table 1.1 gives an overview of the exact units of observation used in the several chapters of this book.

Table 1.1. Units of observation covered in this book

Chapter	Spatial unit	Sectoral unit	Time unit
2	23 OECD countries	-	1976-1996
3	21 OECD countries	Two sectors	1970-1998
4	17 European countries	-	1989-1994
5	40 Dutch regions: NUTS 3 level	Five sectors	1987-1995 [1]
6	59 British regions: NUTS 3 level	-	1980-1998 [1]
7	36 GEM parti-cipating countries	-	1994-2003 [1]
8	6 OECD countries	15 industries, ranging from 2-digit level to 4-digit level	1994-2000 [1]
9	23 OECD countries	-	1972-2002

[1] As far as time is concerned, the data samples in these studies are cross-sections instead of panels; the time periods refer to the fact that (lagged) growth is measured over a multi-year period, and/or that separate (cross-sectional) estimations have been performed for different periods.

Chapter 2

ECONOMIC DEVELOPMENT AND BUSINESS OWNERSHIP

2.1 Introduction [6]

Joseph Schumpeter's contribution to our understanding of the mechanisms of technological progress and economic development is widely recognized. In *The Theory of Economic Development* he emphasizes the role of the entrepreneur as prime cause of economic development. He describes how the innovating entrepreneur challenges incumbent firms by introducing new inventions that make current technologies and products obsolete. This process of *creative destruction* is the main characteristic of what has been called the Schumpeter Mark I regime. In *Capitalism, Socialism and Democracy*, Schumpeter focuses on innovative activities by large and established firms. He describes how large firms outperform their smaller counterparts in the innovation and appropriation process through a strong positive feedback loop from innovation to increased R&D activities. This process of *creative accumulation* is the main characteristic of what has been called the Schumpeter Mark II regime.

The extent to which either of the two Schumpeterian technological regimes prevails in a certain period and industry varies. It may depend upon the nature of knowledge required to innovate, the opportunities of appropriability, the degree of scale (dis)economies, the institutional environment, the importance of absorptive capacity, demand variety, etc. Industries in a Schumpeter Mark II regime are likely to develop a more concentrated market structure in contrast to industries in a Schumpeter Mark I regime where small firms will proliferate.

Most of the 20th century can be described as a period of accumulation. From the Second Industrial Revolution till the 1970s the large firm share was on the rise in most industries and the economy as a whole. It was the period of "scale and scope" (Chandler, 1990). It was the

---

[6] This chapter is reprinted from: Carree, M.A., A.J. van Stel, A.R. Thurik and A.R.M. Wennekers (2002), Economic Development and Business Ownership: An Analysis Using Data of 23 OECD Countries in the Period 1976-1996, *Small Business Economics* 19 (3), pp. 271-290, with kind permission of Springer Science and Business Media, Inc. (http://www.springeronline.com).

era of the hierarchical industrial firm growing progressively larger through exploiting economies of scale and scope in areas like production, distribution, marketing and R&D. The conglomerate merger wave of the late 1960s seemed to have set the case. The period has the characteristics of the Schumpeter Mark II regime. However, from the 1970s onwards times have changed. There is ample evidence that the share of small businesses in manufacturing in Western economies has started to rise (Acs and Audretsch, 1993; Thurik, 1999). Large firms have been downsizing and restructuring in order to concentrate on "core business" again. In the meantime the entrepreneur has risen from the dead. High-technology innovative small firms have come at the forefront of technological development in many (new) industries. Piore and Sabel (1984) claim that an "Industrial Divide" has taken place. Jensen (1993, p. 835) considers it the period of the "Third Industrial Revolution". The last quarter of the 20th century may therefore be characterized as a period of creative destruction in the sense of the Schumpeter Mark I regime. Audretsch and Thurik (2001) refer to a change from "a managed to an entrepreneurial economy".

In the present chapter we discuss why this change happened and what its consequences have been for economic progress and the rate of business ownership. We develop a model relating the regime switch to economic development and present empirical evidence. In Section 2.2 we discuss a variety of theoretical considerations on the relation between business ownership rates and economic development. It is followed by Section 2.3 where we present our two-equation model. The first equation explains the change in the business ownership rate while the second equation explains economic growth. The notion of an equilibrium business ownership rate, being a function of the level of economic development, is crucial in the analysis. In Section 2.4 we present the data of 23 OECD countries and in Section 2.5 we present the estimation results. The final section is used for discussion.

2.2 Theory

In this section we will discuss how business ownership rates and economic development are interrelated. We will pay attention to the role that the "Schumpeterian regime switch" has played in this relationship. We discuss the pre-1970s era of declining self-employment rates and the period thereafter in which the rates have risen in most Western economies. Next we discuss how the business ownership rate at the economy-wide level can be used to determine the extent of structural transformation.

The first three quarters of the 20th century can be characterized as a period of declining small firm presence in most industries. In many

Western countries and industries this decline has ended and even reversed. Many old and large firms have been losing ground to their small, new and more entrepreneurial counterparts. It suggests a switch from a (more) Schumpeter Mark II type of regime towards a (more) Schumpeter Mark I type of regime. Audretsch and Thurik (2001) label this as a regime switch from "a managed to an entrepreneurial economy". We note that the regime labels are rough approximations as the industrial landscape shows a far too great variety to claim that in each and every industry one of the Schumpeter regimes is prevailing. A further complication is that business ownership and entrepreneurship are not synonymous for at least two reasons.

First, entrepreneurial energy is not limited to self-employed individuals. Large companies promote "intrapreneurship" within business units to achieve more flexibility and innovativeness (Stopford and Baden-Fuller, 1994). Second, business owners serve many roles and functions. Many researchers distinguish between Schumpeterian (or real) entrepreneurs and managerial business owners (Wennekers and Thurik, 1999). Entrepreneurs are a small fraction of the business owners. They own and direct independent firms that are innovative and "creatively destroy" existing market structures. After realizing their goals Schumpeterian entrepreneurs often develop into managerial business owners, but some may start new ventures. Managerial business owners dominate in the large majority of small firms. They include many franchisees, shopkeepers and people in professional occupations. They belong to what Kirchhoff (1996) calls "the economic core". Occasionally, entrepreneurial ventures grow out of them. In an empirical context it is difficult to discriminate between managerial business owners and entrepreneurs. Profiles of individual business owners would be required. Moreover, the discrimination is a theoretical one since most business owners are neither pure "Schumpeterians" nor pure "shopkeepers" but share the attitudes associated with these extremes in a varying degree (Wennekers and Thurik, 1999).

Despite these conceptual problems we argue that the secular trend of the business ownership rate declining and afterwards starting to rise again presents a fair indication of the general development of the level of entrepreneurship, at least in modern economies. It shows how the (secular) decline of "mom-and-pop" businesses in traditional sectors like retailing and craft has tended to become compensated for by a rise in new ventures in services and high-tech industries in the period from the 1970s onwards.

The Impact of Economic Development on Business Ownership

The proportion of the labor force that is self-employed has decreased in most Western countries until the mid-1970s. Since then the self-employment rate has started to rise again in several of these economies. Blau (1987) observes that the proportions of both male and female self-employed in the nonagricultural U.S. labor force declined during most of this century. He also observes that this decline bottomed out in the early 1970s and started to rise until at least 1982. The data used in this chapter show that the business ownership rate in the U.S. has continued to rise in the 1980s while stabilizing in the 1990s.[7] More recently business ownership increased in several other countries as well. We will first discuss the period of decline of business ownership (Mark II regime) followed by a discussion of the period of reversal of this trend (Mark I regime).

Decline of Business Ownership

Several authors (Kuznets, 1971; Schultz, 1990; Yamada, 1996) have reported a negative relationship between economic development and the business ownership (self-employment) rate. Their studies use a large cross-section of countries with a wide variety in the stage of economic development.

There are a series of reasons for the decline of self-employment, and of small business presence in general. Lucas (1978) shows how rising real wages may raise the opportunity cost of self-employment relative to the return. Given an underlying "managerial" talent distribution this induces marginal entrepreneurs (in this context Lucas refers to managers) to become employees. This pushes up the average size of firms. Schaffner (1993) takes a different approach. She points out that "over the course of economic development the advantages firm owners derive from being less risk averse (better diversified) than self-employed producers are likely to rise relative to the disadvantages caused by the costliness of circumventing asymmetric information problems" (p. 435). Iyigun and Owen (1998) develop a model implying that economic development is associated with a decline in the number of entrepreneurs relative to the total number of employees. They argue that fewer individuals are willing to run the risk associated with becoming an entrepreneur as the "safe" professional earnings rise with economic development.

Chandler (1990) stresses the importance of investment in production, distribution, and management needed to exploit economies of scale and scope during the period after the second industrial revolution of the second half of the 19th century. It was a period of relatively well-

---

[7] There is considerable controversy about the number of U.S. self-employed. Publications which deal with various issues on estimating the actual number of business owners in the U.S. include Fain (1980), Bregger (1996), Dennis (1997) and SBA (1997), Chapter 3. Most controversy is about measuring the number of incorporated self-employed. In the present chapter we basically follow the approach taken by SBA (2000), p. 5, in which the number of incorporated self-employed is estimated by the number of *employer firms*.

defined technological trajectories, of stable demand and of seemingly clear advantages of diversification.[8]

Reversal of the Trend

Several authors have provided evidence of a reversal of the trend towards less self-employment. Acs et al. (1994) report that of 23 OECD-countries, 15 experienced an increase in the self-employment rate during the 1970s and 1980s. They show that the weighted average of the self-employment rate in OECD-countries rose slightly from 8.4% in 1978 to 8.9% in 1987. Closely related to the development of the self-employment rate is the development of small business presence in general. Some of the other sources showing that the growing importance of large business has come to a halt in Western countries include Carlsson (1989), Loveman and Sengenberger (1991), Acs and Audretsch (1993), Acs (1996) and Thurik (1999).[9]

There are several reasons for the revival of small business and self-employment in Western economies.[10] First, the last 25 years of the 20th century may be seen as a period of creative destruction. Piore and Sabel (1984) use the term "Industrial Divide", Jensen (1993) prefers the term "Third Industrial Revolution", while Freeman and Perez (1988) talk about the transition from the fourth to the fifth Kondratiev wave. Audretsch and Thurik (2000) stress the effects of globalization and the information revolution leading to the demise of the comparative advantage of Europe in many of the traditional industries, such as machine tools, metalworking, textiles and automobile production. The most obvious evidence is the emergence of new industries like the software and biotechnology industries. Small firms play an important role in these new industries. Acs and Audretsch (1987) provide empirical evidence that small firms have a relative innovative advantage over their larger counterparts in such highly innovative industries. Evidence for the comparative advantage of small firms in inventing radically new products is also given in Prusa and Schmitz (1991) and Rothwell (1983, 1984).

Second, new technologies have reduced the importance of scale economies in many sectors. Small technology-based firms started to challenge large companies that still had every confidence in mass production techniques (Carlsson, 1989). Meredith (1987) argues that small firms are just as well, or better, equipped to implement technological advances and predicts the factory of the future to be a small factory.

---

[8] Audretsch and Thurik (2001) characterize this period as one where stability, continuity and homogeneity were the cornerstones and label it the managed economy.

[9] See also the various editions of *The European Observatory for SMEs* that provide an account of the state of small business in Europe, for instance EIM/ENSR (1997).

[10] Brock and Evans (1986) were the first to provide an elaborate overview.

Jensen (1993) argues that "It is far less valuable for people to be in the same geographical location to work together effectively, and this is encouraging smaller, more efficient, entrepreneurial organizing units that cooperate through technology" (p. 842). This is supported by Jovanovic (1993) claiming that: "recent advances in information technology have made market-based coordination cheaper relative to internal coordination and have partially caused the recent decline in firm size and diversification" (p. 221). Others, like Rothwell (1983, 1984), stress that large and small firms complement and succeed each other in the innovation and diffusion process. See also Nooteboom (1994) for an account of this concept of "dynamic complementarity".

Third, deregulation and privatization movements have swept the world. In countries like Australia, Finland, Italy and Sweden there have been strong tendencies to deregulate and privatise (OECD, 1995, pp. 39-49). Phillips (1985) reports that small firms have dominated in both the creation of new businesses and new jobs in deregulated industry sectors in the U.S. in the early 1980s. This confirms some preliminary empirical evidence as provided by Shepherd (1982). Governments have also begun to acknowledge and promote the vital role of small (start-up) firms in achieving economic growth and development. See Storey and Tether (1998), OECD (1998) and EIM/ENSR (1994, 1996).

Fourth, there has been a tendency of large firms to concentrate on "core competences" (Carlsson, 1989). Jovanovic (1993) reports that the 1980s were characterized by corporate spin-offs and divestment. Aiginger and Tichy (1991) blame much of the "back-to-basics" and downsizing (or rightsizing) tendencies on the opportunistic conglomerate merger wave of the late 1960s.

Fifth, the increasing incomes and wealth have enabled individuals to strive for "higher" needs. As a result the demand for variety increases (Jackson, 1984). Cross-cultural influences have also enlarged the demand for variety. Small firms are often the most obvious suppliers of new and specialized products. The decrease in diversification as reported by Jovanovic (1993) suggests that large firms have not been capable of entering into such market niches.

Sixth, self-employment is more highly valued as an occupational choice than before. Roughly one out of four young U.S. workers pursue self-employment according to Schiller and Crewson (1997). Kirchhoff (1996) argues that self-employment is not characterized anymore as under-employment or as mom-and-pop establishments, but as a way to achieve a variety of personal goals. Also, as hypothesized in the social psychology there is a Maslowian hierarchy of human motivations, with physical needs at the bottom and self-realization at the top (Maslow,

1970). A higher level of prosperity will induce a higher need for self-realization and may stimulate entrepreneurship.[11]

Finally, the employment share of the services sector has been well documented to increase with per capita income (Inman, 1985). Given the relatively small average firm size of most services (barring airlines, shipping and some business and financial services) this creates more opportunities for business ownership.

Obviously, some of these factors may have a temporary effect only. For example, it is not unlikely for the outsourcing and deregulation waves to dry up. On the other hand, there are more permanent effects like the impact of new technologies. We refer again to Freeman and Perez (1988). They claim that in the new techno-economic paradigm (fifth Kondratiev wave) the organization of firms will be "networks" of large and small firms. See also Oughton and Whittam (1997) who emphasize the role of external economies of scale when explaining the viability of small firms. Moreover, the introduction of these new technologies is also positively related to the stage of economic development because they cannot be made effective without the necessary skills and other investments. This structural influence of economic development is reinforced by the increasing variety of demand for specialized goods and services and the enhanced valuation of self-realization which are also dependent on the level of prosperity.

An Equilibrium Rate of Business Ownership

In this chapter we investigate whether countries that deviate from the "equilibrium" business ownership rate for comparable levels of economic development suffer in terms of economic growth. For this we develop an error-correction model to determine the "equilibrium" rate of business ownership as a function of GDP per capita. The notion of "equilibrium" appears more akin to neo-classical economic theory than to a Schumpeterian framework. However, in our empirical application the "equilibrium" concerns the labor market and not the product market.

Equilibrium rates of self-employment in the neo-classical framework can be derived by making assumptions about (1) the aggregate production function combining the efforts of business owners and wage-employed individuals and (2) their rational occupational choice between self- and wage-employment. Differences in the assumptions about which factors influence the choice for self-employment lead to different equilibrium models. Two early contributions are Lucas (1978) and Kihlstrom and Laffont (1979). Lucas assumes individuals to have different managerial abilities while Kihlstrom and Laffont assume

---

[11] Entrepreneurial energy as such may not suffice for economic progress. Baumol (1990) stressed the importance of entrepreneurship being led into productive channels.

individuals to differ with respect to their risk attitudes. Calvo and Wellisz (1980) extend the Lucas model by introducing a learning process through which managers acquire the necessary knowledge. Peretto (1999) presents a model in which "development and growth are subsequent stages of the process of structural transformation that economies undergo as they advance from poverty to affluence" (p. 390). This model as well as related models (see for example Lloyd-Ellis and Bernhardt, 2000) suggest that the stage of economic development is the driving force of "equilibrium". For an extensive overview of this type of models, see De Wit (1993).

We hypothesize an "equilibrium" relationship between the rate of business ownership and per capita income that is U-shaped.[12] The U-shaped pattern has the property that there is a level of economic development with a "minimum" business ownership rate.[13] Many forces may cause the actual number of business owners to deviate from the long-term equilibrium rate. Such a "disequilibium" may result from cultural forces, institutional settings (regulation of entry, incentive structures, functioning of the capital market) and economic forces (unemployment, profitability of private enterprise). See Kirzner (1997), Davis and Henrekson (1999) and Henrekson and Johansson (1999).

There are several forces in market economies that contribute to a process of adapting towards the equilibrium. An example may illustrate this. A high labor income share and a structurally low number of enterprises have contributed to structural unemployment in the late 1970s and 1980s in many Western economies. Such high levels of unemployment may have various consequences. First, unemployment may have a direct effect on self-employment, as unemployed are claimed to be more likely to become self-employed than employees. See for instance Storey (1991) and Evans and Leighton (1989). Second, structural unemployment gradually results in wage moderation helping to restore profitability of private enterprise (lower labor income share). In addition, a perceived shortage of business ownership will induce policies fostering entrepreneurship, ranging from better access to financing to competition policies. See OECD (1998). The overall impact of these equilibrating processes are hard to observe directly and may therefore be modelled best using an error correction mechanism.

The Effect of Business Ownership on Economic Growth

There is some evidence on the relation between size class distributions and economic performance. For instance, see Nickell (1996),

---

[12] Schultz (1990) reports having found statistical evidence for a quadratic relationship between the share of wage earners and the stage of economic development.

[13] In case the "minimum" is reached at a level of per capita income exceeding those attained in the data set, the relation can be better described as L-shaped.

Nickell et al. (1997) and Lever and Nieuwenhuijsen (1999) who present evidence that competition, as measured by increased number of competitors, has a positive effect on the rate of total factor productivity growth. Carree and Thurik (1998, 1999a) show that the share of small firms in manufacturing industries in European countries has a positive effect on the industry output growth. Thurik (1996) reports that the excess growth of small firms[14] has had a positive influence on percentage change in gross national product for a sample of 16 European countries in the period 1988 through 1993.[15]

A theoretical endogenous growth model was developed by Schmitz (1989). His model predicts that an increase of the proportion of entrepreneurs in the working force leads to an increase in long-run economic growth. See also Holmes and Schmitz (1990) who develop a model of entrepreneurship in the spirit of T.W. Schultz. They show how specialization in managerial tasks and entrepreneurship – responding to opportunities for creating new products and production processes – may affect economic development. Finally, some evidence of a well-established historical (long-term) relationship between fluctuations in entrepreneurship and the rise and fall of nations has been assembled by Wennekers and Thurik (1999). Also the work of Eliasson (1995) on economic growth through competitive selection is of relevance. He shows (for the Swedish economy) how a lack of industry dynamics affects economic progress not so much on the short term but very strongly so on the long term (from about two decades on).

Another source of evidence on the relation between self-employment and progress is the economic history of the formerly centralized planned economies. A characteristic of these economies was the almost complete absence of small firms (and private ownership of the means of production), and this extreme monopolization constituted one of the major factors leading to the collapse of state socialism (Acs, 1996).

---

[14] The excess growth of small firms in that study is defined as the percentage change in the value-of-shipments accounted for by small firms minus that accounted for by large firms. See also Chapter 4 of this book.

[15] A subset of small firms which are assumed to improve economic performance are the so-called New Technology-Based Firms (NTBFs). Many of the businesses can be found on Science Parks of which the number in many countries has increased strongly during the 1980s and 1990s. Storey and Tether (1998) show that most of the NTBFs are, in fact, small firms. They report the average number of employees to be around 20 both in France and the U.K. The two countries were the first in Europe (in 1969) to establish science parks (Cambridge Science Park in the U.K. and Sophia Antipolis in France). They claim that Italy serves as an example of lagging behind in the establishment of "advanced" science parks and relate this to the relatively low proportion of university research that is financed by the Italian private sector.

The development of small enterprises is considered a vital part of the current transition process in Eastern Europe.[16]

In this chapter we investigate whether deviations between the actual and the equilibrium rate of business ownership will diminish the growth potential of an economy in the medium term. A shortage of business owners is likely to diminish competition with detrimental effects for static efficiency and competitiveness of the national economy. It will also diminish variety, learning and selection and thereby harm dynamic efficiency (innovation). On the other hand, a glut of self-employment will cause the average scale of operations to remain below optimum. It will result in large numbers of marginal entrepreneurs, absorbing capital and human energy that could have been allocated more productively elsewhere.

Iyigun and Owen (1998) show in a dynamic model with two types of human capital (professional and entrepreneurial) that a misallocation of the existing human capital stock between professional and entrepreneurial activities may occur. The nature of the inefficiency, however, is not clear-cut. There may be too much entrepreneurship or too little, depending on how entrepreneurial and professional skills contribute to the level of technology. They find that "a more efficient ratio of professional and entrepreneurial skills will raise the steady state of technology, the wages paid to human capital providers, and therefore, the economy's human capital stock" (p. 457). Their model supports our notion that deviations from the level of "equilibrium" entrepreneurial activity come at a cost of lower economic performance. See also Peretto (1999) who derives a hump-shaped relation between the number of firms and returns to investment and R&D.

2.3 Model

The object of this section is to develop a model of the interrelationship between business ownership and economic development at the macro level. The model consists of two main equations. The first equation deals with the causes of changes in the rate of business ownership whereas the second deals with its consequences. From the first equation we derive the equilibrium rate of business ownership as a function of the stage of economic development. In the second equation we

---

[16] See for example Russia's Shatalin Plan, which "is built on the assumption that society needs small enterprises to orient production to the needs of every person, to fight the dictatorship of monopolies in consumer and production markets, and to create a favourable environment for quick introduction of new scientific and technological ideas" (Nolan, 1995, p. 82).

estimate the effect on economic growth of deviating from this equilibrium rate.

The first equation of the model relates the change in the rate of business ownership E_{it} in country i in year t to the extent to which this rate deviated from the equilibrium rate E_{it}^*, to the unemployment rate U_{it} and to the labor income share LIQ_{it}. The second equation of the model relates the extent of economic growth to the (absolute) deviation of the actual business ownership rate from the equilibrium rate. Economic growth is measured as the relative change in the variable $YCAP_{it}$, the per capita gross domestic product in purchasing power parities per U.S. dollar in 1990 prices in country i and period t. We correct for catching-up effects by including the level of economic development. The equations use the notation $\Delta_4 X_t = X_t - X_{t-4}$. The third equation presents the equation relating the equilibrium business ownership rate to the level of economic development. It is assumed to be a quadratic function of $\ln(YCAP_{it} + 1)$.[17] The model reads as follows:

$$(2.1) \quad \Delta_4 E_{it} = b_1 \left(E_{i,t-4}^* - E_{i,t-4} \right) + b_2 \left(U_{i,t-6} - \overline{U} \right) + b_3 \left(LIQ_{i,t-6} - \overline{LIQ} \right) + \varepsilon_{1it}$$

$$(2.2) \quad \frac{\Delta_4 YCAP_{it}}{YCAP_{i,t-4}} = c_0 + c_1 \left| E_{i,t-4}^* - E_{i,t-4} \right| + c_2 \, YCAP_{i,t-4} + \varepsilon_{2it}$$

$$(2.3) \quad E_{it}^* = \alpha + \beta \ln(YCAP_{it} + 1) + \gamma \ln^2(YCAP_{it} + 1),$$

The symbols stand for the following variables:

E: number of business owners per labor force,
E*:   equilibrium number of business owners per labor force,
YCAP: per capita GDP in purchasing power parities per U.S. $ in 1990 prices,
U: unemployment rate,
$\overline{U}$:   sample average of unemployment rate,
LIQ: labor income share,

---

[17] In Carree et al. (2000) we compare four different specifications of the relationship between the equilibrium business ownership rate and GDP per capita, based upon an earlier version of our business ownership dataset (COMPENDIA 1999; in the present chapter we use COMPENDIA 2000.1, see Section 2.4). The log-quadratic specification adopted in this chapter was found to outperform the other specifications in terms of goodness of fit, although not by much. The estimates of the error-correction parameter b_1 and the growth penalty parameter c_1 did not differ much between the four specifications.

$\overline{LIQ}$:   sample average of labor income share,

$\varepsilon_1, \varepsilon_2$:   disturbance terms in Equations (2.1) and (2.2),

respectively,

Business Ownership Equation

In Equation (2.1), the variable to be explained is the growth in the number of business owners per labor force in a period of four years. The first explanatory variable in the equation, which has the parameter b_1 assigned to it, is an error correction variable describing the difference between the equilibrium and the actual rate of business ownership at the start of the period. The parameter b_1 is expected to have a positive sign. In this version of our model the equilibrium function is U-shaped with respect to per capita income (Equation (2.3) has a quadratic form). Because the parabola should first drop and then rise, we expect the parameter γ to be positive and the parameter β to be negative. In case of absence of economic development ($YCAP_{it}$ =0) the equilibrium function equals α. Since the relative number of business owners cannot be negative or in excess of one, the parameter α should lie between zero and one.

As a second explanatory variable we use lagged unemployment acting as a push factor for business ownership.[18] The expected sign of the parameter b_2 is positive. We choose a lag of six years instead of four for this variable because mental preparation, practical procedures and legal requirements are involved in starting a new enterprise.

As a third explanatory variable we use labor income share. This variable is a pragmatic proxy for the earning differentials between expected profits of business owners and wage earnings. We assume that a relatively high business profitability (as compared to wage earnings) acts as a pull factor for business ownership. The labor income share is defined as the share of labor income (including the "calculated" compensation of the self-employed for their labor contribution) in the net national income. The expected sign of the parameter b_3 is negative. As with the unemployment variable, a time lag has been included.

Economic Growth Equation

In Equation (2.2), the variable to be explained is economic growth in a four-year period, measured as the relative change in gross domestic product per capita. The first determinant of growth is the (absolute) deviation of the actual number of self-employed (business owners) from

---

[18] Audretsch et al. (2005), in an empirical investigation for 23 OECD countries find a positive effect of the (lagged) change of unemployment on the change of the self-employment rate.

the equilibrium rate of business ownership at the start of the period. As explained in a previous section, the deviation variable is expected to have a negative impact on growth.[19]

Next to this deviation variable, we use the level of per capita income at the start of the period as a control variable. It allows to correct for the convergence hypothesis of countries: countries which are lagging behind in economic development grow more easily than other countries because they can profit from modern technologies developed in other countries. The expected sign of the parameter c_2 is negative.

2.4 Data and Estimation Technique

We use data of 23 OECD countries including the fifteen countries of the EU-15, Australia, Canada, Iceland, Japan, New Zealand, Norway, Switzerland and the U.S. and for the period 1976 through 1996.[20] Data are made available for the even years only. The main data sources are the *OECD Labour Force Statistics* and the *OECD National Accounts*. In Table 2.1 some summary statistics values are given for the first and last year of the sample and the mid year 1988 (due to lags only the period 1980-1996 will be used in the estimation procedure).

---

[19] In Carree et al. (2000) we consider an alternative penalty function based on the squared instead of the absolute deviation. For each of the shapes of the equilibrium function the absolute deviation penalty structure outperformed the squared deviation case.

[20] For the unemployment rate and the labor income share we also use data of 1974.

Table 2.1. Summary statistics for the 23 OECD countries

Country	E_{1976}	E_{1988}	E_{1996}	$YCAP_{1988}$	E^*_{1988}
Austria	0.077	0.069	0.074	15,651	0.112
Belgium	0.098	0.109	0.119	15,326	0.113
Denmark	0.081	0.056	0.064	16,263	0.110
Finland	0.059	0.076	0.080	15,456	0.112
France	0.105	0.099	0.088	16,421	0.110
Germany (West)	0.070	0.070	0.082	17,245	0.109
Greece	0.179	0.186	0.196	7,274	0.180
Ireland	0.074	0.091	0.100	9,735	0.145
Italy	0.142	0.169	0.183	15,289	0.113
Luxembourg	0.093	0.075	0.062	21,103	0.107
Netherlands	0.092	0.082	0.102	14,867	0.114
Portugal	0.110	0.116	0.160	8,424	0.161
Spain	0.109	0.122	0.130	10,886	0.135
Sweden	0.068	0.064	0.081	16,632	0.110
United Kingdom	0.074	0.101	0.109	15,590	0.112
Iceland	0.099	0.101	0.130	17,368	0.109
Norway	0.089	0.084	0.071	17,301	0.109
Switzerland	0.069	0.071	0.085	20,133	0.107
United States	0.081	0.107	0.104	21,543	0.107
Japan	0.126	0.123	0.101	16,328	0.110
Canada	0.078	0.106	0.128	18,573	0.107
Australia	0.147	0.164	0.154	16,154	0.111
New Zealand	0.098	0.116	0.133	13,532	0.119
Average	0.096	0.102	0.110	15,526	0.118

Note: The business ownership rates E are per labor force. The business ownership figures are exclusive of the business owners in the agricultural sector. The unit of GDP per capita (YCAP) is purchasing power parities per U.S. $ at 1990 prices. In the last column the estimated equilibrium business ownership rates for 1988 are given, using the estimates of α, β and γ from the "Two yearly" case from Table 2.3. Germany refers to West-Germany for 1976 and 1988. This business ownership data set is referred to as COMPENDIA 2000.1.

From Table 2.1 we see that Australia, Greece and Italy have the highest levels of self-employment (business ownership) in 1988: more than 15% of the labor force. The unweighted sample average level of self-employment in that year is 10%. The countries with the lowest levels of self-employment in 1988 are Denmark and Sweden: six percent of the labor force. Looking at the GDP per capita in 1988, we see that the United States, Switzerland and Luxembourg are the most affluent countries while Greece, Ireland, Portugal and Spain are the least affluent countries in the sample. The unemployment rates are not given in the table but they were highest in the 1980s in Ireland and Spain. Low unemployment rates were found in Japan, Norway, Sweden, Switzerland, Iceland and Luxembourg in that period.

Variables and Sources

The variable definitions and their main sources are given below.

E: self-employment or business ownership. This variable is defined as the number of business owners (in all sectors excluding the agricultural sector), expressed as a fraction of the labor force. Data sources include the OECD Labour Force Statistics 1976-1996 and 1978-1998. EIM completed the missing data by using ratios derived from various other sources. Furthermore, EIM made a unified data set of business owners as the definitions of business owners or self-employed (we use these terms interchangeably) in the OECD statistics are not fully compatible between countries. In some countries business owners are defined as individuals owning a business that is not legally incorporated. In other countries, owner/managers of an incorporated business (OMIBs) who enjoy profits as well as a salary are considered owners too. There are also countries who classify a part of the OMIBs as self-employed and another part as employee. This results from a different set-up of labor force surveys in different countries.[21] By and large, Australia, Japan, Norway and U.S. use a narrow business ownership definition (excluding OMIBs or excluding most OMIBs), while the other countries apply a broader characterization (including OMIBs or including most OMIBs). Business owners in the present report are defined to include OMIBs. For the countries not following this definition, EIM made an estimation of the number of OMIBs using information derived from The European Observatory for SMEs (KPMG/ENSR, 2000), or using information from domestic sources for the non-European countries. Another difference in definition is that for some countries unpaid family workers are included in the self-employment data as well, mostly for early years. For these years,

---

[21] This topic is dealt with in Chapter 5 of *OECD Employment Outlook June 2000.*

the unpaid family workers were removed from the data by using ratios from more recent years for which separate data on unpaid family workers *are* available. Finally, for countries where important unclarified trend breaks occur, these trend breaks were corrected for. Data on the labor force are also from the OECD Labour Force Statistics. Again, some missing data have been filled up from various other sources.[22]

YCAP: gross domestic product per capita. The underlying variables gross domestic product and total population are from OECD National Accounts 1960-1996, Detailed Tables, and from the OECD Labour Force Statistics 1976-1996 and 1978-1998, respectively. GDP is measured in constant prices. Furthermore, purchasing power parities of 1990 are used to make the monetary units comparable between countries.

U: (standardized) unemployment rate. This variable measures the number of unemployed as a fraction of the total labor force. The labor force consists of employees, self-employed persons, unpaid family workers, people employed by the Army and unemployed persons. The main source for this variable is *OECD Main Economic Indicators*. Some missing data on the number of unemployed have been filled up with help of data from the OECD Labour Force Statistics and the *Yearbook of Labour Statistics* from the International Labour Office.

LIQ: labor income share. Total compensation of employees is multiplied by (total employment/number of employees) to correct for the imputed wage income for the self-employed persons. Next, the number obtained is divided by total income (compensation of employees plus other income). The data on the separate variables are from the OECD National Accounts 1960-1996, Detailed Tables. Some missing data have been filled up with help of data from the OECD Labour Force Statistics.

When estimating the model, we weight the observations with population. We consider larger countries such as the U.S. and Japan to be more important in establishing the relationship between business ownership and economic growth than small countries. When the data of, for example, Luxembourg or Iceland would call for a different relation, we would not want this to have a big impact on the estimation results.

---

[22] See also Chapter 9 of this book for more information about these business ownership data.

2.5 Estimation Results

To estimate the Model (2.1)-(2.3) we substitute Equation (2.3) into Equation (2.1):

(2.4)
$$\Delta_4 E_{it} = a_0 - b_1 E_{i,t-4} + b_2 U_{i,t-6} + b_3 LIQ_{i,t-6} + a_4 \ln(YCAP_{i,t-4}+1) + a_5 \ln^2(YCAP_{i,t-4}+1) + \varepsilon_{1it}$$

We apply (weighted) least squares to this equation and then find estimates for the equilibrium relation parameters through:

(2.5) $\qquad \hat{\alpha} = (a_0 + b_2\overline{U} + b_3\overline{LIQ})/b_1 \qquad \hat{\beta} = a_4/b_1 \qquad \hat{\gamma} = a_5/b_1$.

These coefficients are substituted into Equation (2.3) so that we can calculate E*. This variable is incorporated into Equation (2.2). This equation is then also estimated using (weighted) least squares.

We consider two samples. The first is the "Two yearly" case in which data for all the even years are used (1980, 1982, 1984, 1986, 1988, 1990, 1992, 1994 and 1996). The total number of observations then equals 207. As an alternative we use the "Four yearly" case in which data for the years 1980, 1984, 1988, 1992 and 1996 are used. The total number of observations then equals 115. The reason for removing observations from the sample is that the observation periods for two consecutive even years overlap. This may lead to a downward bias in the estimated standard errors of the coefficients.

Weighting with population (in the year t-4) implies that all variables (including constants and dummies) are multiplied with the square root of population before the least squares procedure is run. A more detailed description of the weighting of observations can be found in the Appendix to this chapter.

The estimation results of Model (2.1)-(2.5) are given in Table 2.2.

Table 2.2. Estimation results of Model (2.1)-(2.5)

Parameter	Two yearly	Four yearly	Parameter	Two yearly	Four yearly
a_0	0.049	0.038	α	0.538	0.254
	(1.1)	(0.6)		(0.6)	(0.2)
b_1	0.050	0.049	β	-0.127	0.104
	(2.8)	(1.8)		(0.2)	(0.1)
b_2	0.066	0.057	γ	-0.004	-0.050
	(4.5)	(2.8)		(0.0)	(0.3)
b_3	-0.030	-0.034	c_0	0.222	0.205
	(2.2)	(1.8)		(7.5)	(5.6)
a_4	-0.006	0.005	c_1	-0.488	-0.349
	(0.2)	(0.1)		(3.0)	(1.9)
a_5	-0.000	-0.002	c_2	-0.008	-0.007
	(0.0)	(0.3)		(5.3)	(3.8)
R_1^2	0.224	0.197	R_2^2	0.504	0.569
N	207	115	N	207	115

Note: Absolute t-values are between brackets.

From Table 2.2 we see that most coefficients are significant with the expected signs: unemployment has a positive effect on self-employment and the effect of labor income share is negative (coefficients b_2 and b_3, respectively). Furthermore, the hypothesized error-correction process and the negative impact on growth of deviating from equilibrium also seem to be supported: coefficients b_1 and c_1 are significantly positive and negative, respectively. The speed of adjustment is low: 5%. However, the results on the error-correction process and the growth penalty should be interpreted with caution, since the estimated equilibrium relation between the business ownership rate and per capita income appears not well determined: coefficients α, β and γ have very low t-values.

Special Position of Italy

The low t-values for the equilibrium relation coefficients may be caused by the existence of certain (large) countries with specific developments in the business ownership rate not covered by our model. This could influence the estimates towards implausible results. The country we suspect may deviate most from the other countries is Italy.

Looking at Table 2.1, we see that Italy combines a high level of self-employment with a near average level of per capita income. This is not in accordance with what we would expect: the countries with a high rate of self-employment (business ownership) are generally in a less advanced stage of economic development (for example Greece). Italy can be divided in two different economies: a well-developed economy (Northern Italy) and a less developed economy (Southern Italy or the Mezzogiorno). Italy might not fit well in our model because it basically consists of two different economies. A closer inspection of the data for Northern and Southern Italy[23] shows that Northern Italy in particular deviates from the expected pattern, i.e. the U-shaped trend of the relative number of business owners set out against per capita income. Here, a high self-employment rate is combined with a relatively high value of GDP per capita. Small and medium-sized firms seem to play a bigger role in (Northern) Italian manufacturing than in other industrialized countries.[24] A notable feature of the organization of Italian small and medium-sized firm production is its high geographical concentration in small areas or industrial districts (Piore and Sabel, 1984). The geographical distribution also shows that the majority of small and medium-sized manufacturing firms is located in Northern and Central Italy (Acs and Audretsch, 1993). They often have a strong family component.

The Italian model of extensive small and medium-sized firm production differs from that in other countries in similar stages of development. It may have positive and/or negative effects on economic growth. Many of the Italian firms are highly specialized and are organized on a flexible basis, so as to meet specific customer needs, and produce well designed and fashionable goods, aimed at the richest segments of the market. Another characteristic of the Italian model is that Italian R&D expenditures as a percentage of GNP are by far the lowest among the largest OECD-countries. They amount to only half of that in Germany, the U.S. and Japan over a long period (Klomp and Pronk, 1998, p. 167). Hence, the number of business owners in Northern Italy is higher than one would expect on the basis of the advanced stage of economic development. The data for Southern Italy seem to be in conformity with the general pattern: there is also a high level of self-employment but combined with a low value of the GDP per capita.

Looking again at the Italian data in Table 2.1, we see that Italy not only has a relatively high self-employment rate but also that self-employment in Italy continues to rise. Therefore we suspect that the

---

[23] Separate data for Northern and Southern Italy are obtained from *Eurostat Regions Statistical Yearbook*.

[24] The size of newly established firms in Italy is very small in comparison with the size of incumbent firms (see Santarelli and Sterlacchini, 1994).

hypothesized error-correction process does not apply to the Italian economy. We approach this problem by introducing a dummy variable D_{ITA} that is 1 for the Italian observations and 0 elsewhere. That is, we have the error term in Equation (2.1) equal to $\varepsilon_{1it} = a_{0,ITA} D_{ITA} + \eta_{it}$.

The estimation results of the model including the "Italy-dummy" are given in Table 2.3.

Table 2.3. Estimation results of Model (2.1)-(2.5), including dummy for Italy in (2.4)

Parameter	Two yearly	Four yearly	Parameter	Two yearly	Four yearly
a_0	0.109	0.098	α	0.863	0.743
	(2.5)	(1.5)		(2.5)	(1.5)
b_1	0.120	0.120	β	-0.494	-0.398
	(5.4)	(3.6)		(2.0)	(1.1)
b_2	0.063	0.055	γ	0.081	0.062
	(4.5)	(2.8)		(1.7)	(0.9)
b_3	-0.011	-0.014	c_0	0.182	0.183
	(0.8)	(0.7)		(8.9)	(7.6)
a_4	-0.059	-0.048	c_1	-0.571	-0.576
	(1.9)	(1.0)		(2.7)	(2.4)
a_5	0.010	0.007	c_2	-0.006	-0.006
	(1.6)	(0.9)		(5.3)	(4.5)
$a_{0,ITA}$	0.011	0.011			
	(4.9)	(3.4)			
P-value of Wald test on $\beta = \gamma = 0$				0.002	0.042
Minimum value of E* at $-\beta / 2\gamma$				3.06	3.22
				(12.5)	(5.2)
R_1^2	0.307	0.274	R_2^2	0.500	0.575
N	207	115	N	207	115

Note: Absolute t-values between brackets.

We see that the t-values of the estimated coefficients of the hypothesized U-shape of the equilibrium rate of business ownership in Table 2.3 are higher than those presented in Table 2.2. Also, the coefficients are in accordance with our expectations. The estimates of β and γ have the predicted signs and that of α lies between zero and one.

However, the t-values of β and γ are still not high. This is not surprising, considering the high correlation between the linear and the quadratic $\ln(YCAP_{it}+1)$ variables. Indeed, the Wald test for the hypothesis that β and γ are jointly zero is rejected. Furthermore, an analysis of $-\beta/2\gamma$ (which is the minimum of the parabola in terms of $\ln(YCAP_{it}+1)$) shows that this expression *does* have a high t-value, implying that the log-quadratic specification performs reasonably well. Further investigation of the parabola shows that for the "Two yearly" case the minimum value is reached for a level of per capita income of 20,398 U.S. dollar (in purchasing power parities) at 1990 prices. The minimum level of equilibrium business ownership is 10.7% of the labor force. In Figure 2.1 we show the equilibrium curve and the actual data for the G7-countries. In this figure also the (YCAP; E) combinations for the "out-of-sample" years 1972, 1974 and 1998 are incorporated. For the "Four yearly" case the value of the minimum is 0.103 and it is attained at a level of 23,930 U.S. dollar. We will concentrate on the results of the "Two yearly" case as they are similar to the "Four yearly" one.

The last column of Table 2.1 presents the equilibrium business ownership rates in the year 1988. Greece has the highest equilibrium rate, 0.180. Most of the countries are close to the minimum of the curve, though. The two richest countries, Luxembourg and the United States, have an equilibrium rate which is close to the minimum of the curve. These countries have reached a level of per capita income in 1988 which just exceeds the GDP per capita level at which the equilibrium rate reaches its minimum. For the interpretation of this parabola describing the equilibrium rate of business ownership given a certain stage of economic development, it should be noted that the relation is based upon a limited range of values of GDP per capita. For values of per capita income far outside our sample range -for example less developed countries or GDP per capita levels twice as high as attained in the richest countries in our sample- the equilibrium rate of business ownership may not be described properly by the quadratic function. Furthermore, U-shaped equilibrium functions cannot be distinguished from L-shaped functions in a statistical sense, because the majority of the GDP per capita values in our sample lie below the level associated with the minimum of the parabola.

As before, we find that the hypothesized error-correction process of the number of business owners towards the equilibrium rate is supported: the estimate of b_1 is significantly positive. The speed of adjustment is not high: the deviation from equilibrium at a certain point in time decreases with 12 percent in a period of four years. The low value of the speed of adjustment is not surprising. The convergence process of the actual business ownership rate towards the equilibrium rate is intrinsically slow because it involves structural changes on the supply side (setting up enterprises, investments in physical and human capital, divestments, etc.)

as well as cultural and institutional changes. Note that the estimate of b_1 is higher than in Table 2.2, in which the "Italy-dummy" was excluded from the model. It shows that Italy is an exception to the general pattern of the business ownership rate adjusting towards the equilibrium level. The lack of error-correction for Italian self-employment is also clear from Figure 2.1.[25]

The estimate of b_2 points at a positive impact of unemployment on self-employment: every percent point rise in the unemployment rate leads to a rise of 0.06 percent point in the self-employment rate in the succeeding six years. This is in accordance with evidence in some earlier studies: unemployment is a push factor for self-employment. The other variable explaining the change in self-employment, the labor income share, has the expected effect: the estimate of b_3 is negative. The effect is insignificant, though. This means that we fail to find evidence for our variable of business profitability to act as a pull factor for business ownership. The remaining variable in the business ownership equation, the "Italy-dummy", shows a significant positive coefficient. The rate of business ownership in Italy rises faster *ceteris paribus* than in other countries.

Another important characteristic of the estimation results is the deviation of the actual number of business owners from the equilibrium rate having a negative impact on economic growth: the estimate of c_1 is significantly negative.[26] This implies that economies with a business ownership rate below the equilibrium may benefit from stimulating new start-ups. In case this rate exceeds the equilibrium, it suggests that there are important impediments to growth for small and medium-sized enterprises. In the growth equation, the per capita income parameter c_2 is estimated to be negative. This might reflect the convergence of countries

---

[25] We have also run a regression of Equation (2.4) with dummy-variables included for *all* countries in the sample. We found the error-correction effect to increase to 0.20 and the growth penalty to become insignificant (t-value below unity). Because one possible interpretation of such a regression is that every country has its own unique equilibrium level, these results are not surprising. However, this type of country-specific equilibrium levels is not the focus of this chapter, since we are investigating a "universal" equilibrium function which should be valid for all countries. Indeed, as we described earlier, we do not even interpret the "Italy-dummy" as reflecting a country-specific equilibrium. Instead, we interpret it as an autonomous additional rise in the number of business owners, not necessarily favouring economic growth.

[26] We do not include country-specific dummies in Equation (2.2). However, when including such dummies the coefficient of c_1 remains negative and the value of the estimate barely changes, both in the "Two yearly" case and the "Four yearly" case. This is also found for both cases when the "Italy-dummy" in the first equation is excluded (as in Table 2.2). Likelihood ratio test statistics testing whether or not to include country-specific dummies in Equation (2.2) have values between 34.0 and 46.5 for the four cases of Table 2.2 and 2.3. These values are close to the critical values at 5% (33.9) and 1% (40.3).

hypothesis. However, it may also be a within (regression-to-the-mean) effect: a higher value of GDP per capita in a certain year leads to a smaller economic growth in the subsequent period. Finally, the constant term c_0 is positive.

A comparison of the third and sixth column of Table 2.1 shows that in 1988 most countries had too few self-employed relative to the equilibrium value. An obvious exception is Italy. It indicates that the high level of self-employment in Italy is not efficient: it has a relatively large negative impact on economic growth.[27] Another exception is Australia. But as opposed to Italy, Australia moved in the direction of equilibrium between 1988 and 1996, as can be seen from the fourth column of Table 2.1. Countries which experienced very low business ownership rates compared to the equilibrium include the Scandinavian countries. These economies are chacterized by a large public sector, relatively low entry and exit rates and high taxes. Eliasson (1995) blames part of Sweden's relatively bad economic performance in the 1980s on limited private initiative and a lack of structural adjustment. Another country with a relatively low business ownership rate is Germany. In Figure 2.1 it is shown that, at least until recently, Germany has failed to restructure where for example the United Kingdom has. Klodt (1990) blames (West) German industrial policy for repressing structural change in supporting large-scale industries with subsidies. An important reason for the lack of a vibrant sector of new firms and industries in Germany up till the mid 1990s has been the high barriers to innovative activity (Audretsch, 2000). An example of important economic reforms transforming an economy from a regulated one to a market-orientated one with increasing business ownership rates is New Zealand (see e.g. Evans et al., 1996). Carlsson (1996) shows the strong increase in the number of firms as a result of the reforms, certainly when compared to countries like Sweden. After a painful transition period the New Zealand's reforms appear to ultimately have generated economic growth (McMillan, 1998). The data in Table 2.1 suggest that, indeed, business ownership rates were below equilibrium values for New Zealand before the start of the reforms in 1984. The increase in business ownership rates has been fierce in the period thereafter and may be "overshooting", making some "shake-out" of newly entered entrepreneurs likely.

---

[27] In Italy, research and development expenditures are by far the lowest among the largest OECD countries as a percentage of gross national product. This is in line with the idea that when there are too many business owners, the scale advantages in research and development are not utilized. See Cohen and Klepper (1996).

Figure 2.1. The actual and equilibrium rate of business ownership for G7-countries, 1972-1998

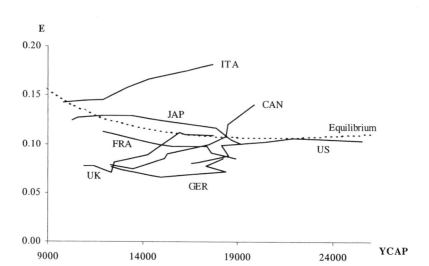

2.6 Discussion

Business ownership has received considerable attention from policy makers in European countries. The high unemployment rate coupled with limited economic growth in Europe has triggered a plea by policy makers for rethinking the policy approach that fostered prosperity during the post-war era. In two ways globalization has reduced the ability of the European countries to generate economic growth and create jobs. On the one hand the advent of new competition from low-cost countries in Asia and Central and Eastern Europe has flooded the EU markets. On the other hand, the telecommunications and computer revolutions have drastically reduced the cost of shifting capital and information out of the high-cost locations of Europe and into lower-cost locations around the globe (Audretsch and Thurik, 2000).

It is deeply embedded in the current European policy approach that the creativity and independence of the self-employed contribute to higher levels of economic activity. In modern economies a great variety of organizations is involved in making innovative products. This is the case particularly in niche markets like in the ICT sector. The more organizations are active in such markets, the greater the chance that an innovation takes place. Variety and selection play a dominant role in this mechanism. Therefore, major funds of governmental institutions and independent donor organizations are being channeled towards young and small firms. The present chapter aims at achieving some first insights into whether such policies are justified in different phases of economic development.

We seek to explain the interrelationship between economic progress and the size class structure of firms. This chapter zooms in on one specific linkage: that between the number of business owners and economic development. Three aspects of this linkage are investigated. First, we investigate whether there is a long-term equilibrium relation between the number of business owners and the stage of economic development. This conjecture arises from analysing empirical and theoretical work in this area. The relation is hypothesized to initially be a decreasing function of economic development in that the self-employment rate is high in low-developed economies whereas more highly developed countries where mass production and scale economies thrive have lower self-employment rates. A large literature points at a still later phase of economic development where the business ownership rate is increasing again. This phase is characterized by "the reversal of the trend" towards increasing economies of scale and scope. Therefore we formulate the equilibrium business ownership to have a U-shaped relation with respect to economic development. Second, we investigate whether there is a correction mechanism when the rate of business ownership is out of equilibrium and compute the speed of convergence. Deviations from equilibrium can occur due to exogenous shocks and institutional divergences, for instance, because "government regulation of market activity is likely to obstruct and frustrate the spontaneous, corrective forces of entrepreneurial adjustments" (Kirzner, 1997, p. 81). Third, we investigate whether deviating from the equilibrium rate of business ownership leads to lower economic growth. The three aspects are tested using a two-equation model. The first equation explains the growth of the number of business owners using the deviation between the actual and the equilibrium rate of business ownership, unemployment as a push factor and the labor income share as a measure of business profitability. The second equation explains economic growth using the deviation between the actual and the equilibrium rate of business ownership, and the per capita income level. The model is tested using a data panel of 23 OECD countries.

We find evidence for a long-term equilibrium relation between economic development and business ownership. However, U-shaped equilibrium functions cannot be distinguished from L-shaped functions in a statistical sense. In fact, the large majority of countries has levels of economic development smaller than that at which the U-curve reaches its "minimum", making the "equilibrium function" largely L-shaped.

We find evidence for an error correction mechanism between the actual rate of business ownership and the equilibrium rate. Lagged unemployment appears to be a significant push factor of business ownership. Italy plays an exceptional role in our sample of 23 OECD countries in that there appears to be an additional autonomous increase of the rate of self-employment which may have frustrated economic growth.

The rate of business ownership is found to influence economic growth through deviations from the equilibrium rate. This result supports the view that size distribution differences across countries matter when explaining economic performance (Davis and Henrekson, 1999). As a consequence, economies can have both too few or too many business owners and both situations can lead to a growth penalty. By and large, a five percent point deviation implies a growth loss of three percent over a period of four years.

An important policy implication of our exercises is not only that "To induce dynamic entrepreneurial competition we require the fulfillment of only one condition: guaranteeing free entrepreneurial entry into any market where profit opportunities may be perceived to exist" (Kirzner, 1997, p. 74), but also that exit free of stigma and financial burdens has to be safeguarded. Low barriers to entry and exit of business owners are a necessary condition for the equilibrium seeking mechanisms which are vital in our model of the relation between business ownership and economic development.

The results presented in this chapter should be interpreted with caution. The very concept of the economy-wide rate of business ownership entails several difficulties of interpretation. For example, it is impossible to make the rates perfectly statistically comparable across countries. In addition, the composition of the rates are unclear: high-tech start-ups are indistinguishable from old mom-and-pop businesses in the retail sector (with the same number of employees). Nevertheless, we argue that this chapter may provide a good starting point for a promising line of research. As an important issue we mention that while the present research is based upon country-wide composites, sectoral diversity between countries probably plays a role when explaining differences in equilibrium situation and differences in the equilibrium restoring mechanism.

2.A Appendix: Weighted Regressions

Estimation results are obtained by weighting the observations with the number of inhabitants. In this appendix we provide the rationale. For simplicity we consider the case of cross sectional data (i.e. no time dimension).

Suppose that there are N regions in L countries with $L \ll N$. In our case, L would be 23 because we have 23 countries in our data set. We assume that these N regions are all of the same size. Thus, for example, the U.S. would have many regions the size of Luxembourg. If we would dispose of data per region, we would propose the following model for a linear relationship between two variables x and y:

(2.A1) $y_{R,i} = \beta x_{R,i} + \varepsilon_{R,i}$, $i = 1,\ldots,N$ (regions).

The subscript R is used to denote that the data are assumed to be available at the regional level. The OLS-estimator of β in (2.A1) is then

$$b_{OLS}(A1) = \frac{\sum_{i=1}^{N} x_{R,i} y_{R,i}}{\sum_{i=1}^{N} x_{R,i} x_{R,i}}.$$

However, we have data at the aggregated level of countries and not at the level of regions. Given our assumption that the regions are equally large, we write the model with the variables x and y at the country level (subscript C) as

(2.A2) $y_{C,j} = \beta x_{C,j} + \varepsilon_{C,j}$, $j = 1,\ldots,L$ (countries),

where

$$y_{C,j} = \sum_{D_{i,j}=1} y_{R,i} / N_j \text{ and } x_{C,j} = \sum_{D_{i,j}=1} x_{R,i} / N_j.$$

The variable $D_{i,j}$ is defined as follows: $D_{i,j} = 1$ if region i lies in country j and 0 otherwise. Furthermore, N_j denotes the number of regions in country j ($\sum_{j=1}^{L} N_j = N$). Hence, we assume that the variables x and y at the country-level can be written as the averages of the variables over the regions of the country. When we translate these country-level variables $y_{C,j}$ and $x_{C,j}$ in (2.A2) back to the regional level variables $y_{R,i}$ and $x_{R,i}$ in (2.A1), we obtain the following observations for our original Model (2.A1) at the regional level:

Observations for which:

$D_{i,1} = 1$: $y^*_{R,i} = y_{C,1}$ $x^*_{R,i} = x_{C,1}$ (N_1 observations)

.

$$D_{i,L} = 1: \qquad \overset{*}{y}_{R,i} = y_{C,L} \qquad \overset{*}{x}_{R,i} = x_{C,L} \qquad (N_L \text{ observations})$$

Writing the data at the regional level in this manner, it is implicitly assumed that *within* countries, the various regions are identical. With these observations, the OLS-estimator can be written as:

$$\overset{*}{b}_{OLS}(A1) = \frac{\sum\limits_{i=1}^{N} \overset{*}{x}_{R,i}\overset{*}{y}_{R,i}}{\sum\limits_{i=1}^{N} \overset{*}{x}_{R,i}\overset{*}{x}_{R,i}} = \frac{\sum\limits_{j=1}^{L} N_j x_{C,j} y_{C,j}}{\sum\limits_{j=1}^{L} N_j x_{C,j} x_{C,j}}.$$

Thus, here it is assumed that there are N observations where for every observation (region) within a country, the variables have identical values. However, we have only L observations and then the OLS-estimator of β from (2.A2) reads as

$$b_{OLS}(A2) = \frac{\sum\limits_{j=1}^{L} x_{C,j} y_{C,j}}{\sum\limits_{j=1}^{L} x_{C,j} x_{C,j}}.$$

We see that this estimator is different from $\overset{*}{b}_{OLS}(A1)$, which we would like to have. The estimator $b_{OLS}(A2)$ does not take into account that different countries have different numbers of regions, or stated differently, that the various countries are not equally large. Therefore, we weight the observations by premultiplying the variables x_C and y_C from (2.A2) with the square root of the number of regions. The (weighted) least squares estimator $b_{WLS}(A2)$ reads as

$$b_{WLS}(A2) = \frac{\sum\limits_{j=1}^{L} \sqrt{N_j} x_{C,j} \sqrt{N_j} y_{C,j}}{\sum\limits_{j=1}^{L} \sqrt{N_j} x_{C,j} \sqrt{N_j} x_{C,j}}.$$

We see that the WLS-estimator of (2.A2) is exactly the same as the OLS-estimator of (2.A1), $\overset{*}{b}_{OLS}(A1)$. Clearly, we do not know the number of regions per country. We use the population size as a proxy.

Chapter 3

BUSINESS OWNERSHIP AND SECTORAL GROWTH

3.1 Introduction [28]

The empirical growth literature has generated a long list of regressors assumed to affect economic growth. The regressors range from schooling to climate and from the extent of democracy to life expectancy (see e.g. Bleaney and Nishiyama, 2002). These factors are of considerable importance and it is for example unlikely to find a non-democratic country with an extreme climate to show fast economic growth, except when oil or other natural resources come into play. However, little attention in the empirical growth literature has been devoted to entrepreneurship and competition usually considered vital to economic progress. The lack of economic progress in (formerly) centralized planned economies has been at least partly due to the absence of these private initiatives. A characteristic of these economies was the almost complete absence of small firms and this extreme monopolization was a major factor leading to the collapse of state socialism (see e.g. Acs, 1996). The incorporation of entrepreneurship and competition into empirical growth models has been hampered by the problem of measurement. However, a small literature has developed that investigates the effect of the industry structure in terms of the share of small firms on economic progress. Examples include Nickell (1996), Carree and Thurik (1998), Audretsch et al. (2002a) and Carree (2002a).

Recently, Carree et al. (2002) introduced a model that describes the interrelationship between the rate of business ownership (or interchangeably self-employment) and economic development. This model consists of two equations, which are estimated successively. In the first equation, an "equilibrium" relation is derived between the rate of business ownership and the level of economic development of a country. In the second equation the impact on economic growth of deviating from the "equilibrium" rate is estimated. The basic idea behind the model is

---

[28] This chapter is reprinted from: Van Stel, A.J. and M.A. Carree (2004), Business Ownership and Sectoral Growth: An Empirical Analysis of 21 OECD Countries, *International Small Business Journal* 22 (4), pp. 389-419, with kind permission of Sage Publications Ltd. (http://www.sagepub.com).

that there can be too many or too few self-employed in an economy. A consequence of a *too* high business ownership rate in a country is that economies of scale and scope are not benefited from and that R&D expenditures may be relatively low. A consequence of a *too* low business ownership rate is that new private initiatives and radical new innovations may be less present than in other countries at comparable levels of economic development. Carree et al. present empirical evidence for the "equilibrium" rate of business ownership to depend upon the stage of economic development and that deviating from the "equilibrium" implies a lower economic growth rate.

The paper by Carree et al. suffers from an important limitation. It studies the relationship between business ownership rates at the economy-wide level without taking into consideration the sectoral structure of the economy. It is well-known that business ownership rates are much higher in the service sector when compared to the manufacturing sector. It is therefore possible that the penalty on deviating from the "equilibrium" business ownership rate is *not* a problem of having too few or too many self-employed, but a problem of having a too small or a too large share of the service sector. Carree et al. find that the "equilibrium" business ownership rates tend to increase with the level of economic development for the highly most developed countries (in terms of GDP per capita). This might be caused by increased interest for the option of self-employment as such across the sectors in the economy, but may also be explained from an employment shift in modern economies away from the manufacturing sector towards the service sector. The current chapter examines the importance of the *sectoral* component in the Carree et al. model, using data for 21 OECD countries. The 21 countries include 16 European countries, the United States, Canada, Japan, Australia and New Zealand.

There is a lot of debate about the reasons behind the increase in self-employment rates in developed countries in the last quarter of the 20th century. On the one hand, Audretsch and Thurik (2000) consider it to be a reflection of the shift from a "managed" towards an "entrepreneurial" economy. They claim that there is more room for business ownership in the latter type of economy because of, among others, increasing variety of demand and rapidly changing economic circumstances in which small firms have a comparative advantage with regard to their larger counterparts. These phenomena particularly apply to fully industrialized economies and therefore, this upward trend of business ownership would only be observable in countries at higher stages of economic development. On the other hand, other economists will say that this upward trend of the macro business ownership rate in modern economies is just a reflection of the (employment) share of the service industries increasing at the cost of the manufacturing industries' share. According to these economists it does not imply that also *within* sectors there would be an upward trend in business ownership. The current analysis gathers business ownership data on the sectoral level and applies the model of Carree et al. at this level. In this way, we can determine whether or not the structural changes in business ownership do also apply *within* sectors. In particular, we will estimate the model for two sectors: manufacturing and services.

In Section 3.2 we will discuss the Carree et al. model and adapt it to make it applicable at the sectoral level. We also discuss the relevant literature. In Section 3.3 we discuss the data for the OECD countries. This is followed by the empirical results in Section 3.4. Section 3.5 is left for discussion.

3.2 Theory and Model

Carree et al. (2000, 2002) introduced a model consisting of two equations with one additional equation defining the "equilibrium" rate of business ownership in period t, E_t^*. The dependent variables of the two equations are the four-year change in the business ownership rate, $E_t - E_{t-4}$, and the four-year growth rate of GDP, $(Y_t - Y_{t-4})/Y_{t-4}$. We use the same model configuration in our analysis but adapt it somewhat to apply it to the sectoral level. The model reads as follows.

$$(3.1) \quad \begin{aligned} E_{ijt} - E_{ij,t-4} &= b_1 \left(E_{ij,t-4}^* - E_{ij,t-4} \right) + b_2 \left(U_{i,t-4} - \overline{U} \right) + \\ & \quad b_3 Y\_share_{ij,t-4} + b_{ITA} D_{ITA} + \varepsilon_{1ijt} \end{aligned}$$

$$(3.2) \quad \begin{aligned} \frac{\Delta_4 Y_{ijt}}{Y_{ij,t-4}} &= c_0 + c_1 \left| E_{ij,t-4}^* - E_{ij,t-4} \right| + c_2 YCAP_{i,t-4} + c_3 Y\_share_{ij,t-4} + \\ & \quad c_4 \overset{\circ}{WT}_t + c_5 \overset{\circ}{WT}_{t-2} + c_6 \overset{\circ}{WT}_{t-4} + \varepsilon_{2ijt} \end{aligned}$$

$$(3.3) \quad E_{ijt}^* = f \left(YCAP_{it} \right) \times (1 + b_{OMIB} D_{OMIB})$$

The symbols in these equations stand for the following variables:

E :	number of business owners as fraction of total employment in sector (sectoral business ownership rate),
E^* :	sectoral equilibrium business ownership rate,
Y :	sectoral GDP,
$YCAP$:	GDP per capita (macro level),
U :	unemployment rate,
$\overline{U}$:	sample average of unemployment rate,

Y_share :   sectoral GDP as fraction of total GDP,

$\overset{\circ}{WT}$:   relative growth of world trade (yearly basis),

D_{ITA} :   dummy for Italy,

D_{OMIB} :   dummy for countries for which number of business owners is
                defined inclusive of owner/managers of incorporated
                businesses (OMIBs),

$\varepsilon_1, \varepsilon_2$:   disturbance terms in Equations (3.1) and (3.2), respectively,

i, j, t :   indices for country, sector, and year, respectively.

The variables E, E^* and Y are defined at the sectoral level and $YCAP$ and U are defined at the macro level. In the current chapter business ownership is defined to include both the self-employed (the unincorporated as well as the incorporated) and the unpaid family workers. More details about this definition and the data sources used are given in Section 3.3. In the remainder of the current section we will describe the three equations in the model in some detail. A more elaborate discussion can be found in Carree et al. (2002). Because the concept of an "equilibrium" rate of business ownership is central to the model, we start with Equation (3.3).

Equilibrium Business Ownership Equation

The (sectoral) equilibrium business ownership rate is assumed to be a function f of (macro) economic development as measured by $YCAP_{it}$. For *low* levels of economic development, we expect the function f to be declining. Several authors (e.g. Kuznets, 1971; Schultz, 1990) have reported a negative relationship between economic development and the business ownership (self-employment) rate. Their studies use a large cross-section of countries with a wide variety in the stage of economic development. There are a series of reasons for the decline of self-employment, and of small business presence in general, during the early phases of industrialization. Chandler (1990) discusses the importance of investment in production, distribution, and management needed to exploit economies of scale and scope during the period after the second industrial revolution of the second half of the 19th century. It was a period of relatively well-defined technological trajectories, of stable demand and of seemingly clear advantages of diversification.

For *high* levels of economic development the function f may be increasing. Acs et al. (1994) report that a majority of OECD-countries experienced an increase in the self-employment rate during the 1970s and 1980s. Further evidence of a recent increase in self-employment in many OECD countries appears from EIM's data set COMPENDIA. For instance, for the United Kingdom, the number of non-agricultural self-employed (including the incorporated self-employed) as a fraction of total labour force increased from 7.8% in 1972 to 10.5% in 2000, and in the United States this fraction increased from 8.0% to 10.0% in the same period (see Van Stel, 2003).

There are several reasons for the revival of small business and self-employment in Western economies. First, the last thirty years can be considered a period of industrial restructuring away from traditional manufacturing industries and towards the electronics, software and biotechnology industries. Jensen (1993) uses the term "Third Industrial Revolution" to describe this development. Small firms play an important role in these new industries. Second, new technologies have reduced the importance of scale economies in many sectors. This increases the comparative advantage of small firms relative to large firms (see e.g. Meredith, 1987). Third, from a certain level of economic development onwards, higher income and wealth increase consumer demand for variety (see Jackson, 1984) creating new market niches. Fourth, self-employment has become more highly valued as an occupational choice. This "supply side" reason may be derived from a supposed hierarchy of human motivations, ranging from physical needs at the bottom to self-realization at the top (Maslow, 1970). Once the main material needs have been satisfied, a still higher level of prosperity will induce a growing need for self-realization. Because it provides more autonomy and independence, entrepreneurship then becomes more highly valued as an occupational choice than at lower income levels.

Based on these trends in self-employment (business ownership), we expect the equilibrium relation to be U-shaped (first declining and then rising business ownership rates). However, we will also consider L-shaped relationships (ownership rates continuously declining towards an asymptotic minimum rate).[29] We have chosen a parametric approach and have used four different equilibrium functions, two of which are U-shaped and two of which are L-shaped. These are given in Equations (3.3a) through (3.3d). For ease of presentation we do not show the correction factor $(1 + b_{OMIB} D_{OMIB})$.

(3.3a) $\quad E_{ijt}^{*} = \alpha + \beta YCAP_{it} + \gamma YCAP_{it}^{2}$ $\qquad\qquad$ Quadratic

(3.3b) $\quad E_{ijt}^{*} = \alpha - \beta \dfrac{YCAP_{it}}{YCAP_{it} + 1}$ $\qquad\qquad$ Inverse

(3.3c) $\quad E_{ijt}^{*} = \alpha + \beta \ln(YCAP + 1)_{it} + \gamma \ln^{2}(YCAP + 1)_{it}$ $\qquad$ Log-Quadratic

---

[29] Carree et al. (2002) concluded that U-shaped functions cannot be statistically discriminated from L-shaped functions.

(3.3d) $E_{ijt}^{*} = \alpha - \beta \dfrac{\ln(YCAP+1)_{it}}{\ln(YCAP+1)_{it}+1}$ Log-Inverse

The equilibrium rate of business ownership equals α when GDP per capita ($YCAP$) is zero in each of the four equations (3.3a) through (3.3d). In Equation (3.3a) the relation between the level of development and the equilibrium rate of business ownership is quadratic. We expect β to be negative as initially economic development is negatively correlated with the business ownership rate. This decline is expected to become smaller over time, so γ is expected to be positive. The minimum of the U-shaped curve is reached for GDP per capita equal to $-\beta/2\gamma$. Another U-shaped relation can be found in Equation (3.3c). Again we expect β to be negative and γ to be positive. In this log-quadratic case the rise of the curve after the minimum has been reached is less steep than the decline beforehand. Equations (3.3b) and (3.3d) give L-shaped equilibrium relations. The equilibrium rate is predicted to decline from α to $\alpha - \beta$ as the level of economic development rises from zero to high levels. We call this equilibrium relation the inverse and log-inverse cases. We compare the four different equilibrium functions on the basis of the explanatory powers in Equations (3.1) and (3.2). That is, we compare the extent to which the change in the rate of entrepreneurship and the sectoral growth rate can be explained from deviations of the actual business ownership rate from the equilibrium business ownership rate.

The functional form of $YCAP$ in Equation (3.3) is multiplied by a factor $(1 + b_{OMIB} D_{OMIB})$. This correction is necessary because the self-employment definitions in our data set vary across countries. In Section 3.3 we will go into detail about these differences in definition. Summarized, one group of countries have self-employed defined as individuals *inclusive* of owner/managers of incorporated businesses (OMIBs) and other countries have a definition *exclusive* of OMIBs. It is clear that this creates an upward bias for the first group of countries as regards the number of self-employed. As these differences in definition are likely to (erroneously) affect the estimated equilibrium functions, we apply the raise-factor $(1 + b_{OMIB} D_{OMIB})$. The implicit assumption is that for a given sector the number of OMIBs as a fraction of the total number of business owners is constant for all levels of economic development. Obviously, the estimated b_{OMIB} should be positive.

Business Ownership Equation

The dependent variable in Equation (3.1) is the growth in the fraction of business owners (self-employed and unpaid family workers) in total sector employment in a period of four years. The first explanatory variable in the equation, which has the parameter b_1 assigned to it, is an error correction variable describing the difference between the equilibrium and the actual rate of business ownership (at sector level) at the start of the period. The parameter b_1 is expected to have a positive sign. There are several forces in market economies that may contribute to a process of adapting towards the equilibrium. An abundance of self-employed will lead to low profits and lack of desire to continue family business given that the government does not provide extraordinary support measures to self-employed. A relative shortage of self-employed may indicate entrepreneurial opportunities that will lead to high (net) entry rates given that the government regulations do not result in high barriers to potential entrepreneurs. The existence of a sound entrepreneurial climate and a well-developed (venture) capital market are instrumental in this respect.

The second explanatory variable is the lagged unemployment rate acting as a push factor for business ownership.[30] The expected sign of the parameter b_2 is positive. The third explanatory variable is the sectoral share in GDP. It is likely that scale advantages rank as an important competitive advantage in a sector in case the sectoral share in an economy is relatively high. Opportunities for new small ventures may be less present in later stages of the life cycle of industries in which scale economies in production or R&D have become key sources of competitive strength (see e.g. Klepper, 1996). Hence, the expected sign of parameter b_3 is negative. Finally, we follow Carree et al. in incorporating a dummy for Italy. Italy, especially Northern Italy, is exceptional in the sense that a relatively high value of GDP per capita is combined with a high and rising self-employment rate.[31]

Economic Growth Equation

The dependent variable in Equation (3.2) is sectoral economic growth, measured as the relative change in sectoral gross domestic product in a four-year period. The first determinant of sectoral growth is

---

[30] The empirical evidence on the effect of unemployment on business formation is mixed. Evans and Leighton (1989) present evidence that unemployed workers are more likely to enter self-employment than employees. Carree (2002b) finds no effect of unemployment rates on the number of establishment in low entry barrier retail and consumer service industries.

[31] We do not include dummies for *all* countries in the sample. An implication of such a specification is that every country has its own unique equilibrium level. However, this type of country-specific equilibrium levels is not the focus of this chapter, since we are investigating a "universal" equilibrium function which should be valid for all countries. Also, deviations from country-specific equilibrium levels have quite a different interpretation than deviations from a "universal" equilibrium level, as the former type of deviation ignores the cross-country variation in business ownership rates.

the (absolute) deviation of the actual rate of business ownership from the equilibrium rate of business ownership at the start of the period. The deviation is expected to have a negative impact on growth, or $c_1 < 0$. A shortage of business owners is likely to diminish competition with detrimental effects for static efficiency and competitiveness of the national economy. It will also diminish variety, learning and selection and thereby harm dynamic efficiency (innovation). On the other hand, a glut of self-employment will cause the average scale of operations to remain below optimum. It will result in large numbers of marginal entrepreneurs, absorbing capital and human energy that could have been allocated more productively elsewhere.

The second determinant is the (economy-wide) level of per capita income at the start of the period. It allows us to correct for the convergence hypothesis of countries. Countries lagging behind in economic development may show faster economic growth than more highly developed countries because they can profit from modern technologies developed in these countries. The expected sign of the parameter c_2 is negative. Similarly, we include the sectoral share of GDP to capture regression-to-the-mean effects at a sectoral level. Countries in which a certain sector is already quite large are expected to be confronted with less sectoral output growth than countries in which a sector has a smaller share of the economy. The parameter c_3 is also expected to be negative. The fourth determinant is (current and lagged) growth of world trade. Value added growth of exporting firms is dependent on the developments in world trade. The hypothesized effect of growth of world trade is positive, or $c_4, c_5, c_6 > 0$. This holds especially for manufacturing as there are, in general, more exporting firms in manufacturing compared to services.

3.3 Data

In this section we deal with the data used in the current chapter. The section is split up in two parts. First, we discuss the sectoral classification and the required sectoral variables number of business owners, total employment and real value added. Second, we provide an overview of definitions and sources for the variables, either at the sectoral level or at the macro level.

3.3.1 Sectoral Data

We estimate the model for the two main private sectors in a modern economy: manufacturing and services. For these sectors we need data on the number of business owners, total employment and real value added. We have collected these variables for 21 OECD countries for the years 1970-1998, as far as the data were available according to uniform definitions. This has resulted in the so-called "BLISS Oeso Sectoraal" data set, which is operated by EIM. The main data source for "BLISS Oeso Sectoraal" is *OECD National Accounts 1983-1995, Detailed Tables.* Where possible, missing data are supplied from other sources. Below we describe the sector classification used in the data set and describe the above-mentioned variables in some more detail.

Sectoral Classification

The sector manufacturing is a one-digit industry in OECD National Accounts. For services four one-digit industries in the OECD National Accounts have been aggregated: (1) Wholesale and retail trade, restaurants and hotels; (2) Transport, storage and communication; (3) Finance, insurance, real estate and business services; (4) Community, social and personal services. We realise that our definition of the service sector is very broad. The four underlying sectors may be substantially different in structure, so ideally we would want to distinguish between these sectors. However, the composition of these four underlying sectors is quite different for different countries, visible in the numerous country notes on this matter to the statistical tables in the OECD National Accounts.[32] Hence, we cannot compare the numbers of business owners in the four underlying service sectors between different countries. These differences in composition do not apply to the aggregate data of the four underlying sectors. Therefore, despite its limitations, we prefer to work with the broad definition of the service sector.[33]

Number of Business Owners

Collecting harmonized data on the number of business owners at sectoral level for a large number of countries and over a long period of

---

[32] For example, for a number of countries the sub-sector Business services, which is part of sector Finance, etc., is included in Community, social and personal services, see OECD (1997a), pp. 100, 212, 351, 368 and 600. For some countries the sub-sector Restaurants and hotels, which is part of Wholesale, etc., is included in Community, social and personal services, see OECD (1997a), pp. 100, 148 and 368. For Italy, a distinction between Finance, etc., and Community, social and personal services has not even been made in the statistical tables of OECD National Accounts. Only aggregate data of these two sectors are included in the tables, see OECD (1997a), p. 431.

[33] A similar problem applies to the one-digit manufacturing sector. In some countries the one-digit sector mining is included in the manufacturing sector. In prevailing cases, we did correct for it with help of data from the Labour Force Statistics. Also, with help of data from other sources, we made a correction in the GDP data for manufacturing to exclude the mining part in these figures.

time is not easy for at least three reasons.[34] First, business owners (self-employed) are not defined uniformly across countries. In some countries owner/managers of incorporated businesses (OMIBs) are counted as self-employed whereas in other countries they are counted as employee. This is because formally an owner/manager of an incorporated business is an employee of his own firm. The different statistical treatment results from a different set-up of labor force surveys in different countries.[35] Second, the big interest for entrepreneurship dates only from recent times. This is the reason that consistent measuring of the self-employed also dates from recent times. For some countries reliable data on the number of self-employed are not available, especially for early years and at a sectoral level. Third, and directly related to the second problem, in some countries major revisions in the way of measuring the self-employed have taken place in the past. Hence, for these countries numbers of self-employed are not readily comparable over time.

From the description above it becomes clear that we cannot measure the number of self-employed in a uniform fashion for all the 21 countries and for all years in our sample period. Instead, we have made definitions as uniform as possible and work with an unbalanced panel.[36] We end up with two groups of countries, using different self-employment definitions. This is explained below.

Three Types of Self-Employed

Based on legal status, self-employed individuals may be split up in three different types: unincorporated self-employed, incorporated self-employed, and unpaid family workers. For each group we have to decide whether or not we want to include them in our self-employment definition. The most common group of self-employed individuals are the *unincorporated self-employed* and this group is obviously included in our self-employment count. We also want to include the *incorporated self-employed* in our count because they are not fundamentally different from the unincorporated self-employed, as far as "entrepreneurial spirit" is involved: both types of self-employed have chosen to "be their own boss". However, as mentioned earlier, in some countries the incorporated self-employed are treated as employee in the statistical tables, and for those countries it is not possible to measure their numbers. Because we include

---

[34] Measurement problems concerning comparability of new firm formation rates across seven economically advanced countries are identified in a special issue of *Regional Studies*, see Reynolds et al. (1994a).

[35] See Chapter 5 of *OECD Employment Outlook June 2000*.

[36] This means that the data are not available for the same period of time for all countries and sectors. Instead we work with the maximum amount of data that we were able to collect for each country and sector.

the incorporated self-employed in our definition, we generally speak of 'business owners' throughout this chapter (in order to distinguish from 'self-employed' which is often understood to include only the unincorporated self-employed).

As far as *unpaid family workers* are concerned, we would rather not include them in our self-employment count. Family workers who work in a family member's firm often have little influence on the 'entrepreneurial' decisions taken. Usually they would not start a business in case this family member would not run one already. Therefore, we would have liked not to include them in our count of self-employed. However, although there is information at the *macro* level about the proportions of unpaid family workers in total self-employed in various countries (see the various issues of the *OECD Labour Force Statistics*)[37], there is no information about these proportions at the *sectoral* level. Because sectoral self-employment data in OECD National Accounts are inclusive of unpaid family workers and we cannot (in a plausible way) exclude the unpaid family workers from the available figures, we were left no choice but to include them in our self-employment count.

Definitions

As mentioned earlier, the way in which the self-employed are defined in OECD National Accounts is different across countries. Specifically, in some countries the owner/managers of incorporated businesses are counted as self-employed and in other countries they are counted as employee. We do not correct for the difference in definitions in our *data*, as we do not dispose of country- and sector-specific information about the proportions incorporated/unincorporated self-employed. Instead, we correct for the differences in our *model*, by means of a so-called OMIB-dummy.

For the construction of the OMIB-dummy, we must know which countries use the narrow definition of self-employed (excluding the incorporated self-employed), and which countries use the broader one (including the incorporated self-employed). In *OECD Employment Outlook June 2000*, the countries that use the narrow definition and the ones that use the broad definition are given. That is, the definitions as applied in OECD Labour Force Statistics (LFS) are mentioned. In principle, the definition used in LFS is also the definition used in OECD National Accounts. But this is not necessarily true for all countries. Based on (1) a comparison between the total number of non-agricultural self-employed (including unpaid family workers) according to OECD Labour

---

[37] In earlier studies that we performed at the macro level, we have in fact used self-employment data exclusive of unpaid family workers (Carree et al., 2000, 2002). These studies make use of EIM's data set COMPENDIA, see Chapter 9 of this book.

Force Statistics and OECD National Accounts; (2) the definition used in each country in OECD Labour Force Statistics as reported by OECD Employment Outlook June 2000, p. 158; and (3) the country-notes in OECD National Accounts 1983-1995; we have been able to distinguish two groups of countries in our dataset: countries using a broad self-employment definition (including OMIBs) and countries using a narrow definition (excluding OMIBs). The countries having a self-employment definition including OMIBs are Belgium, Denmark, France, West-Germany, Greece, Ireland, Italy, Portugal, Spain, United Kingdom, United States and New Zealand. The countries having a self-employment definition excluding OMIBs are Austria, Finland, Netherlands, Sweden, Iceland, Norway, Japan, Canada and Australia. In terms of Equation (3.3), the value of D_{OMIB} is 1 for the first group of countries and 0 for the second group.[38]

Supplementary Sources and Corrections

As mentioned earlier, the main source for the sectoral data is OECD National Accounts 1983-1995.[39] The number of self-employed (in persons) is derived from country tables 15: employment by kind of activity, as the difference between employment of *all persons* and employment of *employees*. Where possible, missing data (including the years 1996-98) are supplied from various other sources, including OECD Labour Force Statistics and *OECD National Accounts 1988-98*. Corrections are made to ensure that data from different sources correspond. In some cases country-specific data sources are used to make data comparable with other countries. For example, in OECD National Accounts the data for the Netherlands are expressed in man-years instead of persons. Therefore, we used information from the Dutch national accounts (published by *Statistics Netherlands*), to obtain a time series in persons. Also, for the United States, we constructed a series inclusive of

---

[38] Two remarks concerning the United States are required here. First, the definition in OECD National Accounts for the U.S. is exclusive of OMIBs. Instead of using these data and classifying the U.S. in the second group of countries (i.e. excluding OMIBs), we made an exception for the U.S. and made an approximation of the number of OMIBs based on information from *The State of Small Business*. The exception was made because we would like to include the number of OMIBs in our definition and we consider the U.S. too important to settle for a definition excluding OMIBs in our data set. Second, the United States is also exceptional in the sense that the self-employment data from OECD National Accounts are exclusive of unpaid family workers, see OECD (1997a), p. 73. Since in the U.S. the number of unpaid family workers is very low (0.1% of total non-agricultural employment in 1996; compare this with, for example 4.1% in Turkey, see OECD, 1997b), this discrepancy in definition with regard to the other countries is very small.

[39] This publication also provides data for years prior to 1983, by means of accompanying disks.

OMIBs, making use of information from *The State of Small Business*, issues 1986 and 1996.

Sectoral business ownership data are reported in Table 3.1. Greece and Italy have the highest business ownership rates (1998) for *manufacturing*, while the Scandinavian countries and the United States have relatively low business ownership rates. Strong increases of the business ownership rate in manufacturing during the period 1970-1998 are found for Ireland, United Kingdom, United States, Canada, Australia and New Zealand, while Denmark, France, Norway, and especially Japan experienced strong decreases in business ownership rates during this period. Belgium, Greece, Italy, Portugal and Spain have the highest business ownership rates (1998) for *services*, while relatively low rates are found for the Netherlands, Sweden, Norway, the United States and Australia. The high proportions of self-employed for the former five countries are partly explained by the relatively high numbers of unpaid family workers in these countries. According to Table 4.2 of *OECD Employment Outlook July 1992*, the proportion of unpaid family workers in non-agricultural civilian employment in 1990 varies from 3.4% (Belgium) to 5.4% (Greece) for these countries. For comparison, this proportion was 0.2% for the United States and Canada in 1990. Strong increases in the business ownership rate during the period 1970-1998 are again found for the United Kingdom, Canada and New Zealand, while Denmark, France and Japan also experienced strong declines in business ownership rate for the service sectors.

Table 3.1. Sectoral business ownership rates for 21 OECD countries, 1970-1984-1998

Country	Manufacturing			Services		
	1970	1984	1998	1970	1984	1998
Austria [b]	0.051 [1976]	0.044	0.040	0.166 [1976]	0.141	0.138
Belgium [a]	0.057	0.062	0.065	0.309	0.280	0.283
Denmark [a]	0.067	0.048	0.032	0.214	0.173	0.144
Finland [b]	0.031	0.028	0.027	0.133	0.145	0.138
France [a]	0.062	0.049	0.041	0.238	0.171	0.138
West-Germany [a]	0.054	0.042	0.049	0.220	0.165	0.176
Greece [a]	0.320 [1972]	0.300	0.307	0.359 [1972]	0.349	0.335
Ireland [a]	0.038	0.048	0.078	N.A.	N.A.	N.A.
Italy [a]	0.139	0.155	0.164	0.425	0.459	0.437
Netherlands [b]	0.043	0.045	0.053	0.165	0.131	0.123
Portugal [a]	0.056 [1974]	0.051	0.055	0.365	0.324	0.381
Spain [a]	0.089 [1972]	0.123	0.123	0.411 [1972]	0.398	0.314
Sweden [b]	0.029	0.027	0.031	0.159	0.107	0.124
United Kingdom [a]	0.019 [1972]	0.033	0.059	0.133 [1972]	0.150	0.158
Iceland [b]	0.048	0.026	0.044	0.175	0.133	0.138
Norway [b]	0.051	0.037	0.032	0.126	0.106	0.093
United States [a]	0.022	0.030	0.037	0.117	0.114	0.103
Japan [b]	0.153	0.120	0.070	0.265	0.200	0.137
Canada [b]	0.029 [1976]	0.032	0.040	0.097 [1976]	0.105	0.130
Australia [b]	0.039	0.051	0.089	0.119	0.131	0.123
New Zealand [a]	0.072 [1972]	0.080	0.127	0.135 [1972]	0.140	0.157
Average	0.070	0.068	0.075	0.217	0.196	0.189

Source: "BLISS Oeso Sectoraal". Note: business ownership rates are per total sector employment. Except for U.S., business owners include unpaid family workers. Labels [a] and [b] indicate that owner/managers of incorporated businesses are included ([a]) or excluded ([b]). In case data for the year 1970 are not available, the first year available in the data set is reported.

Total Employment

Data on total employment (in persons) are also obtained from OECD National Accounts 1983-1995 (country tables 15: employment of all persons). Total employment includes self-employed (including OMIBs and unpaid family workers) as well as employees. Again, where possible, missing data are obtained from other sources, including OECD Labour Force Statistics and the Dutch national accounts.

Real Value Added

Sectoral data on real value added are obtained from OECD National Accounts 1983-1995, country tables 12: gross domestic product by kind of activity. The value added data are transformed into data expressed in millions of purchasing power parities per US $ at 1990 prices. This enables valid comparison of value added between countries and over time. Again, where possible, missing data are obtained from various other sources, including *OECD Stan*, *OECD Statistical*

Compendium (on CD-ROM), and, for Portugal, unofficial statistics from the *Bank of Portugal*.[40]

3.3.2 Model Variables and Data Sources

The variables incorporated in the model have the following definitions and sources.

E : sectoral business ownership rate: number of business owners in sector as a fraction of total employment in sector. Counts of number of business owners and total employment are described in Section 3.3.1.

Y : sectoral GDP in purchasing power parities per U.S. $ in 1990 prices. This variable is described in Section 3.3.1.

YCAP : per capita GDP in purchasing power parities per U.S. $ in 1990 prices (macro level). The underlying variables gross domestic product and total population are from OECD National Accounts, Detailed Tables, and from OECD Labour Force Statistics, respectively. GDP is measured in constant prices. Furthermore, purchasing power parities of 1990 are used to make the monetary units comparable between countries.

U : (standardized) unemployment rate. This variable measures the number of unemployed as a fraction of total labor force. The labor force consists of employees, self-employed persons, unpaid family workers, military and unemployed persons. The main source for this variable is *OECD Main Economic Indicators*. Some missing data on the number of unemployed have been filled up with help of data from the OECD Labour Force Statistics and the *Yearbook of Labour Statistics* from the International Labour Office.

Y_share : sectoral GDP as fraction of macro GDP. Both sectoral GDP and macro GDP are taken from OECD National Accounts 1983-1995, country tables 12: gross domestic product by kind of activity. We correct for different value added definitions at *sectoral* level in different countries, i.e. market prices, factor costs, or base prices. The differences result from a different statistical treatment of the items import duties, value added tax, and other indirect taxes. For some countries these items are ascribed to sectors, while for other countries, they are not. We correct for this by taking GDP exclusive of these three items (i.e. the item 'Subtotal') as denominator of Y_share.

ΔWT : growth of world trade (yearly basis). These data are taken from Appendix A4 ("Kerngegevens 1970-2002") of the publication

---

[40] We are grateful to Jose Mata for providing us with the last-mentioned data.

Central Economic Plan (CEP) 2001, item "relevante wereldhandel",
by CPB Netherlands' Bureau for Economic Policy Analysis.

D_{ITA}: dummy for Italy: this variable has value one for Italy, and zero
otherwise.

D_{OMIB}: dummy for countries defining the number of business owners
inclusive of owner/managers of incorporated businesses (OMIBs):
this variable gets value one for the countries Belgium through New
Zealand (as mentioned in Section 3.3.1), and value zero for the
remaining countries.

3.4 Results

The current section is split up in two parts. In the first part we
present separate results for manufacturing and services. We also discuss
the methods employed to compute the regression models. In the second
part we present a model where business ownership rates in manufacturing
and services, as well as sector structure are assumed to simultaneously
explain growth at the macro level (growth of GDP per capita).

3.4.1 Methods and Sector Results

Equations (3.1) and (3.2) are estimated successively. For a given
specification of E^* (Equation 3.3a, 3.3b, 3.3c or 3.3d), we substitute the
expression into Equation (3.1). This leads to an expression which is
nonlinear in the parameters. Therefore we estimate the regression equation
using non-linear least squares.[41] After having estimated Equation (3.1),
we are able to compute E^*, and hence $\left|E^* - E\right|$, using the parameter
estimates of the equilibrium function (3.3). After computing $\left|E^* - E\right|$, we
are able to estimate Equation (3.2), using OLS.

When estimating the model, we weight observations with
population. We consider larger countries such as the U.S. and Japan to be
more important in establishing the relationship between business
ownership and economic growth than small countries like New Zealand
and Iceland. Weighting with population (in the year t-4) implies that all
variables (including constants and dummies) are multiplied with the
square root of population before the least squares procedure is run. A
more detailed description of the weighting of observations can be found in
Appendix 2.A. Both for manufacturing and services, the regressions are

---

[41] We use the LSQ command in TSP 4.5.

computed using unbalanced panels. This is caused by missing data for certain countries and years in our sectoral data base. Furthermore, as in Carree et al., uneven years are removed.[42] Our sample contains 245 observations for the manufacturing sector and 231 observations for services. For the exact construction of these samples we refer to the appendix. The estimation results are presented in Tables 3.2 and 3.3.

---

[42] The removal of uneven years has the advantage of diminishing the potential danger of a downward bias in the estimated standard errors of the coefficients that may arise due to overlapping observation periods for consecutive years. The key variables like business ownership rate and GDP per capita change only slowly over time. Hence, it is unlikely that the results will alter much in case the uneven years would have been included.

Table 3.2. Estimation results Model (3.1)-(3.2)-(3.3), Manufacturing (245 observations)

Eq. (3.1)+(3.3), dependent variable four-year growth of sectoral bus. own. rate

	Quadratic	Inverse	Log-quadr.	Log-invers
Error correction (b_1)	0.084	0.087	0.086	0.085
	(5.32)	(5.61)	(5.16)	(5.60)
Unemployment (b_2)	0.054	0.055	0.054	0.053
	(3.08)	(3.30)	(3.07)	(3.21)
Sectoral GDP share (b_3)	-0.039	-0.037	-0.038	-0.039
	(-2.71)	(-3.00)	(-2.59)	(-3.16)
OMIB-correction (b_{OMIB})	0.293	0.281	0.287	0.293
	(1.70)	(1.65)	(1.64)	(1.76)
Italy-correction (b_{ITA})	0.0083	0.0087	0.0086	0.0084
	(3.26)	(3.68)	(3.20)	(3.55)
α	0.320	1.40	0.697	1.10
	(3.79)	(4.27)	(1.27)	(4.29)
β	-0.019	1.36	-0.320	1.31
	(-1.69)	(4.07)	(-0.75)	(4.04)
γ	0.00041		0.042	
	(1.12)		(0.52)	
Adjusted R^2	0.302	0.305	0.302	0.305
LR Test $\delta = 0$ (5% crit. value 3.84)	0.076		0.118	
LR Test $\beta = \gamma = 0$ (crit. value 5.99)	0.056		0.117	

Eq. (3.2), dependent variable four-year growth of sectoral GDP

	Quadratic	Inverse	Log-quadr.	Log-invers
Constant (c_0)	0.145	0.143	0.144	0.145
	(2.67)	(2.65)	(2.66)	(2.68)
Deviation E from E* (c_1)	-0.454	-0.490	-0.479	-0.472
	(-3.77)	(-4.00)	(-3.95)	(-3.96)
GDP per capita (c_2)	-0.0012	-0.0011	-0.0011	-0.0011
	(-0.71)	(-0.63)	(-0.66)	(-0.68)
Sectoral GDP share (c_3)	-0.493	-0.497	-0.493	-0.488
	(-3.75)	(-3.79)	(-3.76)	(-3.72)
World trade (c_4)	0.410	0.411	0.409	0.406
	(1.89)	(1.90)	(1.88)	(1.87)
World tr., 2 year lag (c_5)	1.234	1.237	1.235	1.233
	(5.81)	(5.84)	(5.83)	(5.82)
World tr., 4 year lag (c_6)	0.559	0.564	0.563	0.562
	(2.85)	(2.89)	(2.88)	(2.88)
Adjusted R^2	0.446	0.450	0.449	0.449

EXTRA: Test of robustness

	Quadratic	Inverse	Log-quadr.	Log-invers
Deviation E from E* (c_1)	-0.252	-0.291	-0.280	-0.278
	(-2.46)	(-2.79)	(-2.72)	(-2.75)
Growth of empl. (c_7)	0.863	0.859	0.859	0.859
	(10.3)	(10.3)	(10.3)	(10.3)
Adjusted R^2	0.612	0.615	0.614	0.615

Note: T-values in parentheses. The extra equation uses the same control variables as Equation (3.2).

Table 3.3. Estimation results Model (3.1)-(3.2)-(3.3), Services (231 observations)

Eq. (3.1)+(3.3), dependent variable four-year growth of sectoral bus. own. rate				
	Quadratic	Inverse	Log-quadr.	Log-inverse
Error correction (b_1)	0.164 (9.11)	0.162 (8.98)	0.162 (9.01)	0.159 (8.79)
Unemployment (b_2)	0.111 (4.13)	0.093 (3.62)	0.106 (3.95)	0.088 (3.45)
Sectoral GDP share (b_3)	-0.003 (-0.14)	0.014 (0.94)	-0.001 (-0.04)	0.016 (1.04)
OMIB-correction (b_{OMIB})	0.130 (0.99)	0.307 (1.15)	0.129 (0.91)	0.383 (1.13)
Italy-correction (b_{ITA})	0.048 (9.21)	0.047 (8.95)	0.048 (9.16)	0.046 (8.77)
α	0.556 (4.80)	1.87 (5.13)	1.94 (3.60)	1.33 (4.42)
β	-0.050 (-4.83)	1.92 (5.29)	-1.22 (-3.25)	1.73 (4.64)
γ	0.0014 (4.04)		0.203 (2.88)	
Adjusted R^2	0.402	0.385	0.398	0.377
LR Test $\delta = 0$ (5% crit. value 3.84)		0.369	3.33	
LR Test $\beta = \gamma = 0$ (crit. value 5.99)		7.02	12.2	
Eq. (3.2), dependent variable four-year growth of sectoral GDP				
Constant (c_0)	0.173 (4.82)	0.163 (4.48)	0.172 (4.71)	0.162 (4.46)
Deviation E from E* (c_1)	-0.110 (-2.39)	-0.053 (-1.22)	-0.087 (-1.94)	-0.051 (-1.16)
GDP per capita (c_2)	-0.0051 (-3.75)	-0.0047 (-3.40)	-0.0051 (-3.66)	-0.0046 (-3.39)
Sectoral GDP share (c_3)	0.058 (0.73)	0.059 (0.74)	0.057 (0.71)	0.060 (0.75)
World trade (c_4)	-0.302 (-2.35)	-0.303 (-2.34)	-0.302 (-2.34)	-0.303 (-2.34)
World tr., 2 year lag (c_5)	0.405 (3.20)	0.417 (3.27)	0.410 (3.23)	0.417 (3.27)
World tr., 4 year lag (c_6)	0.374 (3.19)	0.390 (3.31)	0.382 (3.26)	0.391 (3.31)
Adjusted R^2	0.788	0.783	0.786	0.782
EXTRA: Test of robustness				
Deviation E from E* (c_1)	-0.051 (-1.19)	-0.0057 (-0.14)	-0.032 (-0.76)	-0.0030 (-0.075)
Growth of empl. (c_7)	0.542 (7.07)	0.559 (7.30)	0.549 (7.16)	0.559 (7.31)
Adjusted R^2	0.819	0.817	0.818	0.817

Note: T-values in parentheses. The extra equation uses the same control variables as Equation (3.2).

Equilibrium Equation (3.3)

In Tables 3.2 and 3.3 estimation results are given for the four different specifications of the sectoral equilibrium rate of business ownership (3.3a)-(3.3d). Based on likelihood ratio tests we try to identify which specification fits the data best. To test the quadratic specification versus the inverse specification, we estimate an additional equation (3.1), where the equilibrium function is now specified as $E_{ijt}^*=\alpha+\beta YCAP_{it}+\gamma YCAP_{it}^2+\delta YCAP_{it}/(YCAP_{it}+1)$. The quadratic and inverse specifications are special cases of this (artificial) function: the quadratic equilibrium function corresponds to $\delta=0$, while the inverse specification corresponds to $\beta=\gamma=0$. In other words, the quadratic and inverse models are *nested* in the model and, hence, standard likelihood ratio tests apply. This holds analogously for the log-quadratic versus the log-inverse model. The LR test statistics are given in the tables.

For *manufacturing* both null hypotheses $\delta=0$ and $\beta=\gamma=0$ cannot be rejected. This means that U-shaped equilibrium functions cannot be distinguished from L-shaped functions in a statistical sense. The inverse specification has the highest adjusted R^2 values, although the differences are small. The implied asymptotic value of 0.04 for this specification seems plausible. For *services* the likelihood ratio tests point in the direction of a U-shape: the null hypothesis $\delta=0$ is not rejected while the null hypothesis $\beta=\gamma=0$ is. This holds for both types of comparisons: quadratic versus inverse and log-quadratic versus log-inverse. So, after having reached a minimum level, the business ownership rate starts to rise again with increasing wealth (i.e. increasing GDP per capita). For the quadratic specification, the minimum $-\beta/2\gamma$ is reached at 18,129 U.S. dollar (1990 prices). The minimum business ownership rate equals 0.099. Based on this analysis, we will discuss the other estimation results for the specifications with the best statistical fit: L-shape for manufacturing (inverse or log-inverse) and U-shape for services (quadratic or log-quadratic).

Equation (3.1)

From Tables 3.2 and 3.3 we see that error-correction processes are statistically significant for both manufacturing and services. However, the speed of adjustment is low: 16% for services and 9% for manufacturing. A speed of adjustment of 16% means that a deviation of the number of business owners from equilibrium at a certain point in time decreases with 16% in the succeeding four years. The low value of the speed of adjustment is not surprising. The convergence process of the actual business ownership rate towards the equilibrium rate is intrinsically slow because it involves structural changes on the supply side (setting up enterprises, investments in physical and human capital, divestments, etc.) as well as cultural and institutional changes. As some of these processes are especially slow in manufacturing, the lower speed of adjustment for this sector compared to services is not surprising. For instance, it is more difficult to start a business in the manufacturing sector than in the service sector, because on average more start-up capital is required.

We find evidence for the unemployment push hypothesis. For services, every percent point rise in the unemployment rate leads to a rise of 0.11 percent point in the self-employment rate in the succeeding four years. For manufacturing this effect is 0.06 percent point. Again, the smaller effect for manufacturing may be explained by higher set-up costs for starting a new business. A significantly negative sign of sectoral GDP share (parameter b_3) is found only in case of the manufacturing sector. High shares of manufacturing in a country's economy are associated with subsequently lower business ownership rates. This may reflect the importance of economies of scale in manufacturing.

The estimated correction factor for the number of OMIBs, b_{OMIB}, is plausible, both for manufacturing and services. In the equilibrium functions, the number of OMIBs as a proportion of other self-employed (unincorporated self-employed and unpaid family workers) equals 0.28 and 0.13 for manufacturing and services, respectively. The additional (unexplained) rise in business ownership for Italy is supported by our estimations: parameter b_{ITA} is significantly positive. The effect is much stronger for services though: the parameter is about five times higher for services compared to manufacturing.

Equation (3.2)

According to the significantly negative estimate of c_1, deviations between actual and equilibrium business ownership rates come at a cost of forgone growth. The effect is stronger for manufacturing than for services. Each percent point difference between E and E^* is associated with a loss of 0.5 percent point subsequent growth in value added (on a four year basis) in manufacturing. For services this effect is only 0.1 percent point. This suggests that deviating from the "optimal" firm size distribution is more important for manufacturing when compared to services. Either having too few or too many entrepreneurial ventures in manufacturing appears to be more damaging to economic performance than when this occurs in the service sector. When there are too few entrepreneurs this may come at the cost of the rate of radical innovations and consequently, economic growth. When there are too many entrepreneurs economies of scale may not be benefited from enough. In Figures 3.1 and 3.2 it is shown that for manufacturing the number of business owners is generally too *low* (consistent with a lack of incentives to innovate), while for services the number of business owners is generally too *high*. The latter observation implies that in many countries there are a lot of 'marginal' entrepreneurs, whose efforts and energy could be allocated more effectively working as wage earners. This is especially true for Italy.

The estimations also find evidence for the convergence of countries: GDP per capita has a negative impact on subsequent growth (parameter c_2), although the effect is significant only for services. For manufacturing there is a regression-to-the-mean effect: the parameter of sectoral GDP-share (c_3) is significantly negative. For services the latter effect is not found. Finally, we find a significant positive impact of the growth of world trade on sectoral growth. Looking at the combined effect (the sum of parameters c_4, c_5 and c_6) the effect is larger for manufacturing. Again, this is not surprising, given the bigger orientation on export in this sector.

Test of Robustness

As a test of robustness, we also estimated the sector growth equation with employment growth included as an extra explanatory variable. See the last parts of Tables 3.2 and 3.3. Note that, by and large, we thus measure labour productivity growth instead of production growth. Although t-values become lower, the estimates of c_1 (growth penalty) remain negative. This gives us some confidence about the robustness of the growth penalty. The coefficient of employment growth c_7 is smaller than one, which suggests decreasing returns to scale. However, this is not necessarily the case. As employment is measured in persons, the low coefficient may reflect a relative increase in part-time workers (compared to full-time workers). This phenomenon may be stronger for services, considering the low value of the estimated coefficient c_7.

Equilibrium Curves

In Figures 3.1 and 3.2, we show the equilibrium curves and the actual data for the G7-countries. For the equilibrium curves we choose the specification with the best statistical fit: "Inverse" for manufacturing and "Quadratic" for services. For manufacturing, all G7-countries –except for Italy- are well below the "equilibrium" rate.[43] According to the significant negative parameter estimate of c_1 in Equation (3.2), these deviations from equilibrium are penalised in the form of lower growth rates. So,

---

[43] In Van Stel and Carree (2002) we provide additional empirical evidence for the validity of the equilibrium curve depicted in Figure 3.1. In particular, we show that allowing for *country-specific* (hence lower) equilibrium functions is unattractive, both statistically and theoretically. We find no growth penalty any more because structural differences between countries are removed and only time-specific deviations are left.

apparently, there are too few self-employed in the manufacturing industries. Perhaps the low numbers of competitors and new entrepreneurial initiatives result in a lack of innovation incentives and therefore, in lower growth rates. Japan and Italy have been relatively close to the equilibrium curve. According to our model, the relatively high business ownership rate for manufacturing in these countries has favoured economic growth.

Figure 3.1. Actual and equilibrium business ownership rate for G7 countries, 1970-1998, Manufacturing

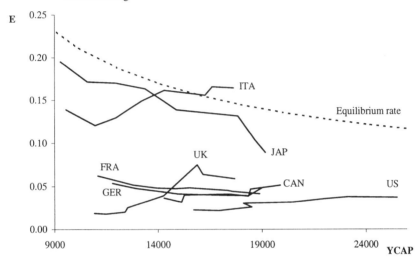

Note: Actual and equilibrium business ownership rates are per total sector employment. Business owners include unpaid family workers and owner/managers of incorporated businesses. Equilibrium rate according to "Inverse" specification in Table 3.2. Data for Japan and Canada are raised by the estimated factor $(1 + b_{OMIB}) = 1.281$ to facilitate valid comparison of E and E^*. Per capita income $YCAP$ expressed in purchasing power parities per U.S. $ at 1990 prices.

Contrary to manufacturing, the business ownership rates in most of the G7-countries are above equilibrium for services, the United States being the exception. The U-curved equilibrium function, which was clearly preferred over an L-shape, does not show in the actual business ownership rate data for the G7-countries. Only the United Kingdom and Canada have increasing business ownership rates. Note, however, that most countries still have levels of GDP per capita corresponding to the decreasing part of the curve. That is, they did not yet reach the per capita income corresponding to the minimum level of the parabola. For services, the business ownership rate of Italy lies far above equilibrium. The extremely low scale of operations in Italian service industries appears clearly sub-optimal. It suggests that the majority of these marginal self-employed individuals could work more effectively as wage-earners.[44]

Figure 3.2. Actual and equilibrium business ownership rate for G7 countries, 1970-1998, Services

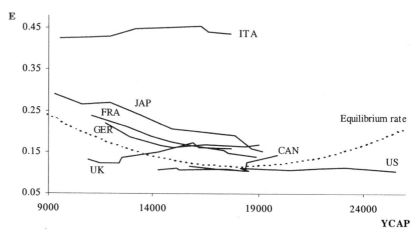

Note: Actual and equilibrium business ownership rates are per total sector employment. Business owners include unpaid family workers and owner/managers of incorporated businesses. Equilibrium rate according to "Quadratic" specification in Table 3.3. Data for Japan and Canada are raised by the estimated factor $(1 + b_{OMIB}) = 1.130$ to facilitate valid comparison of E and E^*. Per capita income $YCAP$ expressed in purchasing power parities per U.S. $ at 1990 prices.

3.4.2 Effect on Macro Growth

In the previous sections we analysed the relationship between business ownership and economic growth for manufacturing and services separately. We related deviations between the actual business ownership rate E and the equilibrium or optimal business ownership rate E^* in one sector to value added growth of that same sector. In this section we look at the effect of deviations at the sectoral level to growth at the macro level. In this way we can determine whether deviations in one sector are more harmful to growth than deviations in another sector. We also consider (deviations from the average) sector structure as a possible determinant of

---

[44] Note that the large distance from equilibrium for Italy (Figure 3.2) is consistent with the high value of the Italy-dummy in Table 3.3, while the small distance from equilibrium for manufacturing (Figure 3.1) is consistent with the low value of the Italy-dummy in Table 3.2.

economic growth at the macro level. In Table 3.4 we report the sector shares of manufacturing and services in economy-wide GDP for the 21 countries in our data set, for three years in the period 1970-1998.

Table 3.4. Sector share in total economy (GDP) for 21 OECD countries, 1970-1984-1998

Country	Manufacturing			Services		
	1970	1984	1998	1970	1984	1998
Austria	0.23	0.23	0.23	0.40	0.46	0.49
Belgium	0.22	0.23	0.21	0.52 [1976]	0.52	0.54
Denmark	0.20	0.21	0.17	0.46	0.44	0.45
Finland	0.22	0.23	0.29	0.34	0.37	0.38
France	0.25	0.24	0.22	0.41	0.47	0.51
West-Germany	0.38	0.33	0.27 [1996]	0.35	0.41	0.50 [1996]
Greece	0.17	0.17	0.14	0.37	0.41	0.47
Ireland	0.19 [1976]	0.21	0.30 [1994]	N.A.	N.A.	N.A.
Italy	0.18	0.21	0.22	0.42	0.47	0.50
The Netherlands	0.21	0.20	0.19	0.48	0.52	0.57
Portugal	0.21	0.23	0.26	0.48	0.43	0.48
Spain	0.23	0.23	0.21	N.A.	0.49 [1986]	0.50
Sweden	0.24	0.23	0.25	0.37	0.39	0.42
United Kingdom	0.30	0.23	0.20	0.45	0.46	0.53
Iceland	0.23 [1980]	0.20	0.16	0.39 [1980]	0.42	0.44
Norway	0.23	0.15	0.11	0.49	0.46	0.44
United States	0.20	0.18	0.22 [1996]	0.48	0.56	0.59 [1996]
Japan	0.26	0.26	0.27	0.42	0.48	0.53
Canada	0.20	0.19	0.18	0.38	0.44	0.48
Australia	0.18 [1974]	0.16	0.13	0.60	0.63	0.68
New Zealand	0.21 [1978]	0.22	0.18	0.51 [1978]	0.50	0.55
Average *	0.23	0.22	0.21	0.44	0.47	0.50

Source: EIM, based on OECD. Note: When 1970 or 1998 data are not available, the earliest or the most recent year available in the data set, are reported. *Excluding Ireland and Spain.

The Average Sector Structure

In order to investigate the effect of sector structure on economic growth we introduce the concept of an average sector structure. Like the sectoral equilibrium business ownership rate equations (3.3), we choose a specification in which sector structure is dependent on GDP per capita. Because the two sectors manufacturing and services comprise almost all economic activity in most countries, we simply use GDP share of services in a country's total GDP as indicator of sector structure. We choose a log-linear specification for the average sector structure function:

$$(3.4) \quad Y\_share_{i,services,t} = \varsigma + \eta \ln(YCAP+1)_{it} + \varepsilon_{3it},$$

where Y_share and $YCAP$ are as defined in Section 3.2, and ε_3 is a disturbance term. It is well-known that the share of services in an economy rises with GDP per capita. Hence, the expected sign of η is positive. As parameter ς is interpreted as the share of services when per capita income equals zero, this parameter should also be positive. Equation (3.4) is estimated as a separate equation (again using weighted least squares) and residuals are interpreted as deviations from the average sector structure.[45] Next, the absolute values of the residuals are inserted in the macro growth equation as an independent variable. Like deviating from an equilibrium business ownership rate, it could be the case that deviating from an average sector structure may hamper economic growth.[46] However, this is far from certain because countries might also benefit from "specialization".

For our macro growth equation we use the equilibrium relations with the best statistical fit found in Section 3.4.1: inverse for manufacturing and quadratic for services. Next we estimate Equation (3.4), to obtain a function for the average industry structure. Finally, the variables thus obtained (deviations for sectoral business ownership rates and industry structure) are used as independent variables in the macro growth equation. This equation reads as follows.

(3.5)

$$\frac{\Delta_4 YCAP_{it}}{YCAP_{i,t-4}} = c_0 + c_1 \left| E^*_{i,manuf,t-4} - E_{i,manuf,t-4} \right| +$$

$$c_2 \left| E^*_{i,serv,t-4} - E_{i,serv,t-4} \right| +$$

$$c_3 \left| Y\_share^*_{i,serv,t-4} - Y\_share_{i,serv,t-4} \right| +$$

$$c_4\, YCAP_{i,t-4} + c_5\, \overset{\circ}{WT}_t + c_6\, \overset{\circ}{WT}_{t-2} + c_7\, \overset{\circ}{WT}_{t-4} + \varepsilon_{2ijt}$$

where the subscripts *manuf* and *serv* stand for manufacturing and services, respectively, and where the variable Y_share^* is formed by the fitted values of Equation (3.4). Equation (3.5) is chosen such that results of our macro growth equation are comparable to the sector results presented earlier. In Equation (3.5) we explain macro-economic growth (growth of GDP per capita) from deviations between actual and equilibrium business ownership rate in both manufacturing and services.

---

[45] Because Equation (3.4) is estimated separately (i.e. not in an error-correction type of equation like (3.1)), the estimated function should not be interpreted as an equilibrium, but rather as an average.

[46] Empirical evidence of the impact of sectoral composition on economic growth can be found in Fagerberg (2000) and Carree (2003). They find evidence of countries which have a relatively large or growing share of the electronics industry to show relatively high subsequent productivity growth in manufacturing.

Furthermore we include deviations from the average industry structure as an independent variable. Results are presented in Table 3.5.

In Table 3.5, the results of the first estimated equation are taken from Tables 3.2 and 3.3. Based on these equilibrium functions, deviations between actual and equilibrium business ownership rates are calculated. These deviation variables are used in the third estimated equation, along with the deviation from the average industry structure (residuals of Equation (3.4)). The estimation results of this latter equation are also in Table 3.5. The statistical fit of the average sectoral GDP-share of services is high with an adjusted R^2 of 0.979. The estimated share of services in macro-GDP rises with per capita income as η is estimated to be positive.

Table 3.5. Estimation results Model (3.1)-(3.3)-(3.4)-(3.5), Macro level

Eq. (3.1)+(3.3), dependent variable four-year growth of sectoral bus. own. rate		
	Manufacturing: inverse case (245 observations)	Services: quadratic case (231 observations)
Error correction (b_1)	0.087 (5.61)	0.164 (9.11)
Unemployment (b_2)	0.055 (3.30)	0.111 (4.13)
Sectoral GDP share (b_3)	-0.037 (-3.00)	-0.0027 (-0.14)
OMIB-correction (b_{OMIB})	0.281 (1.65)	0.130 (0.99)
Italy-correction (b_{ITA})	0.0087 (3.68)	0.048 (9.21)
α	1.40 (4.27)	0.556 (4.80)
β	1.36 (4.07)	-0.050 (-4.83)
γ		0.0014 (4.04)
Adjusted R^2	0.305	0.402
Eq. (3.4), dependent var. GDP-share services in macro-GDP (227 observations)		
ς		0.011 (0.32)
η		0.171 (13.6)
Adjusted R^2		0.979
Eq. (3.5), dependent var. four-year growth of GDP per capita (227 observations)		
Constant (c_0)		0.307 (3.96)
Deviation E from E*, manufacturing (c_1)		-0.248 (-1.03)
Deviation E from E*, services (c_2)		-0.150 (-0.99)
Deviation from 'optimal' industry structure (c_3)		-0.329 (-1.04)
GDP per capita (c_4)		-0.011 (-3.64)
World trade (c_5)		-0.444 (-1.22)
World tr., 2 year lag (c_6)		-0.024 (-0.067)
World tr., 4 year lag (c_7)		-0.083 (-0.25)
Adjusted R^2		0.100

Note: T-values in parentheses. Estimations of Equations (3.4) and (3.5) include all observations for which data of manufacturing and services are simultaneously available.

Estimation of the macro growth equation (3.5) results in negative parameter estimates for all three deviation variables. However, absolute t-values are around one.[47] Although they are not significantly different from zero, the fact that all three coefficients are negative provides an indication that deviating from equilibrium business ownership rates or average sector structure might have a negative impact on per capita income growth. Of course, they are no more than indications because t-values are low.

3.5 Discussion

In this chapter we investigate the development of business ownership (self-employment) rates over time and the effect of business ownership on economic growth, both at the sectoral level. In an earlier exercise, Carree et al. (2002) presented a two-equation model to analyze the interrelationship between economy-wide business ownership rates and economic development. They apply the model to a data set of 23 OECD-countries for the period 1976-96. The paper showed empirical evidence for a (slow) error-correction process for business ownership rates: countries with business ownership rates more or less than the "equilibrium" value for the specific stage of economic development of these countries showed, on average, convergence towards the "equilibrium". In addition, it was found that the "equilibrium" relationship between business ownership rate and stage of economic development (as proxied by GDP per capita) was declining for the larger part of the range of GDP per capita but had the tendency to rise for the highest levels of GDP per capita. The study also provided evidence that countries that had an out-of-equilibrium value of business ownership rate suffered in terms of economic growth foregone.

The analysis performed by Carree et al. (2002) raises an important research question: to what extent do differences in business ownership at the economy-wide level reflect differences in the sectoral structures of economies or differences in business ownership rates at the sectoral level? It is well known that the average business ownership rate in the service sector is much higher than that in the manufacturing sector. Data in the current chapter show that the average rate (including unpaid family workers) for OECD-countries was almost 20% in 1984 for the service sector, while it was less than 7% for the manufacturing sector. This has important consequences for the analysis previously performed. The tendency of business ownership rates to increase may be due just to a shift of economic activity from the manufacturing sector towards the service

---

[47] This is not caused by multicollinearity as mutual correlations between the three variables are low.

sector in the course of economic development. As a consequence, the penalty found for deviating from the "equilibrium" value of (economy-wide) business ownership may really be a penalty for deviating from a certain structural composition of the economy. This study investigates the "equilibrium" relationship between business ownership rates and economic development, the speed of the error-correction process and the existence (and severity) of the growth penalty when deviating from "equilibrium" for both the manufacturing sector and the service sector for the OECD-countries in the period 1970-98.

The chapter develops an adjusted two-equation model relating business ownership rates and economic growth rates at the sectoral level. Specific attention in the model is paid to whether national statistical agencies have reported to include owner/managers of incorporated business into the data. Four different types of "equilibrium" relations between business ownership rate and GDP per capita are investigated, two of which have a U-shape (first declining and then rising ownership rates) and two of which have an L-shape (ownership rates continuously declining towards an asymptotic minimum rate). We have collected data for 21 OECD-countries for the years 1970-1998, as far as the data were available according to uniform definitions. The data show that, on average for OECD-countries, business ownership rates in manufacturing have been largely stable at 7%, while they have, on average, been decreasing for the service sector from 22% in 1970 to 19% in 1998. However, in several important industrial economies such as the United Kingdom, the United States, Canada and Australia, business ownership in manufacturing has gone up. Ownership rates in manufacturing remain lower than ownership rates in services though. This confirms that at least part of the increase in the economy-wide share of business ownership is due to the sectoral shift towards the service sector in developed economies.

Results show that the empirical fit of the four different types of "equilibrium" relationships is not too different, both for the case of manufacturing and that of services. However, results for the speed of error-correction are hardly affected by which type is chosen. The estimated speed of error-correction for the manufacturing sector is about 8.5% for a four-year period. This estimated speed is twice as high in the service sector: about 16%. Both in the manufacturing sector and for services there is a positive effect of (lagged) unemployment: countries with high unemployment show higher subsequent business ownership rates both in manufacturing and services. The results show that there is a significant penalty of the business ownership rate deviating from "equilibrium" for manufacturing for each of the four types of the "equilibrium" relationship. For the service sector also a negative effect on growth is found, but it is not always significant and it is far smaller than that for manufacturing.

The analysis confirms the empirical evidence provided by Carree et al. (2002) that differences in business ownership rates matter and disappear over time slowly. The general idea behind the model is that there can be both too many and too few businesses. Too many businesses may mean that economies of scale and scope are not benefitted enough from and that there are probably many "marginal" ventures. Too few business may imply that there is not enough entrepreneurial activity.

The results presented in the current chapter make a contribution to the international debate on increasing entrepreneurship as a route to economic growth. For instance, one of the major objectives of the *Global Entrepreneurship Monitor* research program is to gain more insight in the systematic relationship between entrepreneurship and national economic growth (Reynolds et al., 2002). Based on correlation analysis of nation-wide measures of entrepreneurship and economic growth, Reynolds et al. (2002) state that "evidence continues to accumulate that the national level of entrepreneurial activity has a statistically significant association with subsequent levels of economic growth" (p. 6).

The current analysis shows that entrepreneurial activity as far as embodied in self-employment rates *may* benefit economic growth, but is *not always* a route to growth. Our analysis suggests not only that economies can have too few or too many businesses, but also that the extent to which there are too many or too few businesses varies by sector. In particular, the estimated equilibrium curves suggest that having too few businesses is the more likely problem in manufacturing, while having too many businesses is the more likely problem in the service sector. It would suggest that, not only, the economic benefits of government promoting new (and small) business may be country-specific, but also sector-specific. Such promotion seems most beneficial in the manufacturing sector of countries with very low business ownership rates (like the Scandinavian countries). It may be counter-productive to have similar promotion in the service sector of countries with very high business ownership rates (like Italy).

3.A Appendix: Data Availability

The various estimations in this chapter were performed using data from the data base "BLISS Oeso Sectoraal". As this is an unbalanced panel, different numbers of observations per country are used for different estimations. The exact data per country used in the various estimations are reported in this appendix.

In Table 3.A the construction of the estimation samples used for the various estimations in this report is given. For manufacturing, there are 245 observations in total, and for services 231 (see Tables 3.2, 3.3 and

3.5). The maximum number of observations for a country is 13 (1974-98; only even years).[48] For countries having less than 13 observations the exact years available are reported in the table.

Table 3.A. Number of observations per country used for sector estimations

Country	Manufacturing		Services	
Austria	10	(1980-98)	10	(1980-98)
Belgium	13	.	10	(1980-98)
Denmark	13		13	
Finland	13		13	
France	13		13	
West-Germany	13		13	
Greece	12	(1976-98)	12	(1976-98)
Ireland	8	(1980-94)	-	
Italy	13		13	
The Netherlands	13		13	
Portugal	11	(1978-98)	13	
Spain	12	(1976-98)	5	(1990-98)
Sweden	13		13	
United Kingdom	12	(1976-98)	12	(1976-98)
Iceland	8	(1984-98)	8	(1984-98)
Norway	13		13	
United States	12	(1974-96)	12	(1974-96)
Japan	13		13	
Canada	10	(1980-98)	10	(1980-98)
Australia	11	(1978-98)	13	
New Zealand	9	(1982-98)	9	(1982-98)
TOTAL	245		231	

Note: Maximum number of observations is 13 (1974-98).

As we saw in Table 3.5, the number of observations used for the macro estimations is 227. This number is obtained by taking the intersection of the manufacturing and services samples. In Table 3.A, compared to the services sample of 231 observations, only for Portugal and Australia there are missing observations for manufacturing (viz. 1974 and 1976, for both countries).

---

[48] Note that in these cases the actual number of available years is 15 (1970-98), due to the four-year lag in the model.

Chapter 4

IMPEDED INDUSTRIAL RESTRUCTURING: THE GROWTH PENALTY

4.1 Introduction [49]

Explanations for economic growth have generally been restricted to the realm of macroeconomics (Romer, 1990; Krugman, 1991). However, a different scholarly tradition linking growth to industrial organization dates back at least to Schumpeter (1934). According to this tradition, performance, measured in terms of economic growth, is shaped by the degree to which the industry structure most efficiently utilizes scarce resources. But what determines this optimal structure? There is a long-standing tradition in the field of industrial organization devoted towards identifying the determinants of industry structure. As early as 1948, Blair stated that technology is the most important determinant of industry structure.[50] Scherer and Ross (1990) and Chandler (1990) expand the determinants of optimal industry structure to include other factors as well as the underlying technology. Dosi (1988, p. 1157), in his systematic review of the literature in the *Journal of Economic Literature*, concludes that "Each production activity is characterized by a particular distribution of firms."

When the determinants of the underlying industrial structure are stable, the industry structure itself would not be expected to change. However, a change in the underlying determinants would be expected to result in a change in the optimal industry structure. Certainly, Chandler (1990) and Scherer and Ross (1990) identified a shift in optimal industry structure towards increased centralization and concentration throughout

---

[49] This chapter is reprinted from: Audretsch, D.B., M.A. Carree, A.J. van Stel and A.R. Thurik (2002a), Impeded Industrial Restructuring: The Growth Penalty, *Kyklos* 55 (1), pp. 81-98, with kind permission of Helbing and Lichtenhahn Verlag (http://www.helbing.ch).

[50] See Blair (1948, p. 121): "The whole subject of the comparative efficiency of different sizes of business has long raised one of the most perplexing dilemmas in the entire body of economic theory....But a beginning must be made sometime in tackling this whole size-efficiency problem on an empirical basis. The first step in any such undertaking would logically be that of studying the underlying technological forces of the economy, since it is technology which largely determines the relationship between the size of plant and efficiency."

the first two-thirds of the previous century as a result of changes in the underlying technology along with other factors.

More recently, a series of studies has identified a change in the determinants underlying the industry structure that has reversed this trend. The most salient point of this change is that technology, globalization, deregulation, labor supply, variety in demand, and the resulting higher levels of uncertainty have rendered a shift in the industry structure away from greater concentration and centralization towards less concentration and decentralization. So, the industry structure is generally shifting towards an increased role for small enterprises. However, the extent and timing of this shift is anything but identical across countries. Rather, the shift in industry structures has been heterogeneous and apparently shaped by country-specific factors (Carree et al., 2002; Thurik, 1996). Apparently, institutions and policies in certain countries have facilitated a greater and more rapid response to globalization and technological change, along with the other underlying factors, by shifting to a less centralized industry structure than has been the case in other countries. An implication of this high variance in industry restructuring is that some countries are likely to have industry structures that are different from "optimal".

While the evidence suggests that the restructuring paths of industry vary considerably across countries, virtually nothing is known about the consequences of lagging behind in this process. Do countries with an industry structure that deviates considerably from the optimal industry structure forfeit growth more than countries deviating less from the optimal industry structure? This question is crucial to policy makers, because if the opportunity cost, measured in terms of forgone growth, of a slow adjustment towards the optimal industry structure is low, the consequences of not engaging in a rapid adjustment process are relatively trivial. However, if the opportunity cost is high the consequences are more alarming. The purpose of this chapter is to identify the impact of deviations in the actual industry structure from the optimal industry structure on growth.

In the second section of this chapter, the shift in industry structure away from more to less concentrated production is documented and underlying explanations provided. In the third section, we use a data base linking industry structure to growth rates for a panel of 18 European countries spanning five years to test the hypothesis that deviations from the optimal industry structure result in reduced growth rates. Finally, in the last section conclusions are provided. In particular, we find that deviations from the optimal industry structure, measured in terms of the relative importance of small firms, have had an adverse effect on economic growth rates.

4.2 The Shift in Industry Structure

A wide range of studies identified systematic evidence documenting two imposing characteristics of industry structure over the first two-thirds of the previous century (Scherer and Ross, 1990; Chandler, 1990). The first is that the degree of centralization of production was steadily increasing over time. The second is that production was at its highest point of centralization and concentration in the 1970s. This reflected underlying technological and demand characteristics rendering large-scale production and organization more efficient.

Until 1970s: Large Businesses as the Engine of Growth

Giant corporations were seen as the sole and most powerful engine of economic and technological progress in the early post war period. Schumpeter (1950) provided an image of large corporations gaining the competitive advantage over small and new ones and of giant corporations ultimately dominating the entire economic landscape. This advantage would be due to scale economies in the production of new economic and technological knowledge. These scale economies would result from the organization of teams of highly trained specialists working on technological progress in a routinized fashion. The large corporation was thought to have both superior production efficiency and superior innovative efficacy. Galbraith (1956) pointed out that in his world of countervailing power large corporations are superior to small ones in nearly every aspect of economic behavior like productivity, technological advance, compensation and job security. In his world all major societal institutions contributed to the maintenance of the stability and predictability needed for mass production. In these worlds of Schumpeter and Galbraith there is little room for small scale, experimenting firms thriving on the uncertainty of technological advance, whimsical markets and the individual energy of an obstinate entrepreneur. Only large industrial units were thought to be able to compete on global markets producing global products.

The exploitation of economies of scale and scope was thought to be at the heart of dictating an industry structure characterized by concentration and centralization (Teece, 1993). Chandler (1990) stresses the importance of investment in production, distribution, and management needed to exploit economies of scale and scope. Audretsch (1995) stresses the influence the image of the East-European economies and the perceived Soviet threat had on Western policy makers. An important concern in the late 1950s and early 1960s was the assumed strong technological progress emerging from huge and concentrated research and development programs being assembled in the Soviet Union and Eastern Europe. It was a period of relatively well-defined technological trajectories, of a stable demand and of seemingly clear advantages of diversification. Audretsch and Thurik (2001) characterize this period as one where stability, continuity and homogeneity were the cornerstones and label it the managed economy. Small businesses were considered to be a vanishing breed.

From 1970s on: Shift in Economic Activity toward Small Firms

Perhaps it was the demise of the economies of Central and Eastern Europe and the former Soviet Union that made it clear that concentration and centralization were no longer the cornerstones of the most efficient industry structure. At the same time, more and more evidence became available that economic activity moved away from large firms to small, predominantly young firms. Brock and Evans (1989) provided an extensive documentation of the changing role of small business in the U.S. economy. They were the first to understand these new developments filling the void of economic research concerning formation, dissolution and growth of businesses and concerning the differential impact of regulations across business size classes. The new role of small firms and their new interaction with large ones is described in Nooteboom (1994). Various authors have provided empirical evidence for this new role. Blau (1987) showed that the proportion of self-employed in the U.S. labor force began to rise in the late 1970s. Acs and Audretsch (1993) and Carlsson (1992) provided a survey of evidence concerning manufacturing industries in countries in varying stages of economic development. Acs (1996) shows that the self-employment rate in OECD countries declined until 1977 and increased between then and 1987. Carree et al. (2002) show that for a sample of 23 OECD countries the average business ownership rate increased from 9.6% in 1976 to 11% in 1996. See also Van Stel (2003).

There has been considerable documentation of the shift in the structure of American industry. Carlsson (1989) showed that the share of the Fortune 500 in total manufacturing employment dropped from 79% in 1975 to 73% in 1985. In the same period the share of these firms in total manufacturing shipments dropped from 83% to 78%. More recently, he shows that the employment share of the Fortune 500 dropped to 58% in 1996 and the latter to 75% (Carlsson, 1999). Unfortunately, similar documentation for Europe has not been possible due to the absence of systematic data that is comparable across countries. However, Eurostat has begun to publish yearly summaries of the firm size distribution of EU-members at the two-digit industry level for the entire private sector, see Eurostat (1994, 1996). The efforts of Eurostat are currently being supplemented by the European Network of SME Research (ENSR), a co-operation of 18 European institutes. This organization publishes a yearly report of the structure and the developments of the enterprise and establishment populations in the countries of the European Union.[51]

Explaining the Shift in Industry Structure

Carlsson (1992) offers two explanations for the shift in the industry structure away from large corporations and towards small enterprises. The first deals with fundamental changes occurring in the world economy from the 1970s onwards. These changes relate to the intensification of global competition, the increase in the degree of uncertainty and the growth in market fragmentation. The second deals with changes in the character of technological progress. He shows that flexible automation has had various effects resulting in a shift from large to smaller firms. The shift in the nature of technological progress particularly involving flexible automation facilitated product differentiation and led to a new division of labor involving more cooperation and less competition between large and small firms. Piore and Sabel (1984) argue that in the 1970s firms and policy makers were unable to maintain the conditions necessary to preserve mass production. Mass production was based upon the input of special-purpose machines and of semi-skilled workers and the output of standardized products. A fundamental change in the path of technological development led to the occurrence of vast diseconomies of scale. This market instability resulted in the demise of mass production and promoted flexible specialization. Piore and Sabel use the term *Industrial Divide* for the "reversal of the trend" from that toward more large firms to that toward more small ones. Jensen (1993) refers to the *Third Industrial Revolution* when describing the same phenomenon. Meredith (1987) discusses the advantages of a range of recently developed flexible production techniques for small-scaled enterprises. Audretsch and Thurik (2000) point at the role knowledge plays when explaining the shift from the managed economy to the entrepreneurial economy.

This shift away from large firms is not confined to manufacturing industries. Brock and Evans (1989) show that this trend has been economy-wide, at least for the United States. They offer four additional reasons as to why this shift has occurred: (1) the increase of labor supply; (2) changes in consumer tastes; (3) relaxation of (entry) regulations and (4) the fact that we are in a period of creative destruction. Loveman and Sengenberger (1991) stress the influence of two other trends of industrial restructuring: decentralization and vertical disintegration of large companies and the formation of new business communities. Furthermore,

---

[51] See the various editions of *European Observatory* which provide an account of the state of small business in Europe like, for instance, EIM/ENSR (1997).

they emphasize the role of private and public policies promoting the small business sector.[52]

The Effect of the Shift

The extent to which this shift in industry structure has influenced economic performance has received limited attention. This has to do with a persistent lack in knowledge of market structure dynamics (Audretsch, 1995). In other words, there is a lack in knowledge concerning questions like who enters and exits, what determines this mobility and what are its effects, in particular on economic performance. Here we are concerned with a key question in economics: why do industries or economies grow? As discussed earlier, traditionally, the prevalent assumption was that large enterprises are at the heart of the process of innovation and creation of welfare. This assumption is generally referred to as the *Schumpeterian Hypothesis*. Recently, the focus of attention has shifted towards whether the process of decentralization and deconcentration, which virtually every industrialized country has experienced in the last two decades, has had positive welfare implications. Audretsch (1995) calls this shift in orientation of our social-economic thinking 'the new learning'.

The link between the shift in the industry structure and subsequent growth can be investigated in two distinct ways. First, by investigating the range of consequences of the shift in the locus of economic activity. For instance, one may study whether this shift has been favorable to the rejuvenation of industries and the process of (radical) innovation.[53] Alternatively, one may focus on the importance of the role of small firms in enhancing competition.[54] A yet different perspective on the link between the shifting industry structure and performance has been to examine the relationship between small firms and job creation.[55] Lastly, the role of small firms as a vehicle for entrepreneurship has been the focal point for a series of studies. For example, Baumol (1990) provides an

---

[52] See also Carree et al. (2002) for a survey of the determinants of the shift away from a managed and toward an entrepreneurial economy. An important consequence of the shift in consumer tastes and the decentralization and vertical disintegration of large companies has been the increased share of the service sector. Because enterprises in the service sector are, on average, much smaller than in the manufacturing industry, this implies an increased share of small firms at the economy-wide level.

[53] See Acs and Audretsch (1990), Audretsch (1995) and Cohen and Klepper (1996).

[54] See Audretsch (1995), Oughton and Whittam (1997) and You (1995). Nickell (1996), Nickell et al. (1997) and Lever and Nieuwenhuijsen (1999) present evidence that competition, as measured by an increased number of competitors, has a positive effect on the rate of total factor productivity growth.

[55] Davis et al. (1996) and Carree and Klomp (1996) provide some insights in the relationship between small firms and job creation.

extensive account of the role that entrepreneurial activities and their consequences for prosperity play throughout history. Acs (1992) brings it all together in a short descriptive manner in a survey of some consequences of the shift of economic activity from large to smaller businesses. He claims that small firms play an important role in the economy as they are agents of change by their entrepreneurial activity, as they are a source of considerable innovative activity, as they stimulate industry evolution and as they create an important share of the newly generated jobs.

A second way to answer the question of how changes in the industry structure impact performance is to circumvent the intermediary variables of technological change, entrepreneurship, competitiveness and job generation to investigate a direct link between the shift and performance measures at the industry or economy-wide level. Some preliminary empirical results of the relation between changes in the firm size distribution and economic growth are presented in Thurik (1996). His analysis lacks a theoretical component but provides some indication of an increase in the economy-wide share of small firms positively affecting subsequent growth. Schmitz (1989) presents an endogenous growth model relating entrepreneurial activity and economic growth. An important implication of his model is that the equilibrium fraction of entrepreneurs is lower than the social optimal level, providing a rationale for policies stimulating entrepreneurial activity. Some evidence of a well-established historical (long-term) relationship between fluctuations in entrepreneurship and the rise and fall of nations is assembled by Wennekers and Thurik (1999). In this respect we also mention the work of Eliasson (1995) on economic growth through competitive selection. He demonstrates that such a relation may be characterized by significant time lags up to a couple of decades.

The evaluation of the various consequences of the shift in the locus of economic activity is necessary to establish whether it is desirable and whether it should be promoted by economic policy. However, this evaluation is complicated because none of these consequences is, in fact, independent of the other three and because the evaluation offers something of a series of trade-offs. Audretsch and Thurik (2001) contrast the most fundamental elements of the newly emerging entrepreneurial economy with those of the managed economy by identifying fifteen trade-offs that are essential for these two polar worlds. For instance, while total employment may rise due to new start-ups and declining average firm sizes, the lower average wages that small firms pay, may at least partly offset the welfare effect induced by the employment growth. By following the second way we are able to investigate whether there has been an *overall* growth-enhancing effect of the shift in the locus of economic activity from 'large' to 'small'. This is the subject of Section 4.3.

4.3 Estimating the Growth Penalty

In this section we test the hypothesis that the extent of the gap between the actual industry structure and the optimal industry structure influences subsequent growth. We start with the assumption that a country's growth can be decomposed into two components: (i) growth that would have occurred with an optimal industry structure, and (ii) the impact on growth occurring from any actual deviations from that optimal industry structure. This can be represented by

$$(4.1) \quad \Delta GNP_{cp} = \Delta GNP_{cp}^* - \gamma \left| SFP_{cp-1} - SFP_c^* \right|,$$

where the dependent variable is the actual rate of economic growth. ΔGNP_{cp}^* is the rate of economic growth in country c in the case where the actual industry structure, summarized by small firm presence (SFP_{cp}), is at the optimal level at the start of the period p. For ease of exposition we assume that the optimal industry structure in a country remains constant for the total period under investigation. This is not vital to our analysis. Since we are considering only short-term periods (maximum five years) this may be a reasonable assumption.

Industry structure is multidimensional and spans a broad array of characteristics that defy measurement by a single statistic. However, as explained elsewhere (Audretsch and Thurik, 2000, 2001), the most salient characteristic driving the shift in industry structure from the managed to the entrepreneurial economy is that the relative role of small and entrepreneurial firms has increased. Thus, we capture changes in industry structures by changes in the relative importance of small firms.

In Equation (4.1) the parameter γ is positive. Deviations of the actual industry structure from the optimal industry structure negatively affect economic growth, both when the industry structure consists of too few or too many small firms. In either case there is a deviation from the optimal industry structure and number of small firms. Taking the first difference of Equation (4.1) we obtain

$$(4.2) \quad \Delta GNP_{cp} = \Delta GNP_{cp-1} + \Delta\Delta GNP_{cp}^* - \gamma \left(\left| SFP_{cp-1} - SFP_c^* \right| - \left| SFP_{cp-2} - SFP_c^* \right| \right).$$

In case both SFP_{cp-1} and SFP_{cp-2} are above the optimal small-firm share, the expression between brackets reduces to ΔSFP_{cp-1}. Indeed, in case the small-firm share is too high, adding small firms to the industry structure reduces economic growth. In case both SFP_{cp-1} and SFP_{cp-2} are below the optimal small-firm share, the expression between brackets reduces to $-\Delta SFP_{cp-1}$. An increase in the small firm share when this presence is below optimal enhances economic performance. Therefore, the sign of the parameter of ΔSFP_{cp-1} reflects whether the small firm presence is below or above the optimal levels for the countries under consideration. In case the parameter is negative, the industry structure consists of too many small firms. In case the parameter is positive, the reverse holds and the industry structure consists of too few small firms.

We will denote the parameter of ΔSFP_{cp-1} as κ. Note that this is not the same parameter as γ, since the sign of κ is dependent on whether the actual small-firm share is above or below the optimal one. So, κ can be both positive and negative whereas γ is necessarily positive.

We make some further assumptions to transform Equation (4.2) into an equation that can be estimated using the data at hand. First, we approximate ΔSFP_{cp-1} by $\Delta SF_{cp-1} - \Delta LF_{cp-1}$, the difference between the growth of small firms and large firms in terms of value-of-shipments. Second, we assume that ΔGNP_{cp}^{*} is idiosyncratic with respect to time and country. Therefore country dummies and time dummies (the last to correct for European wide business cycle effects) are included. Thus, $\Delta\Delta GNP_{cp}^{*}$ is approximated by time dummies only because the country dummies drop out when taking first differences. Third, we add an error term e_{cp}. Summarizing we have

$$(4.3) \quad \Delta GNP_{cp} = \Delta GNP_{cp-1} + \sum_{p=1}^{P}\beta_{p}D_{p} + \kappa(\Delta SF_{cp-1} - \Delta LF_{cp-1}) + e_{cp},$$

where D_{p} denote dummy variables for periods $p = 1,...,P$. Factors specific to each time period are reflected by β_{p}. A high value of this parameter indicates an unexplained increase in the extent of economic growth. In case of a low β_{p} the reverse holds. The contribution of the shift in the size class distribution of firms to the percentage growth of GNP is represented by κ. The influence of this shift on GNP growth is lagged. This implies that $p = 1,...,P$ runs from 1990 through 1994 when applying Equation (4.3) to our European data set.

To estimate Equation (4.3), we use data provided by the *European Observatory* (EIM/ENSR, 1993, 1994, 1995, 1996, 1997). The European Observatory provides data on the annual percentage growth of real gross value added of the (non-primary) private sector, the annual percentage growth of value-of-shipments of small- and medium-sized firms (with employment less than 250 employees), as well as the annual percentage growth of value-of-shipments of large firms (with employment of at least 250 employees).[56] These data are available for five years (1989 through 1993) for all fifteen member countries of the European Union (Europe-15), Iceland, Norway and Switzerland (including Liechtenstein).[57]

Hence, our European data set consists of a total of 90 (18 countries times five years) observations. However, Germany had to be omitted for the entire period. Germany's then recent unification led to specific economic perturbations that render it inappropriate for inclusion in the estimation model. The remaining 85 observations are used for computing the regression coefficients. The lowest values of $\Delta SF_{cp} - \Delta LF_{cp}$ in the data set are -2.5%-point (Finland, 1993) and -1.8%-point (Norway, 1989), while the highest values are 2.1%-point (Finland, 1989) and 1.9%-point (United Kingdom, 1989). The mean value is -0.2%-point. The period 1990-1994 is characterized by relatively vehement cyclical movements with 1992 being a recession year and 1994 being a year with an exceptional strong recovery.

In Table 4.1 the regression results for the period 1990-1994 are presented. Equation (4.3) does not contain country dummies. The 'mean' country effect is reflected by coefficient α while D_{1991} is left out of all computations to avoid full multicollinearity.[58] The two dummy variables with a significant contribution are D_{1993} and D_{1994}. This reflects the strong economic recovery after the recession of 1992. We present both results with all time dummies included and with the two insignificant dummies excluded. In the first part of Table 4.1 weighted least squares results are presented, with total employment as the weighting variable. In the second part of the table ordinary least squares results are presented.

In each of the cases we find a significantly positive coefficient (at the 5% significance level) for κ. Its value ranges from 0.55 for the first column of Table 4.1 to 0.92 for the last column.[59]

---

[56] The European Observatory data are corrected for the so-called size distribution fallacy, i.e. the phenomenon that firms may cross size-class boundaries between year t and year t+1 (see e.g. Kleijweg and Nieuwenhuijsen, 1996).

[57] The European Observatory database is largely based on the Eurostat publication *Enterprises in Europe*, which contains harmonised information for each of the countries listed above on the number of enterprises, employment, turnover, value added and labour costs, by industry and size class. For some countries, estimates have been made in case of incomplete data.

[58] Instead of estimating coefficients for all P time dummies as suggested by Equation (4.3), we actually estimate P-1 dummy coefficients and a constant term α.

[59] To control for possible country selection effects, we have run the regression 17 times independently, each time with one country excluded from the sample and with a model specification with only dummies for the years 1993 and 1994 in Equation (4.3). The

The empirical evidence suggests that the consequences for economic growth of not shifting the industry structure away from large business towards smaller ones are rather large. However, this result is qualified by the large standard deviation of the coefficient for κ. Another important qualification to these results is that measurement of the variables includes a number of estimates. Follow-up studies are required for corroboration of these results.[60] Still, the estimated κ is found to be significantly positive in all computations. We conclude, based on the empirical findings, that there is evidence that on average those countries that have experienced a shift in their industry structures away from large firms and towards small firms have also experienced greater economic growth, at least for a sample of Western European countries over a recent time period. Since our interpretation is that this shift is an indicator of the stage of the transition of the economy from a managed one to an entrepreneurial one, we conclude that European countries that progress on this transition track seem to have been rewarded with additional growth. [61]

One has to be careful interpreting the estimation results for different countries. The estimated positive value of κ must be viewed as an average value of the (unobserved) κ_c's of the different countries. So, the positive value found for κ does not mean that in *all* countries in the sample an increase in small-firm presence is rewarded with additional growth. There may be countries in the sample where small-firm presence

---

estimates of κ range from 0.53 (t-value 1.71) to 0.68 (t-value 2.67) using weighted least squares and from 0.73 (t-value 1.63) to 1.01 (t-value 2.43) using ordinary least squares.

[60] Carree and Thurik (1998 and 1999a) provide complementary analyses showing the consequence of lagging behind in this restructuring process in manufacturing. Using a sample of 14 manufacturing industries in 13 European countries and 13 manufacturing industries in 12 European countries, respectively, they find that, on average, the employment share of large firms in 1990 has had a negative effect on growth of output in the subsequent four-year period.

[61] It is conceivable that there is reversed causality, i.e. that the degree of industry restructuring is dependent on the level of economic growth. To correct for business cycle effects, we estimate the following equation: $\Delta SF_{cp} - \Delta LF_{cp} = \mu + v \Delta GNP_{cp} + \varepsilon_{cp}$ for the period 1989-1993. The estimated residuals of this equation, $\hat{\varepsilon}_{cp}$, can be seen as the variable $\Delta SF_{cp} - \Delta LF_{cp}$, corrected for business cycle effects. Equation (4.3) is now estimated for the period 1990-1994 (note that there is lag in (4.3)), with $\Delta SF_{cp} - \Delta LF_{cp}$ replaced by $\hat{\varepsilon}_{cp}$. The estimate of v is 0.00 (t-value 0.01) using WLS and –0.04 (t-value –1.43) using OLS. As a consequence, the estimated value of κ in Equation (4.3) is the same as in Table 4.1 using WLS and is 0.62 (t-value 1.45) using OLS (only dummies for 1993 and 1994). After correcting for reversed causality, the estimate of κ equals 0.6 in all four versions of Table 4.1. We conclude that omission of the option of reversed causality hardly influences the size and sign of the effects as represented in Table 4.1.

is indeed above the optimal level and consequently, a further increase in the number of small firms leads to a growth penalty instead of a growth reward. The estimation results do indicate, however, that for the majority of countries in the sample, the number of small firms was too low in the period under consideration. In translating the positive value of κ in terms of implications for different countries, policy makers should compare small-firm presence in their own country with that in surrounding countries. If *SFP* is relatively low, small-firm presence may be expected to be below optimum, given the positive value of κ. On the other hand, if *SFP* is relatively high, small-firm presence might exceed optimum, despite the estimated κ being positive.

Table 4.1. Regression results for Equation (4.3): relating growth to structure[1,2]

	Weighted least squares[3]		Ordinary least squares	
α	-0.93	-0.79	-1.22	-0.97
	(-2.30)	(-3.38)	(-1.84)	(-2.56)
β_{1990}	0.52		0.39	
	(0.89)		(0.41)	
β_{1992}	-0.08		0.37	
	(-0.14)		(0.39)	
β_{1993}	1.32	1.20	2.19	1.94
	(2.26)	(2.50)	(2.32)	(2.53)
β_{1994}	4.35	4.25	4.72	4.48
	(7.40)	(8.74)	(4.91)	(5.65)
κ	0.55	0.63	0.91	0.92
	(2.14)	(2.58)	(2.20)	(2.27)
R^2	0.441	0.422	0.318	0.317
Adjusted R^2	0.406	0.401	0.275	0.291
DW	2.05	2.04	1.72	1.72
N	85	85	85	85

[1] Regression for 17 European countries over the period 1990-1994.

[2] DW is the Durbin-Watson statistic. T-values between parentheses.

[3] Weighting variable for WLS is total employment.

The regression results are illustrated using Figure 4.1. We have grouped the growth-acceleration observations, $\Delta\Delta GNP = \Delta GNP_{cp} - \Delta GNP_{cp-1}$, on the basis of the degree to which the value-of-shipments shifted from large to small firms. That is, the $\Delta\Delta GNP$ observations have been sorted in order of the values of the (lagged) structural change variable, $\Delta SF - \Delta LF$. Both variables have been computed in deviation of the mean per year in order to correct for specific year effects. The 85 sorted observations have been divided into five groups of 17 observations. The averages of both $\Delta SF - \Delta LF$ and $\Delta\Delta GNP$ are displayed in Figure 4.1. We see that, on average, a larger shift toward smallness is associated with a higher growth acceleration.

Figure 4.1. Growth accelerations and the relative shift toward small firms [1]

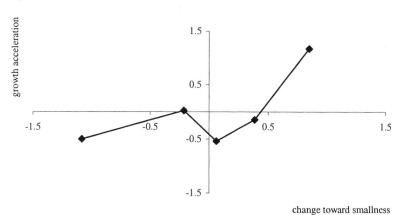

change toward smallness

[1] Averages of five groups of growth acceleration values ($\Delta\Delta$GNP), ordered on the basis of the degree of change toward small firms (ΔSF-ΔLF), both in deviation of yearly country-averages. Both axes are scaled in percentage points.

4.4 Conclusions

An extensive literature has linked the structure of industries to performance. However, little is known about the consequences of deviating from the "optimal" industry structure. The evidence provided in this chapter suggests that, in fact, there is a cost of not adjusting industry structure towards the "optimal". This cost is measured in terms of forgone economic growth.

Most developed countries have experienced a shift towards a more decentralized industry structure in the last several decades. The magnitude of this shift and speed of adjustment varies considerably across countries. The evidence suggests that those countries that have shifted industry structure towards decentralization in a more rapid fashion have been rewarded by higher growth rates.[62]

Our analysis is based upon whether excess growth of small firms over their larger counterparts has led to additional macro-economic growth for member countries of the European Union in the early 1990. The results of this investigation are meant to supplement the intuition of many policymakers that the changes in industrial structure have had some real effects on economic performance.

European public policy has been preoccupied with generating economic growth and reducing unemployment. The resulting policy debate has typically focused on macroeconomic policies and instruments. The results of this chapter suggest that an additional set of instruments may also be valuable in generating growth – policies focusing on allowing the industry structure to adjust. As the evidence shows, just as countries reluctant to shift their industry structures will be penalized by lower growth rates, those nations able to harness the forces of technology and globalization by transforming their industry structures are rewarded by growth dividends.

---

[62] Fagerberg (2000) investigates the impact of a different dimension of industry structure, that of the distribution of economic activity across (manufacturing) industries. Using data for a sample of 37 countries over the 1973-1990 period, he finds empirical evidence for increases in the shares of the electrical machinery industry (containing electronics) in the total manufacturing sector to positively affect productivity growth in manufacturing. Fagerberg argues it to be a consequence of this industry having the highest productivity growth (4.7% per annum), on average, of all manufacturing industries and of technological progress in electronics to spill over to other manufacturing industries.

Chapter 5

KNOWLEDGE SPILLOVERS AND ECONOMIC GROWTH

5.1 Introduction [63]

Spillovers occur if an innovation or improvement implemented by a certain enterprise increases the performance of another enterprise without the latter benefiting enterprise having to pay (full) compensation. In the past decades there has been increasing recognition that spillovers contribute substantially to economic growth. According to the new growth theory (Lucas, 1988; Romer, 1986), spillovers are the engine of growth. Mackun and Macpherson (1997) conclude that the relative importance of firms' in-house R&D compared to external technical activity may be declining. They suggest that external inputs (for example in the form of spillovers) can increase the productivity of in-house initiatives of firms.

There are various types of spillovers (transfers), viz. knowledge spillovers, market spillovers and network spillovers. [64] The new growth theory primarily focuses on knowledge spillovers (Aghion and Howitt, 1992; Aghion et al., 1997; Romer, 1986). Knowledge (obtained via, for example, R&D activities) accumulates, and this generates innovations in enterprises. Since enterprises benefit from each other's innovations and ideas, an economy may grow even in the event of maximum input of labour and capital. In other words, spillovers explain part of the phenomenon that economies grow faster than might be expected on the basis of labour and capital input growth. [65] The increasing role of knowledge and small firms in the modern economy (Audretsch and

---

[63] This chapter is reprinted from: Van Stel, A.J. and H.R. Nieuwenhuijsen (2004), Knowledge Spillovers and Economic Growth: An Analysis Using Data of Dutch Regions in the Period 1987-1995, *Regional Studies* 38 (4), pp. 393-407, with kind permission of Taylor and Francis Group (http://www.taylorandfrancisgroup.com).

[64] For an extensive elaboration, see Jaffe (1996). In the present chapter, the term spillovers denotes knowledge spillovers, unless stated otherwise.

[65] In the new growth theory, knowledge spillovers are considered an example of *(technological) external economies of scale*. For an individual firm, average costs per unit of output decrease with growing output at the *industry-wide level*. An increase in industry output increases the stock of knowledge through positive information spillovers for each firm, leading to an increase in output at the firm level (Van Oort, 2002, p. 42).

Thurik, 2000, 2001) motivates the investigation of the effect of knowledge spillovers, as small firms usually are more dependent upon knowledge spillovers than large firms are.[66]

Knowledge spillovers appear to be a local phenomenon (Audretsch and Feldman, 1996). Interaction between people and enterprises located in each other's proximity produce the highest likelihood of spillover effects. This seems surprising, considering the current state of information technology, where information can be diffused throughout the world at practically zero cost. Audretsch and Thurik (1999) refer to a paradox, which they explain by distinguishing between information and (tacit) knowledge. Information consists of facts and may be diffused simply and free of charge, with examples being the gold price in Tokyo, or the weather in New York. Knowledge, contrastingly, may not simply be coded. This is because knowledge is often highly specific in nature (think for instance of technical knowledge), and therefore difficult to transmit through formal means of communication. This makes that face-to-face contacts are important for the diffusion of knowledge. Knowledge diffusion primarily emerges by means of social contacts, for example during meetings or sales transactions.[67] It may also emerge in a more structured fashion, as part of public-private initiatives explicitly focusing on knowledge dissemination between clustering firms. We describe a case study of such an initiative in Section 5.2.

The contribution of knowledge spillovers to economic growth has been demonstrated by several authors (e.g. Griliches, 1992; Soete and Ter Weel, 1999). There are, however, various conflicting theories as regards the exact mechanisms of spillovers, with debates focusing on two questions. First, do spillovers primarily emerge within one sector or, alternatively, do spillovers emerge between different sectors? Second, how does local competition influence the amount of innovative activity and hence, economic growth?

The present chapter focuses on these questions, using a model of regional growth based on Glaeser et al. (1992). The model examines three possible determinants of regional sectoral growth, viz. specialization, diversity and competition. Specialization is hypothesized to facilitate spillovers between firms from the same sector, while diversity is hypothesized to facilitate spillovers between firms from different sectors.

---

[66] Some authors investigate the relation between various aspects of innovation and firm performance, while taking size-class differences in the relation into account. See e.g. De Kok (2002) and Folkeringa et al. (2004).

[67] The distinction between knowledge and information as used in this paragraph is also known in the literature as the distinction between tacit and codified knowledge or that between implicit and explicit knowledge.

The impact of specialization and diversity on growth, therefore, indicates the importance of *intra*-sectoral and *inter*-sectoral spillovers, respectively. The third variable, competition, may have both positive and negative effects on the amount of innovative activity and hence on economic growth. In fact, this involves a trade-off between internalization of innovation externalities (local monopoly) and the necessity to innovate to remain competitive in the market (local competition). By including local competition as a possible determinant of economic growth, this trade-off can be tested.

The model is estimated using data of 40 Dutch regions (spatial NUTS3 aggregation level), that provide information on the number of businesses, employment and real value added for six sectors, viz. mining, manufacturing, construction, the trades, transport&communication and financial services. The 40 regions cover the entire Netherlands. The data cover the period 1987-1995.

We remark that the present study focuses on inter-firm spillovers, i.e. knowledge spilling over between different firms. Our focus is not on knowledge produced by universities or public research institutions spilling over toward private firms. Wever and Stam (1999) show that for their sample of Dutch high technology SMEs, "by far the most important external innovation impulses came from other firms ... (instead of knowledge centres such as universities)" (p. 396).

The remainder of this chapter is set up as follows. In Section 5.2 three theories on knowledge spillovers and local competition are discussed. Also, to illustrate how spillovers may come about in practice, we describe a case study on 'knowledge-intensive industrial clustering' in the Netherlands. Section 5.3 outlines the model which the theories are tested with. Also the hypotheses to be tested, the construction of the model variables, and the differences between the present chapter and the study of Glaeser et al. (1992), are dealt with. Section 5.4 discusses the modelling of spatial externalities. Section 5.5 describes the data employed. In Section 5.6 we present the estimation results. The final section contains a summary and some conclusions.

5.2 Theory

The model of Glaeser et al. (1992) departs from the assumption that knowledge spillovers at the regional level are of major significance as regards innovation and economic growth. More precisely formulated, Glaeser et al. assume that sectors in different regions may have different growth rates because knowledge spillovers work out more effectively in one region than in another. This is because different *types* of knowledge spillovers may emerge in different regions, viz. *intra*-sectoral spillovers versus *inter*-sectoral spillovers. Furthermore, the intensity of local competition may differ between regions. The model examines three theories as to the impact of knowledge spillovers and local competition on regional growth. In this section these theories are discussed. Also, we describe how knowledge spillovers between firms may come about in practice, by means of a case study on 'knowledge-intensive industrial clustering'.

Three Theories on Knowledge Spillovers and Local Competition

The first theory is developed by Marshall (1890), Arrow (1962) and Romer (1986), abbreviated as MAR. They assume that knowledge spillovers are most effective between homogeneous enterprises. So, spillovers primarily emerge within one sector. For a given region, this would imply that specialization in a limited number of activities may contribute to spillovers and growth. An example of this type of within-industry spillovers would be the microchip manufacturing industry in Silicon Valley (Glaeser et al., 1992, p. 1130). The MAR economists further assume that the situation of a local monopoly is beneficial for economic growth, since in that case, the vast share of the yields generated by innovation benefits the innovator itself. That is, the externalities associated with innovation are internalized by the innovator. This would produce an additional incentive to innovate. In the MAR theory, regional sectoral growth is maximized if the sector is dominant in the region, and if local competition is not too strong.

The second theory is that of Porter (1990), who agrees with MAR that knowledge spillovers between firms in specialized sectors (sectors which are concentrated in certain regions) stimulate economic growth. In contrast to MAR, however, Porter assumes that local competition has a positive impact on growth. In his view, competition accelerates imitation and upgrades innovation. Although competition decreases the relative benefits for the innovator (due to larger spillovers flowing to competitors), the amount of innovative activity will increase, because enterprises are "forced" to innovate: enterprises that fail to improve products and production processes in due time will lose ground to their competitors and will ultimately go bankrupt. An example of fierce competition to innovate, resulting in growth, would be the Italian ceramics and gold jewelry industries (Glaeser et al., 1992, p. 1128). So, while MAR emphasize the negative effect of competition on the amount of innovative activity, Porter assumes that the positive effect is dominating.

The third theory elaborating on the significance of local knowledge spillovers was developed by Jacobs (1969). Jacobs' theory departs from the assumption that knowledge spillovers work out most effectively among enterprises that practise different activities. Primarily *inter-sectoral* knowledge transfers would thus be of significance. In her view, sectors will grow in regions where, besides the sector itself, various other sectors are important. In this philosophy, regions marked by a high degree of variety (diversity) will thrive.[68] As regards competition, Jacobs agrees with Porter, i.e. Jacobs assumes that local competition accelerates the adoption of new technologies and, consequently, stimulates economic growth.

Knowledge Spillovers in Practice: The Case of Océ [69]

The three theories discussed above all deal with the phenomenon of spillovers flowing between neighbouring firms. But how do these spillovers come about in practice? In the introduction to this chapter we already mentioned that face-to-face contacts are important, for example during meetings or sales transactions. However, this is still somewhat vague. As an illustration of how spillovers may work in practice, below we describe a case study on 'knowledge-intensive industrial clustering'.

In modern economies, many high-tech firms operate in highly competitive markets. In these markets it is crucial to constantly improve upon all parts of the production process. This is particularly important with the advent of low-cost but highly skilled competition in Central and Eastern Europe as well as Asia (Audretsch and Thurik, 2001). Therefore, in some regions, innovative clusters of high-tech firms are formed. Wintjes and Cobbenhagen (2000) describe the case of Océ, a high-tech multinational making specialised copy machines, located in the Eindhoven-Venlo region in the Netherlands. In this region, as a public-private policy initiative, a cluster of (small) local suppliers was formed around Océ with the purpose of benefiting from each other's expertise, by closely working together. Océ, whose core competence is product development (i.e. developing copy machines), outsourced their engineering tasks to the regional suppliers, thereby externalising part of the codification process to the region. The externalities were absorbed, accumulated and cultivated within the regional supplying firms. In this way these firms increased their innovative competences. In particular, the supplying firms, whose innovative capacity traditionally consisted of tacit knowledge built up by years of 'learning by doing', learned how to codify their knowledge. The supplier firms in the cluster used and socialised their tacit knowledge, in order to jointly transform a prototype of a new product or module into a manufacturable one. In this way, in its turn, Océ benefited from the supplier firms as these firms were now better equipped

---

[68] An example of this type of inter-sectoral spillovers would be the following: "A San Francisco food processor invented equipment leasing when he had trouble finding financing for his own capital; the industry was not invented by the bankers" (Glaeser et al., 1992, p. 1132).

[69] The remainder of this section is based on Wintjes and Cobbenhagen (2000).

to codify their tacit knowledge and communicate their codified knowledge to Océ. Wintjes and Cobbenhagen show that proximity is crucial in these kind of processes as "the restructuring of a codification process requires intensive communicative interaction between heterogeneous knowledge resources".

5.3 Model, Hypotheses, Variables, and Earlier Work

In this section the model to be estimated is described. Also the hypotheses to be tested, and the operationalizations of the variables specialization, competition and diversity, which are crucial in the model, are discussed. Finally, at the end of this section, we discuss the surplus value of this chapter with regard to the study of Glaeser et al. (1992).

Model

We use a simple model to test the three theories described above. The model assumes that each individual firm in a certain sector and region has a production function of output which depends on labour input and the overall level of technology. Each firm takes technology, prices and wages as given and sets labour input such that profits are maximized. Furthermore, the overall level of technology is assumed to have both national components and local components. Growth of *local* technology captures technological externalities present in the sector in the region. These externalities can be measured by variables such as specialization, local competion and diversity. Using these assumptions one can derive that growth in a sector in a region depends on wage growth, growth of *national* technology, and these measures of (local) technological externalities. For a formal derivation we refer to the Appendix to this chapter.

The above framework leads us to an equation that we can test empirically by means of regression analysis. The dependent variable is value added growth in a sector in a region. The explanatory variables are specialization (S), local competion (C) and diversity (D), and a constant term. The constant term captures both growth of *national* technology and wage growth (see Equations (5.A9)-(5.A10) in the Appendix). We thus assume a national labour market instead of a local one. By including S, C and D in the regression equation, the empirical validity of the various theories from Section 5.2 can be tested.

In our empirical application, regional sectoral economic growth is measured between 1987 and 1995. Growth is analysed at the mid-term (we use an eight-year period), since it is assumed that the effects of knowledge spillovers are not immediately observable. Newly obtained knowledge has to be implemented in existing structures, etcetera.

Obviously, economic growth cannot entirely be explained by the three variables S, C and D. Therefore, we employ a number of control variables, the most important being national sector-growth. This variable corrects for demand shifts. If the demand for products of a given sector changes (at the national level), then for a given region, the demand for the products of that sector is also likely to change. As a result, growth of that sector in that region will be affected. This has nothing to do with the spillover effects that we want to investigate, so we include *national* sector-growth as a control variable.[70] By including this variable, merely *regional* sector-growth is left to be explained. Indeed, regional sector-growth is exactly what we want to explain (given the assumption that knowledge spillovers are a local phenomenon). So, national sector-growth is a useful control variable. Besides, we also investigate whether there are region-specific effects not covered by the model. For this purpose, we include region-dummies. As the regional dummies *might* be interpreted as an indicator of *inter-regional* spillovers, we use dummies at various spatial aggregation levels to investigate the spatial extent of these inter-regional spillovers. This will be explained in Section 5.4. The model reads as follows:

$$(5.1) \quad \Delta y_{i,r} = \beta_0 + \beta_1 S_{i,r} + \beta_2 C_{i,r} + \beta_3 D_{i,r} + \gamma_1 \Delta y_{i,NL} + \sum_{k=2}^{K} \gamma_k R_k + \varepsilon_{i,r} \, ,$$

where:

Δy : average annual relative growth of real value added in the period 1987-1995

S: specialization in 1987

C: competition in 1987

D: diversity in 1987

R: region-dummy

i: sectoral index (i=1,..,6)

r: regional index (r=1,..,K; K dependent upon spatial aggregation level used)

β :   vector with parameters of main explanatory variables

γ :   vector with parameters of control variables

ε :   disturbance term

NL: indicator for The Netherlands

---

[70] The national sector-growth variable also controls for differences in internal production characteristics across sectors.

Hypotheses

The outlined theories of MAR, Porter and Jacobs as regards the effects of S, C and D may now be expressed in model hypotheses in terms of expected signs of the parameters β_1 to β_3. In MAR's theory, specialization has a positive effect on growth, and local competition a negative effect. According to Porter, both specialization and local competition positively affect growth. According to Jacobs, diversity as well as local competition generate positive effects on growth. In formulas (5.2a) to (5.4b), the various hypotheses are formally expressed in terms of null hypotheses H_0 and alternative hypotheses H_a:

(5.2a) $H_0: \ \beta_1 = 0,$ $H_a: \ \beta_1 > 0$ (specialization; MAR)

(5.2b) $H_0: \ \beta_2 = 0,$ $H_a: \ \beta_2 < 0$ (competition; MAR)

(5.3a) $H_0: \ \beta_1 = 0,$ $H_a: \ \beta_1 > 0$ (specialization; Porter)

(5.3b) $H_0: \ \beta_2 = 0,$ $H_a: \ \beta_2 > 0$ (competition; Porter)

(5.4a) $H_0: \ \beta_2 = 0,$ $H_a: \ \beta_2 > 0$ (competition; Jacobs)

(5.4b) $H_0: \ \beta_3 = 0,$ $H_a: \ \beta_3 > 0$ (diversity; Jacobs).

Note that the alternative hypotheses always assume a specific sign for the parameter value (positive or negative), hence the hypotheses have to be tested by means of one-tailed test procedures.

Operationalization of Variables

It is important how the variables specialization, competition and diversity are defined, as the estimation results of Equation (5.1) may be different for different variable operationalizations. The operationalizations employed in this chapter are discussed below. The three variables are defined at the spatial NUTS3 aggregation level (i.e. 40 regions for the Netherlands).

Specialization is defined as the employment share of the sector in the region, relative to the share of that sector in the whole country (in our case The Netherlands). If a sector is overrepresented in a region (relative to the national employment share of that sector), then there are larger-than-average opportunities for within-sector spillovers to emerge, and according to MAR and Porter, this would stimulate growth of that sector in that region. The expression of specialization (S) reads as follows:

(5.5) $S_{i,r} = \dfrac{Empl_{i,r} / Empl_{tot,r}}{Empl_{i,NL} / Empl_{tot,NL}}$,

where "Empl" stands for employment and "tot" for total. The value of the variable is expressed as a quotient in deviation from one, which figure corresponds to the national average employment share of the sector. Note that the value of S for a given sector is independent of the shares of the other sectors in the same region. That is, for a given region, small sectors may have larger values of S than large sectors. This is because we are only concerned with the relative extent of regional concentration for the sector under consideration. According to formula (5.5), there are many possibilities as regards within-sector spillovers if relatively many employees work in the same sector. This may be the case if in a sector a few relatively large enterprises operate, or, alternatively, if relatively many small enterprises operate.[71]

Competition is defined as the number of businesses in a sector in a region relative to the number of businesses in that sector in the whole country, adjusted for the size of the region. The (economic) size of a region is measured as total employment in that region. The variable assesses whether local (regional) competition is higher or lower than national competition. According to MAR, intensive local competition in a sector impedes economic growth in that sector. In case of intensive competition, MAR assume that enterprises limit their amount of innovative activities (e.g. by cutting down R&D expenses) because too much new knowledge spills over to competitors (i.e. externalities are considered too large). According to Jacobs and Porter, to the contrary, intensive local competition benefits economic growth, because enterprises are "forced" to innovate (the alternative being demise). The expression of local competition (C) reads as follows:

(5.6) $C_{i,r} = \dfrac{B_{i,r} / Empl_{tot,r}}{B_{i,NL} / Empl_{tot,NL}}$,

where B stands for the number of businesses. Local competition of sector i in region r is thus defined as the region-size-adjusted number of businesses in the sector relative to the nation-wide number of businesses in that sector. The value of the variable is expressed as a quotient in deviation from one, which figure corresponds to the nation-wide (adjusted) number of businesses in the sector.

---

[71] Of course, inter-firm spillovers can not occur if one very large enterprise were to operate alone. In that case, the specialization variable would have to be fixed at zero, considering that the variable is used as an indicator of the facilitation for intra-sectoral spillovers. Our dataset does not comprise such a case.

In our approach, specialization and competition are different concepts in that specialization deals with the clustering of workers while competition deals with the clustering of businesses (see formulas 5.5 and 5.6). Since the number of workers and the number of businesses may be positively correlated, the variables specialization and competition may also be correlated. In our dataset, the correlation between specialization and competition is 0.37. This value is low enough to ensure that our model outcomes do not suffer from multicollinearity.

For a given sector in a given region, *diversity* is defined as the employment share of the three smallest sectors in the *remaining* five sectors in the region, adjusted for the employment share in the region of those five sectors.[72] The first factor measures diversity of the region (excluding the sector of analysis). A larger share of the smallest sectors implies a more diverse sector structure. Adjustment for the employment share of the remaining five sectors is required, since large sectors can benefit relatively less from spillovers from the remaining sectors, plainly because these remaining sectors are relatively small compared to the (large) sector of analysis. In other words, assuming an identical structure of the remaining sectors, the potential to benefit from inter-sectoral spillovers is relatively higher for a small sector of analysis than for a large sector of analysis. According to Jacobs, higher degrees of diversity generate higher growth rates. The expression of diversity (D) reads as follows:

$$(5.7) \quad D_{i,r} = 100 \times \frac{\sum_{k=1}^{3} Empl_{-i[k],r}}{\sum_{-i} Empl_{i,r}} \times \frac{\sum_{-i} Empl_{i,r}}{Empl_{tot,r}} = 100 \times \frac{\sum_{k=1}^{3} Empl_{-i[k],r}}{Empl_{tot,r}},$$

where:

$Empl_{-i[k],r}$ Employment of kth smallest sector in region r, sector i excluded,

$\sum_{-i} Empl_{i,r}$ Total employment in region r, sector i excluded.

Formula (5.7) shows that the two factors may be rewritten as one expression: the share of the three smallest sectors (*excluding* the sector of analysis) in total regional employment (*including* the sector of analysis). The variable is expressed in percentages.

Diversity is not to be interpreted as the counterpart of specialization. High levels of specialization may coincide with high levels

---

[72] In this chapter, the (nonagricultural) economy is disaggregated into six sectors.

of diversity. A sector may be relatively dominant in a region, while at the same time the remainder of that region may be characterized by a high degree of diversity. However, because employment of the sector of analysis is part of the denominator in (5.7), there will be some negative correlation between the variables specialization and diversity. In fact, in our dataset, the correlation is -0.26. Again, this does not lead to multicollinearity problems.

Differences between Present Study and Glaeser et al. (1992)

There are several ways to specify the concepts of specialization (S), competition (C) and diversity (D) in model variables. Glaeser et al. (1992), choose an alternative operationalization of local competition. They use the number of businesses per worker for a sector-region combination relative to the number of businesses per worker in the entire sector (whole country). This variable measures the inverse average business size but this may not be appropriate as a measure of local competition.[73] Furthermore, if a positive effect of this inverse business size measure on growth is found, one may have found merely the effect that small firms grow faster than large firms. See for example Kleijweg and Nieuwenhuijsen (1996). Also for specialization and diversity there are alternative operationalizations. Some measures are discussed in Nieuwenhuijsen and Van Stel (2000), pp. 29-37. Besides the operationalizations of the variables S, C and D, there are also other differences between the present study and that of Glaeser et al. (1992). While they investigate employment growth in the United States in the period 1956-1987, the present chapter investigates value added growth in the Netherlands in a more recent, hence more knowledge-intensive period (1987-1995). Furthermore, while Glaeser et al. (1992), consider only large two-digit sectors, we consider firms from all sectoral sizes, albeit at a higher level of aggregation. Consequently, we also include small sectors, which -on average- have a relatively high small firm presence. This is important for the purpose of the present chapter, because small firms usually are more dependent upon knowledge spillovers than large firms are.

5.4 Modelling Spatial Externalities

---

[73] For example, for a given sector in equally large regions, the inverse business size measure cannot distinguish between regions with 100 businesses with on average 5 workers, and regions with 20 businesses, also with on average 5 workers. Clearly, competition is more intense in regions with 100 businesses. The operationalization (5.6) employed in this chapter takes account of that.

In a recently held specialist meeting on the state of the art in modelling spatial externalities, both *scale* (level of spatial aggregation) and *range* (extent of spatial interaction) in the measurement of economic phenomena were identified as important aspects of incorporating space in economic models (Anselin, 2003a).[74] In this section we discuss how we deal with these two aspects in our regression model.

First, we describe the spatial aggregation level at which we measure economic phenomena. Second, we describe a new method to model inter-regional spillovers. This involves the use of regional dummies at various spatial aggregation levels.

Investigating Intra-Regional Spillovers: Which Spatial Aggregation Level to Use?

In this chapter we use a database with sector-information at the spatial level of the 40 Dutch *Corop* regions, covering the period 1987-1995. The 40 regions cover the entire Netherlands. In terms of the international NUTS classification of regions, the *Corop* level corresponds to NUTS3 level.[75] This level is appropriate to assess intra-regional knowledge spillovers, because the *Corop* regions are constructed so that most regions are characterized by some degree of clustering. Furthermore, the scale of *Corop* regions is such that personal contacts *between* regions are likely to occur less frequently than personal contacts *within* regions. Therefore it is plausible to assume that the vast share of spillovers emerges within these regions. Some support for this assumption is provided by Oosterhaven et al. (2001). Using bi-regional input-output data they are able to identify both *intra*-regional and *inter*-regional clusters of interrelated economic activity. They focus on three regions, of which two are defined at the NUTS3 level (Greater Amsterdam and Greater Rotterdam) and one is defined at NUTS1 level (Northern Netherlands). Even for the smaller NUTS3 regions, they find a substantial number of *intra*-regional clusters, including the important sea and air transport sector in Greater Rotterdam.

Modelling Inter-Regional Spillovers

Although we argued above that the NUTS3 level is the appropriate level for investigating *intra*-regional spillovers, we acknowledge that there are also *inter*-regional knowledge spillovers. For

---

[74] The proceedings of this meeting are included in a special issue of the *International Regional Science Review*, Vol. 26, No. 2, April 2003.

[75] For the Netherlands, the NUTS1 classification distinguishes 4 regions (Northern, Eastern, Western and Southern Netherlands), while the NUTS2 classification distinguishes 12 regions (the 12 provinces of the Netherlands). The *Corop* or NUTS3 regions are still smaller.

instance, the above-mentioned study of Oosterhaven et al. (2001) also finds a number of inter-regional clusters, including linkages between Amsterdam business services and trade sectors on the one hand, and several other sectors in the rest of the Netherlands.

A common way of modelling spillovers between regions is using spatial econometric models. This often involves the use of a spatial weights matrix W, which allows for explicit modelling of the spatial dependence structure. Typically, the weights matrix consists of positive elements for "neighbouring" locations, and zero elements for other pairs of regions (Anselin, 2003b). In modelling space, various spatial process specifications circulate, involving the use of spatially lagged dependent variables (Wy), spatially lagged explanatory variables (WX), and/or spatially lagged error terms (Wu).

Concerning spatially lagged error models, different specifications correspond to different assumptions about the spatial extent of spillovers. Anselin (2003b) shows that the spatial covariance structure of the autoregressive model (SAR) corresponds to a *global* range of spatial dependence (all locations are related to each other) while the moving average model (SMA) corresponds to a *local* range of spatial dependence (only neighbouring locations within a limited number of "bands" are related).

Besides the specification of the spatial process, assumptions about the range of spillovers can also be reflected by the choice of the weights matrix W. However, the proper specification of the spatial weights matrix is not always obvious. In this connection, Fingleton (2003a) poses the question "what is the theoretical and empirical basis of assumptions about the spatial reach of externalities, and how can this be enhanced?" (p. 205). More generally, it is often difficult to make a well founded choice concerning the spatial dependence structure. Indeed, at the specialist meeting referred to earlier, it was concluded that "Space is seen as crucial in the conceptualization of interaction and externalities, but the way in which space is modeled requires further consideration" (Anselin, 2003a, p. 150).

We do not have an a priori assumption about the spatial extent of spillovers in the context of our regression model. Therefore, instead of using a spatial econometric model we choose a regional dummy approach to model inter-regional spillovers. Our method makes use of regional dummies at different levels of spatial aggregation, making the range of the spillovers an empirical matter rather than a theoretical one. This is explained below.

We compute regressions using regional dummies at the NUTS1 (4 regions), NUTS2 (12 regions) and NUTS3 (40 regions) levels, and using no regional dummies at all. Next, making use of a standard model selection procedure (Schwarz information criterion), we establish the most

adequate spatial aggregation level at which the regional dummies must be defined.[76] The selected aggregation level may be interpreted as the range or spatial extent of the inter-regional spillovers. This can be seen as follows. Formally, a significant parameter estimate of a regional dummy explains part of the variation in the endogenous variable that can not be explained by the other model variables. Now, when the regional dummy is defined at higher aggregation level than the level at which the 'regular' model variables are defined, a significant parameter estimate indicates that the underlying regions have 'something in common' that explains the regional variation in the endogenous variable.

For example, if the selection procedure chooses the specification with NUTS2 level dummies, then apparently real value added growth 1987-1995 at NUTS3 level is partly explained by a factor that is common for all NUTS3 regions within a NUTS2 region. As *intra*-regional spillovers are captured already by the variables specialization, competition and diversity, it is not implausible to assume that the NUTS2 dummies reflect, among other things, *inter*-regional spillovers flowing between firms from different NUTS3 regions within the same NUTS2 region.

In this line of reasoning, the spatial aggregation level selected by the Schwarz information criterion gives us an indication about the range of the inter-regional spillovers. For example, when a specification with NUTS2 dummies is selected, then apparently the NUTS3 regions are so uniform that the regional variations in economic growth not captured by the 'regular' model variables, can be explained by a common variable (i.e. a NUTS2 dummy). On the other hand the NUTS2 regions apparently are too different from each other to make a NUTS1 dummy specification appropriate. In terms of the range of spillovers, this example would be consistent with spillovers flowing between firms within *the same* NUTS2 region, but not with spillovers flowing between firms from *different* NUTS2 regions.

So, we model inter-regional spillovers by investigating four possible specifications (NUTS1, 2 or 3 level dummies, or no dummies at all). The unexplained variation in the endogenous variable that is common for adjacent NUTS3 regions is captured by a higher level regional dummy. However, a potentially important drawback of using dummies concerns the issue of multicollinearity which may nullify the significance of certain variables of interest. This may be the case especially when variables vary a lot across (larger) regions but not so much across smaller regions within the (larger) regions at which the dummy variables are defined. As Fingleton (2003b) points out: "In the extreme case, consider a

---

[76] The Schwarz information criterion weighs the statistical fit against the number of parameters. The lower the Schwarz information criterion, the more 'efficient' the model specification.

(hypothetical) variable which takes the same value in all regions within a given country, and which takes another value, which is constant across all regions in a second country, and so on across countries. It is then impossible to include this variable in the presence of country dummies because of aliasing due to perfect multicollinearity" (pp. 47-48). As it turns out, our estimation results do not suffer from this particular problem, as we will demonstrate in Section 5.6.

We acknowledge that our method is a second best solution to the problem of spatial interaction. Although it models interaction between regions to some extent (viz. in terms of distance), it does not take account of other types of interaction between regions. For instance, distant regions may interact more than neighbours because they contain important cities and are well connected by communications networks. This type of interaction between regions can be modelled by choosing a proper specification of a weights matrix, whereas these effects are not captured by our dummy approach. Nevertheless, we think that our method does enable straightforward interpretation of estimated coefficients for the *intra*-regional spillover variables specialization, competition and diversity in our model, which is the main interest of the present study.

5.5 Data

In this section we give a description of our data. The regional information is disaggregated into six sectors (excluding agriculture): mining, manufacturing, construction, the trades, transport&communication and financial services. The data are obtained from Statistics Netherlands (CBS) and the Netherlands Association of Chambers of Commerce (VVK). Table 5.1 illustrates the database variables adopted, as well as the respective source and the use in Model (5.1).

Table 5.1. Variables; source and use

Database variable	Years covered	Source	Use in Model (5.1)
Number of establishments	1987	VVK	Competition
Labour volume [1]	1987	CBS: Annual Regional Economic Data	Specialization, competition, diversity
Value added [2]	1987; 1995	CBS: Annual Regional Economic Data	Growth value added
Deflator value added	1987; 1995	CBS: National Accounts	Growth value added

[1] Number of full-time jobs.

[2] Gross value added at factor costs (current prices).

Nominal value added is deflated with help of a value added price index that is sector-specific, not region-specific. The deflator is derived from CBS National Accounts. For more information on the data employed, see Nieuwenhuijsen et al. (1999).

As we see from Table 5.1, enterprises are measured in terms of establishments. This may be a disadvantage, since one enterprise may consist of several establishments, and our study covers inter-firm spillovers and inter-firm competition.[77] The problem is limited though, since the number of establishments and the number of enterprises are highly correlated. Furthermore, we consider *local* competition in the model. Establishments of one firm operating in different regions is not contradictory with the concept of local competition. Since most enterprises operating several establishments probably have their establishments dispersed throughout several regions, the competition variable (5.6) is hardly affected by the use of establishments instead of businesses.

Basically, there are 240 observations available (viz. 6 sectors times 40 regions). However, a number of observations is not used in the determination of the parameter estimates. The sector mining is not used since in many regions there are no mining activities at all. For those regions with some form of mining activities, employment in this sector is

---

[77] In this chapter, we use the terms enterprises, firms and businesses interchangeably.

considered too small. Of the remainder 200 observations, 3 extreme observations (outliers) are removed, leaving 197 observations in the data set. The model is estimated on the basis of these 197 observations. Table 5.2 presents some characteristics of the data set employed.

Table 5.2. Characteristics of model variables (based on 197 observations)

Variable	Mini-mum	Maxi-mum	Average	Median	Standard deviation
Average annual growth real value added (%)	-3.22	9.93	2.84	2.84	2.14
Specialization (national average = 1)	0.43	1.90	0.98	0.95	0.27
Competition (national average = 1)	0.50	2.15	1.07	1.04	0.29
Diversity (%)	10.94	38.00	21.44	20.23	6.12

5.6 Estimation Results

In this section the estimation results are discussed. In the first instance, the model is estimated with data for all sectors included in the estimation sample. We call this the macro-estimation. However, we suspect that the spillover mechanisms may work out differently for different sectors of economy. Therefore, we also present estimation results for the sectors "Industry" and "Services" separately.

Macro Estimates

Model (5.1) is estimated with ordinary least squares (OLS) and the results are in Table 5.3. We have a sample of 197 observations (see Section 5.5). We estimated the four model variants described earlier, i.e. including regional dummies at NUTS1, NUTS2 and NUTS3 level (model variants (5.1b) until (5.1d) in Table 5.3) and no regional dummies at all (model variant (5.1a)). From the Schwarz information criterion we see that NUTS3 level dummies are not appropriate; model variant (5.1d) has the highest value. So, apparently, variations in value added growth not captured by the 'regular' model variables can be explained satisfactorily by higher level regional dummies. This indicates that adjacent NUTS3 regions have 'something in common' explaining growth, and, among other things, this may reflect inter-regional spillovers between firms from these adjacent regions.

On the other extreme, the specification which includes no dummies at all is also not appropriate, as model variant (5.1a) has the second highest value for the Schwarz information criterion. So, at least some regional variation in value added growth is explained by regional dummies, possibly indicating that inter-regional spillovers do not occur at a country-wide level, but rather are restricted to smaller areas.

Table 5.3. Estimation results Model (5.1), all sectors, dependent variable average annual growth real value added; 1987-1995 [1]

Explanatory variable (parameter)	Model (5.1a)	Model (5.1b)	Model (5.1c)	Model (5.1d)
Constant (β_0)	-1.17	-1.17	-1.90 **	-0.97
	(-1.39)	(-1.45)	(-2.45)	(-0.92)
Specialization (β_1)	-0.34	-0.25	-0.11	-0.056
	(-0.70)	(-0.56)	(-0.26)	(-0.13)
Competition (β_2)	0.71 *	0.70 *	0.59	-0.15
	(1.65)	(1.75)	(1.50)	(-0.27)
Diversity (β_3)	0.034 *	0.041 *	0.050 **	0.041 *
	(1.76)	(2.28)	(3.01)	(2.25)
Macro growth sector (γ_1)	1.09 **	1.08 **	1.08 **	1.05 **
	(12.0)	(12.9)	(14.0)	(13.5)
Number of observations	197	197	197	197
Regional aggregation level:[2]				
NUTS1 (4 regions)		X		
NUTS2 (12 regions)			X	
NUTS3 (40 regions)				X
R^2	0.469	0.547	0.640	0.713
Schwarz info criterion	379.3	371.7	370.2	422.0

[1] T-values between parentheses.
[2] The model specifications (5.1a) until (5.1d) use 0, 3, 11, and 39 regional dummies, respectively. Dummy coefficients are not reported due to space limitations.
* Significant at 5% level (one-tailed test).
** Significant at 1% level (one-tailed test).

Model variants (5.1b) and (5.1c) have the lowest Schwarz information criterion values, indicating that specifications which include regional dummies at NUTS1 or NUTS2 level are statistically most efficient. We will now focus on the results for the intra-regional spillover variables specialization, competition and diversity according to the statistically most efficient model variants (5.1b) and (5.1c).

Specialization

From Table 5.3, we see that the estimate of the specialization parameter has a negative sign in both the model variants (5.1b) and (5.1c). This finding is in contrast to the theories of MAR and Porter who predict a positive sign (see hypotheses 5.2a and 5.3a). However, absolute t-values are well below unity. We may conclude that the effect of specialization on (regional) economic growth is small or absent. That is, spillovers between homogeneous enterprises do not contribute significantly to economic growth. By and large, this finding is in line with Wever and Stam (1999) who find that regional clusters of high technology small and medium sized enterprises (SMEs) hardly exist in the Netherlands.[78] They find that, even in regions where high technology SMEs are overrepresented, most of the customers and suppliers that the interviewed high technology SMEs consider relevant for their innovative development are located outside their own region.

The finding that specialization has practically no impact on regional growth seems to contradict the experience that many regions are characterized by high levels of concentration of homogeneous enterprises. But many reasons other than growth opportunities may account for these high concentration levels. Marshall (1890) mentions the possibility to jointly utilize production factors (e.g. highly skilled staff). Henderson (1986) explains a high level of business concentration of a certain sector in a certain region by a relatively high demand for the products of that sector in that region, favouring business startups in such regions because of low transport costs. By and large, the above explanations state that specialization emerges because of the *static* efficiency thus achieved. The present study, however, investigates *dynamic* efficiency (i.e. growth). See also Glaeser et al. (1992), p. 1129.

Competition

The estimate of the competition parameter β_2 is positive in both model variants (5.1b) and (5.1c). We may conclude that MAR's theory on competition is rejected, see hypothesis (5.2b). Enterprises do not limit innovative activity out of fear that their efforts employed will spill over to competitors. Instead, the results seem to confirm the theories of Porter and

---

[78] Wever and Stam define a regional cluster as "a geographical concentration of firms which exhibit a significant degree of intraregional linkages" (Wever and Stam, 1999, p. 393). Like this chapter, they apply the spatial level of the Dutch *Corop* regions (i.e. NUTS3 regions).

Jacobs, i.e. enterprises innovate to a higher extent so as not to incur a backlog compared to competitors. The higher levels of innovation, in turn, lead to higher growth rates. The t-value of the estimate of β_2 is not high though. The parameter estimate is significant at 5% level (one-tailed test) in model variant (5.1b), but only at 10% level in model variant (5.1c). So, we must be cautious when claiming a positive relation between local competition and growth.

As regards the size of the effect, we compute the effect on average annual growth in percent points if competition were to increase by one standard deviation. We do this because the measurement unit adopted for the competition variable is not trivially interpretable (competition is expressed as a quotient in deviation from one), and standard deviations can be interpreted independently of the measurement unit employed. From Table 5.2, we see that the standard deviation of competition in our data set equals 0.29. The estimate of the competion parameter equals 0.70 (variant 5.1b estimate). So, a ceteris paribus increase of one standard deviation has an effect on average annual growth of $0.29 \times 0.70 = 0.20\%$-point.

Diversity

A diverse economic environment of a sector appears to have a positive effect on growth. The estimate of the parameter of diversity is significantly positive at 5% level in model variant (5.1b) and at 1% level in variant (5.1c). This result is consistent with Jacobs' theory on diversity. Higher degrees of regional diversity generate higher spillovers and, therefore, higher growth rates. As many different enterprise types as possible should locate in each other's proximity to enable enterprises to capitalize on ideas they do not develop themselves since they exercise very different business activities. According to the estimation results, a ceteris paribus increase of one standard deviation of the diversity variable has a positive impact of $6.12 \times 0.041 = 0.25\%$-point.

Multicollinearity Issues

For a proper interpretation of estimation results it is important that results are not influenced by model specification problems. In particular, in the context of our model, it is imaginable that certain non-significant results might have been caused by the inclusion of regional dummies, as we described in Section 5.4. When the dummies correlate strongly with the variables of interest, significance might be nullified due to multicollinearity (Fingleton, 2003b). However, our results do not suffer from this, as we will show below.

Consider Table 5.3. The effect of specialization is non-significant in all four variants, *including* variant (5.1a), in which no regional dummies are included. The non-significance is thus not caused by multicollinearity. For the competition variable we see that t-values are more or less the same for model variants (5.1a) until (5.1c) but significance is nullified in variant (5.1d). As in this variant regional dummies are defined at the lowest spatial aggregation level (39 dummy variables), it is likely that the non-significance is indeed caused by multicollinearity. However, as this variant turned out to be statistically inefficient (as indicated by a high value of the Schwarz criterion), we already left this result out of consideration in our interpretation. Finally, results for diversity are not affected by multicollinearity as the parameter estimate is significant in all four variants.

Sector Estimates

It is possible that the spillover mechanisms work differently in different sectors of economy. For example, knowledge spillovers may be more important in manufacturing industries than in service industries, given the –on average- higher levels of R&D in manufacturing. Therefore we want to analyze the different sectors of economy separately. However, it is not possible to obtain separate reliable results for each of the five sectors in our data set, because of too few observations. Therefore, we subdivide our data set in two larger sectors, viz. "Industry" and "Services". The industry-sector contains the observations of manufacturing and construction, while the services-sector contains the trades, transport&communication and financial services. Again, for both samples we computed the four model variants (5.1a) until (5.1d) described earlier. The estimation results are given in Table 5.4. To save space, for each sector we report only the two model specifications with the lowest value for the Schwarz information criterion. This involves variants (5.1a) and (5.1b) for Industry and variants (5.1b) and (5.1c) for Services.[79]

---

[79] As for the results at macro level, it can be shown that these results do not suffer from multicollinearity due to inclusion of regional dummies.

Table 5.4. Estimation results Model (5.1), industry and services, dependent variable average annual growth real value added; 1987-1995 [1]

Explanatory variable (parameter)	Industry: Model (5.1a)	Industry: Model (5.1b)	Services: Model (5.1b)	Services: Model (5.1c)
Constant (β_0)	-1.05	-0.43	-0.49	-0.35
	(-0.52)	(-0.23)	(-0.43)	(-0.33)
Specialization (β_1)	-0.076	-0.61	0.13	-0.30
	(-0.11)	(-0.94)	(0.18)	(-0.48)
Competition (β_2)	1.91 **	1.69 **	-0.44	-0.21
	(2.86)	(2.81)	(-0.81)	(-0.41)
Diversity (β_3)	-0.027	0.011	0.075 *	0.092 **
	(-0.44)	(0.20)	(1.92)	(2.48)
Macro growth sector (γ_1)	0.74 *	0.92 **	0.79 *	0.60 *
	(2.10)	(2.88)	(2.22)	(1.80)
Number of observations	80	80	117	117
Regional aggregation level:[2]				
NUTS1 (4 regions)		X	X	
NUTS2 (12 regions)				X
NUTS3 (40 regions)				
R^2	0.253	0.424	0.421	0.587
Schwarz info criterion	165.1	161.2	216.4	215.7

[1] T-values between parentheses.
[2] The model specifications (5.1a) until (5.1d) use 0, 3, 11, and 39 regional dummies, respectively. Dummy coefficients are not reported due to space limitations.
* Significant at 5% level (one-tailed test).
** Significant at 1% level (one-tailed test).

Table 5.4 illustrates that the results are indeed quite different for different sectors of economy. For the industry-sectors, competition appears to be of particular importance as regards realizing regional economic growth. For the service sectors, on the other hand, diversity appears to have a positive impact on growth.

These results may be interpreted as follows. In industry sectors, R&D expenses are relatively high in comparison with service sectors. Therefore, in industry sectors, growth mainly originates from the amount of firms' own innovative activities, rather than from inter-firm spillovers. Indeed, the estimates of the parameters of both spillover facilitating variables specialization and diversity have t-values below unity, while the estimate of the competition parameter is significantly positive (1% level, one-tailed test). So, in the industry sectors, if local competition is intensive, innovation and rapid adoption of new technologies is required for firms in order to not lose ground to competitors. That is, intensive competition encourages a process that could be characterized as an "innovation race".

In contrast to the industry sectors, knowledge spillovers seem to be important in the service sectors. It concerns spillovers between heterogeneous enterprises rather than spillovers between homogeneous enterprises. Diversity appears to have a positive effect on growth (parameter estimate is significant at 1% level; model variant (5.1c)), while specialization again has a very low t-value. Note that, given the construction of the diversity variable (see formula 5.7), the positive effect of diversity does not necessarily imply that service sectors benefit from spillovers from industry sectors. It is also possible that, for instance, the financial service sector capitalizes on ideas originating from the transport&communication sector. However, given the higher amounts of R&D in the industry sectors, it seems plausible that service sectors benefit from spillovers from industry sectors rather than from other subsectors within the service industries. The non-significant estimate of the competition parameter suggests that it is not crucial for enterprises in these sectors to generate many innovations by themselves. If they were to lag behind in that field, they will not directly incur a critical backlog compared to their competitors. The combination of non-significant parameter estimates for specialization and competition and a significantly positive estimate for diversity suggests that innovation processes in service industries are more or less accidental in nature: there appears to be little competition in innovation and few spillovers originating from within the own sector. Instead, innovations or improvements at firms in the service sectors seem to be dependent on innovation-generating firms (which apparently are in the industry sectors) located nearby. So, for service industries, a high degree of diversity is especially important.

5.7 Summary and Conclusions

In recent decades, the importance of knowledge spillovers for the processes of innovation and economic growth has been widely recognized. Firms can improve their performance by implementing innovative ideas that were not originally developed by themselves. In this way economies may grow without having to use additional labour and capital inputs.

Although the importance of knowledge spillovers is undisputable, little is known about the size of spillover effects and what type of spillovers is more important for achieving growth: spillovers emerging *within* sectors or spillovers emerging *between* sectors. Furthermore, the impact of local competition on innovation and growth is not straightforward. All these issues are investigated in the present chapter, using a regional growth model that is based on Glaeser et al. (1992). In the model mid-term growth at sectoral and regional level is explained by specialization, competition, diversity and some controls. By including these variables in the model, the empirical validity of three theories about knowledge spillovers and innovation can be tested.

The first theory is that of Marshall, Arrow and Romer (MAR). According to these economists, important spillovers primarily emerge among homogeneous enterprises, implying a positive impact of specialization on economic growth. As regards the role of competition, they assume a negative impact, due to the limited possibilities to internalize the externalities associated with innovation in case of fierce competition. The second theory is that of Porter. He assumes, like MAR do, a positive effect of specialization. As regards competition, however, Porter assumes a positive impact on growth, resulting from the sheer necessity for firms to innovate, as the alternative to innovation is demise. The third theory is developed by Jacobs. Like Porter, she assumes a positive effect of local competition. As regards knowledge spillovers, however, she emphasizes the importance of spillovers emerging among heterogeneous enterprises, implying a positive effect of diversity on economic growth.

We use a data set with information at six-sector level and at the spatial level of 40 Dutch (so called *Corop*) regions, covering the entire Netherlands. Regional data are used because geographical proximity is considered important, as face-to-face contacts are assumed a necessary condition for knowledge spillovers to occur.

We find no empirical evidence for a positive relationship between specialization and value added growth, suggesting that specialization contributes to static efficiency rather than to dynamic efficiency (i.e. growth). We find evidence for positive relationships between competition and value added growth and between diversity and value added growth. The empirical evidence supports the theory of Jacobs. It does not support the theories of Marshall, Arrow and Romer, whereas it is inconclusive regarding Porter's theory. The estimation results further imply that local competition is particularly important for achieving growth in the industry sectors while diversity is particularly important for achieving growth in the service sectors. By and large, this can be interpreted as intensive competition in the industry sectors encouraging an "innovation race", and high extents of diversity encouraging spillovers from industry sectors towards service sectors.

There are a number of limitations to our approach which makes that the results presented in this chapter should be interpreted with some caution. First, this chapter investigates only one type of spillovers, viz. knowledge spillovers. As mentioned earlier, there exist other types of spillovers such as network spillovers and market spillovers. The latter type emerges through mutual supplies between firms (for example if a firm purchases a computer). But it is safe to assume that these other types of spillovers do not have a specific regional character, as face-to-face contacts are not crucial for these types of spillovers. If we assume that the network and market spillovers are distributed randomly across regions, we may claim that the model picks up the effects of knowledge spillovers adequately, accounting for growth differences between regions.

Second, the sectoral aggregation level strongly determines the meaning of the variables specialization, competition and diversity. Interpretations of results are conditional upon the aggregation level applied. For example, as regards the competition variable, the question arises whether the six-sector classification adopted in this chapter is appropriate. By defining the entire manufacturing industry as one sector, one implicitly assumes that businesses in, for instance, the metal industry compete with businesses in the food industry. This is implausible. The high sectoral aggregation level even implies that a small proportion of the businesses within these broad sectors might be vertically linked firms instead of local competitors. However, assuming this proportion constant across regions, our competition variable still validly measures regional differences in the amount of local competition.

Despite these limitations, we argue that the present study provides some important insights concerning the effects of knowledge spillovers and innovation at the regional level. Future research should concentrate on performing comparable exercises for more countries as the results of the present study need to be confirmed for other countries as well. Policy makers may want to base policy measures concerning regional firm clustering on the empirical findings of more countries. Furthermore, as the sectoral aggregation level applied is crucial in this type of research, it may be worthwhile to perform the regressions while defining the variables specialization, competition and diversity at lower aggregation levels.

5.A Appendix: Derivation of Model

In this appendix we provide a mathematical derivation of Model (5.1), based on Glaeser et al. (1992).

Suppose that an individual firm in a certain sector and region has a production function of output, f, which depends on labour input, l, and technology, A, as follows:

(5.A1) $f(A,l)=Al^{1-\alpha}, \quad 0<\alpha<1.$

Each firm takes technology, prices, and wages, w, as given and maximizes profits with respect to labour input at time t:

(5.A2) $\max_{l_t} f(A_t,l_t)-w_t\,l_t\,.$

The first order condition reads:

(5.A3) $f'(A_t,l_t)=w_t$, where f' represents the partial derivative with respect to l.

We can rewrite (5.A3) in terms of growth rates as

(5.A4) $\log\left(\dfrac{f'(A_{t+1},l_{t+1})}{f'(A_t,l_t)}\right)=\log\left(\dfrac{w_{t+1}}{w_t}\right).$

This can be rewritten as

(5.A5) $\log\left(\dfrac{A_{t+1}}{A_t}\right)-\alpha\log\left(\dfrac{l_{t+1}}{l_t}\right)=\log\left(\dfrac{w_{t+1}}{w_t}\right).$

The level of technology, A, in a certain sector and region is assumed to have both national components and local components:

(5.A6) $A = A_{local}\,A_{national}$

The technological growth rate will then be the sum of the growth of national technology in the sector and the growth of local technology:

(5.A7) $\log\left(\dfrac{A_{t+1}}{A_t}\right)=\log\left(\dfrac{A_{local,t+1}}{A_{local,t}}\right)+\log\left(\dfrac{A_{national,t+1}}{A_{national,t}}\right).$

The growth of national technology is assumed to capture the changes in the price of the product as well as shifts in nationwide technology in the sector, and the local technology is assumed to grow at a rate exogenous to the firm but depending on the various technological externalities present in the sector and the region. These externalities can be measured by variables such as specialization, local competition and diversity. See Equation (5.A8).

$$(5.A8) \qquad \log\left(\frac{A_{local,t+1}}{A_{local,t}}\right) = g(specialization, local\ competition, diversity) + \varepsilon_{t+1},$$

where ε represents a disturbance term.

Combining (5.A5), (5.A7) and (5.A8), we obtain the following equation:

$$(5.A9) \qquad \alpha \log\left(\frac{l_{t+1}}{l_t}\right) = -\log\left(\frac{w_{t+1}}{w_t}\right) + \log\left(\frac{A_{national,t+1}}{A_{national,t}}\right) + $$
$$g(specialization, local\ competition, diversity) + \varepsilon_{t+1}$$

Assuming that both wage growth and growth of national technology do not differ across regions, Equation (5.A9) implies that employment growth in a sector and region can be explained by a constant and the variables specialization, local competition and diversity.

Next, because the dependent variable in our model is *value added* growth and not *employment* growth, we will show that value added growth in a sector and region can also be explained by a constant and the variables specialization, local competition and diversity.

Growth of production (value added) can be written as

$$(5.A10) \qquad \log\left(\frac{f(A_{t+1}, l_{t+1})}{f(A_t, l_t)}\right) = \log\left(\frac{A_{t+1}}{A_t}\right) + (1-\alpha)\log\left(\frac{l_{t+1}}{l_t}\right).$$

Making use of Equations (5.A7)-(5.A9) and the above mentioned assumptions about wage growth and national technology growth, Equation (5.A10) implies that *value added growth* in a sector and region can be explained by a constant and the variables specialization, local competition and diversity.

Finally, because we estimate our regression equations using pooled data, i.e. regions times sectors, we must control for region- and sector-specific influences. For this we use regional dummies and national sector-growth, respectively. In this way we arrive at Model (5.1) in Section 5.3. This equation can be estimated using OLS.

Chapter 6

THE LINK BETWEEN FIRM BIRTHS AND JOB CREATION

6.1 Introduction [80]

This chapter examines the relationship between new-firm startups and employment change in Great Britain. This relationship is of considerable policy importance, since national and sub-national governments in Britain have, for more than two decades, sought to raise business startup rates in order to enhance wealth- and job-creation. An example of a central government policy was the Enterprise Allowance Scheme (EAS). At its peak in 1987-88, public expenditure on EAS was virtually £200 million, subsidising more than 106,000 unemployed people to start a new business (Storey, 1994). A second example is the Business Birth Rate Strategy initiated in Scotland in the early 1990s, which sought to raise new-firm formation rates. A third example was the Entrepreneurship Action Plan for Wales announced in 2001. Finally, in 2004, the UK government announced that "building an enterprise culture" and "encouraging a dynamic start up market" are the first two of the seven pillars of small business policy. The assumption of a strong positive relationship between increased new-firm startup rates and subsequent employment growth underpinned all such policies.

This chapter tests for that underpinning. It begins by presenting the theoretical arguments for the presence of a relationship between startups and job creation, going on to provide an overview of current evidence. The central theme is that, with the exception of a recent paper by Audretsch and Fritsch (2002) for Germany, the relationship between startups and job creation has previously been examined either with no time-lag or with only a short period lag.

The current chapter claims to make seven advances on prior work. First, to construct and use a long-run (1980-98) data set that facilitates a valid comparison between the results for Great Britain and Germany. A second innovation is the explicit choice of variables. It argues that the appropriate measure of new firm formation is the sectorally adjusted

---

[80] This chapter is reprinted from: Van Stel, A.J. and D.J. Storey (2004), The Link between Firm Births and Job Creation: Is there a Upas Tree Effect?, *Regional Studies* 38 (8), pp. 893-909, with kind permission of Taylor and Francis Group.

number of private sector new firms, normalised by the sectorally adjusted working population. It also argues that the appropriate measure of employment change is the sectorally adjusted private sector employment. Third, it incorporates, for the first time, data on private sector wages in the locality. Fourth, the chapter explicitly incorporates various tests for misspecification which virtually all models pass. Fifth, the chapter explicitly corrects for multicollinearity caused by strong intertemporal correlations between startup rates for different periods. Sixth, it utilises the concept of the "Upas Tree" to see whether Scotland and Wales differ from England in the relationship between startups and job creation. Seventh, it links the findings to changes in Enterprise Policy both for the UK as a whole and for Scotland in particular.

The key results in the chapter call into question the impact of policies seeking to raise new firm formation, so as to enhance employment creation, particularly in areas where new firm formation rates are low. Specifically we find that, in the 1980's when national public policy was focussed on raising new firm formation, there is no evidence that this led to increased employment creation during that decade. Furthermore, although it is non significant for the UK as a whole in the 1980's, it is significantly negative for the North East of England, an area with notably low rates of new firm formation.

In the 1990's, when UK national policy shifts away from stimulating new firm formation, a positive relationship emerges between firm formation and employment creation. Crucially, however, in Scotland which implemented a policy to stimulate new firm births in the 1990's, a significant negative relationship between new firm births and employment creation appears in this decade, although our data do not extend sufficiently in time to imply that Scotland's business birth rate policy led to lower employment.

6.2 The Issues

This section reviews the theoretical basis for believing a relationship exists between the extent to which a geographical area is "entrepreneurial" and the extent to which it is "economically successful". We show there are a priori reasons for expecting a positive relationship, but that there are also reasons for expecting no relationship or, in extreme cases, a negative relationship.

There are three reasons why more "entrepreneurial" areas might generate more jobs- where jobs are a measure of "economic success". The first is that if "entrepreneurial" is reflected in "new-firm formation" then these new firms themselves create jobs directly and so add to the stock of jobs. The second is that the new firms constitute a (real or imagined) competitive threat to existing firms, encouraging the latter to perform better (Disney et al., 2003). Finally, new firms provide a vehicle for the introduction of new ideas and innovation to an economy, which has been shown to be a key source of long-term economic growth (Romer, 1986). Indeed Audretsch and Thurik (2001) argue that the role of new firms in technological development has been enhanced by a reduced importance of scale economies and an increasing degree of uncertainty in the world economy, creating more room for innovative entry.

The reasons for not expecting firm formation rates to be related to job creation are also three-fold. The first is that new firms directly contribute only a very small proportion of the stock of jobs in the economy (5.5% of the stock of UK employment in 1989 was in firms that had been born in the previous two years; Storey, 1994). Secondly, innovation is very much the exception rather than the rule amongst new firms. For example, during the 1990s, twice-yearly Surveys were taken of (primarily) small firms in the West Midlands.The proportion of firms claiming to have introduced a product or service new to the marketplace in the prior twelve months varied from 4% to 17% (Price Waterhouse Coopers, 1999). Third, the scale of job creation in new firms varies considerably from firm to firm. Storey and Strange (1992) show that 2% of all new firms created 33% of jobs in new firms, reflecting the extent of skewness in the distribution of employment. This skewness is taken to reflect differences in the human capital of founders (Frank, 1988) or their ability to learn (Jovanovic, 1982). For these reasons job creation, even in new enterprises, may be more strongly influenced by the human capital of the founders, than by the absolute number of startups (Cooper et al., 1989; Van Praag and Cramer, 2001).

The case for a negative relationship between new firm births and subsequent job creation derives from examining policies to stimulate new firm formation in "unenterprising" areas. Since these are frequently areas where human capital is low, the new firms tend to be in easy to enter sectors such as vehicle-repairing, window cleaning and hairdressing (Storey and Strange, 1992). Subsidising entry means entrants temporarily have a competitive advantage over incumbents who are forced out of business. Once the subsidy is removed, the no-longer subsidised entrants may be forced out either by newly subsidised entrants or by re-entrants. The effect of this 'churn' is to lower customer confidence leading to lower expenditure and hence lower employment (Greene et al., 2004).

6.3 The Evidence

Prior empirical studies of the relationship between "entrepreneurship" and "economic success" have adopted different approaches, yielding different results. Three studies, albeit using very different dependent and independent variables, find a positive relationship. Reynolds et al. (2000) examine the relationship across 21 countries between "Total Entrepreneurial Activity" and per cent growth in GDP. They show that "Entrepreneurship is strongly associated with economic growth. Amongst nations with similar economic structures, the correlation between entrepreneurship and economic growth exceeds 0.7 and is highly significant" (p. 1). Second, Johnson and Parker (1996) find "robust evidence that growth in births (and reductions in deaths) *significantly* lowers unemployment" (p. 686; original emphasis). Finally, taking the period 1981-89, Ashcroft and Love (1996) find new-firm formation to be strongly associated with net employment change in Great Britain.

Fritsch (1996), however, obtains more ambiguous results. In a pioneering study that can be considered as the fore-runner to this study, he examines 74 (former) West German planning regions, 1986-89. He finds "a positive statistical relationship between entry rates and employment change for manufacturing in the longer run, ...(but)... this relationship proves to be negative for the service sector as well as for all sectors together" (Fritsch, 1996, p. 247). A recent paper by Audretsch and Fritsch (2002) provides new insights for (West) Germany. Taking the same 74 planning regions, they present three key findings. First, confirming the Fritsch (1996) findings, startup rates in the 1980s are found to be unrelated to employment change. Second, in the 1990s, those regions with higher startup rates have higher employment growth. Third, and perhaps most interesting, is that regions with high startup rates in the 1980s had high employment growth in the 1990s.

In summary therefore the evidence to date generally points to a significant and positive relationship between new firm formation and measures of employment creation. There seems no prior empirical support for a negative relationship, although some non-significant relationships have been found.

6.4 Modelling Issues

The relationship to be modelled is of the simple form in Equation (6.1) below:

(6.1) $\Delta EMP_t = f\left(BIR_{t-1}, CON\right),$

where ΔEMP_t = change in employment,

BIR_{t-1} = firm birth rate at start of period,

CON = vector of control variables.

Choice of Measures

Whilst, in principle, the model is simple to estimate there are five clear problems of definition. The first relates to the measure of BIR to be used. Given that the units of account are geographical areas that vary in size, BIR needs to be normalised by a size measure. The denominator should both control for the different absolute sizes of the regions concerned, and represent the source from which startups or firm formations are most likely to come (Ashcroft et al., 1991). The two variables normally used as denominators are the stock of existing firms, and the size of the regional workforce (Keeble et al., 1993). This is called the Business Stock (BS) approach and the Labour Market (LM) approach, respectively. The BS approach assumes new firms arise from existing ones, whereas the LM approach assumes that new firms arise from (potential) workers. The choice of measure can be highly significant. For example, for a given number of startups, regions which are equally large in terms of workforce but which are different in terms of average firm size, will have the same startup rate according to the LM approach but different startup rates according to the BS approach. Garofoli (1994) makes a robust case in favour of LM over BS. The latter, he argues, is misleading in areas with small numbers of (generally large) firms. Here small numbers of new firms would provide an artificially high birth rate, primarily because of the small denominator. Audretsch and Fritsch (1994) also show that, in West Germany, the statistical relationship between unemployment and startup activity crucially depends on the BS or LM methods used to measure startup rates.[81] We favour the Garofoli arguments and in this chapter present only results from the LM approach.[82]

Lags

The second key problem relates to the lag structure specified in Equation (6.1). The case for the lag is that the employment impact of new firms is not likely to be immediate. Storey (1985), for example, shows that new manufacturing firms are generally eight or nine years old by the time they reach their peak employment, at which time they are about twice the size they were at the end of Year 1. However, because of their high exit

---

[81] In Audretsch and Fritsch (1994) the business stock approach is called the ecological approach.

[82] Analyses comparing the LM and BS approach are in Van Stel and Storey (2002). In that paper we also pay extensive attention to some other empirical matters discussed later in this section, such as the sector adjustment of the startup rates and the impact of public sector employment on regression results.

rates, total employment in a cohort of new firms is lower in Year 5 than in Year 1. This means that the maximum employment impact of a cohort depends on the scale of these two influences and is an empirical, rather than theoretical, issue.

The above discussion is framed in terms of simple arithmetic, but more complex social processes could also influence the lag. For example, new businesses started in time period t may stimulate the formation of other new firms in period t+1. This may be because the t period firms constitute a market for the t+1 firms; alternatively the success of the t firms could stimulate individuals to seek to emulate them, so the t firms become "role-models". In turn, the t+1 firms stimulate more firms in later time periods, with the result that employment in that economy in t+n is stimulated. Theory, again however, is not helpful in specifying the value of n.

Nevertheless, the above theoretical arguments discourage the use of contemporaneous startup rate variables in the model, i.e. employment change in period t being explained by new-firm startups in period t. Although correlations might be significant, the implied causal relation from births to (immediate) employment growth is potentially misleading. Positive correlations between startup rates and growth in the same period are often due to reversed causality, i.e. regions with high growth attracting new firms.[83] In our empirical work we will include lagged startup rates only, but the precise nature of that lag is the subject of tests.

Sectoral Comparisons

A third problem relates to differences in industrial structure between regions. This raises the question of whether the different sectoral structures of regions should be taken into account, since this influences both the number of startups and also employment change. Taking only the difference between services and manufacturing, startup rates are higher in service industries than in manufacturing (Audretsch and Fritsch, 2002), partly because entry barriers are lower, Minimum Efficient Scale (MES) is also likely to be lower and, for some services, demand is high. For all these reasons, regions with a high share of services in the local economy are more likely to have higher startup rates than regions with a low service share.

But this does not necessarily mean these regions are also more "entrepreneurial", in the sense that startup rates are higher for each sector of the local economy (or most sectors of the local economy). Therefore, to correct for different sectoral structures, the Ashcroft et al. (1991) shift-share procedure is applied to derive a measure of sector-adjusted startup

---

[83] Even if there is a lag in this reversed causality process, the measured correlation is often still positive, because of path dependency in the growth performance of regions.

activity. The sector-adjusted number of startups is defined as the number of new firms in a region that can be expected to be observed if the composition of industries was identical across all regions. Thus, the measure adjusts the raw data by imposing the same composition of industries on each region (Audretsch and Fritsch, 2002). An identical process is used to derive a measure of sectorally adjusted employment change. Appendix 6.A1 provides an illustration of the shift-share procedure.

Another sector issue concerns the impact of the public sector on estimated model coefficients. Ideally, analysis should be restricted to private sector enterprises and private sector employment. Unfortunately, however, both private and state-owned enterprises can be present within some SIC groups. Furthermore, SIC groups with a relatively large employment share of public sector organizations (such as universities and hospitals) may disturb estimations as changes in public sector employment may create a bias in the estimated employment effect of new-firm startups. Therefore, we eliminate SIC groups dominated by state-owned enterprises or other public sector organizations from our analysis.[84]

'Control' Variables

A fourth issue relates to the choice of control variables (CON) used in Equation (6.1). In addition to the sectoral composition effects, noted above, previous studies have shown urban and rural areas differ in both employment change and in new-firm formation rates. In their review of regional variations in firm birth rates, Reynolds et al. (1994b) pointed to urban areas consistently having higher formation rates in the 1980s than non-urban areas. Employment change, however, has been more mixed, with an urban-rural shift in the 1970s and 1980s (Fothergill and Gudgin, 1979) but a more mixed picture in more recent times (Green and Turok, 2000). Account of urban/rural differences is taken by the inclusion of a population density variable, and by Standard Region dummies.[85]

Another control factor is the nature of the labour market, reflected in local wage rates. Rees and Shah (1986) assume the welfare maximising individual chooses between utility in self-employment compared with paid employment, for which wages are taken as the proxy. Hence rises in

---

[84] This involves SIC92 industries L, M, and N (Public administration, defence and compulsory social security; Education; and Health and social work, respectively) for post-1991 data, and SIC80 industry 9 ("other services") for pre-1991 data; we utilise data according to different SICs before and after 1991, see Tables 6.A2b and 6.A3 in Appendix 6.A2.

[85] According to Audretsch and Fritsch (2002, p. 120), who also use population density as a control in their regressions for Germany, "Population density here represents all kinds of regional influences such as availability of qualified labour, house prices, local demand and the level of knowledge spillovers".

wage rates would be expected to lead to movements into wage-employment and out of self-employment, consistent with a positive effect on employment change (which in the present study is defined to include employees only). Furthermore, wage rises may also stimulate labour supply which could also lead to increased employment at the regional level. However, there is also a possible negative effect as a higher price of labour may lead to a lower demand for labour (substitution between capital and labour).[86] These opposite effects make the sign of wage rates indeterminate from theory.

A further control factor relates to the issue of reversed causality discussed earlier. Even if we include lagged startup rates only, the employment impact of new-firm startups might be overestimated, due to positive path dependency in the economic performance of regions (i.e. the business cycle effect). We correct for this by including lagged employment growth.[87]

Public Policy and Region-Specific Effects

The 1980's and 1990's saw radical changes in Enterprise Policy in the UK. Greene (2002) argues that the decade of the 1980's saw, following the election of a Conservative government in 1979, the first explicit attempt to create an enterprise culture in Britain. Policy was directed towards maximising the number of new business starts so as to achieve this 'enterprise culture' and to seek to create jobs so as to offset the high levels of unemployment. In the 1990's, however, British policy changed towards a focus on established business with "growth potential". This we refer to as the policy effect.

In addition we also argue for the presence of region-specific effects reflecting the major cultural differences, within Great Britain, in attitudes towards enterprise and self-employment. We call this the Upas Tree effect. The term was originally used by Checkland (1976) to describe economic change in the city of Glasgow, and was derived from a description of the Upas Tree that was native to Java. According to legend, the Upas Tree was able to destroy other growths for a radius of 15 miles, and Checkland viewed it as analagous to the destructive effect that the

---

[86] For a selection of European countries, Van Stel (1999) estimates the real wage elasticity (the response of labour demand on an exogenous rise in real wages at constant output level and price of capital) to lie between –0.2 and –0.4 in the period 1970-1994.

[87] The concept of using lagged dependent variables to correct for reversed causality is known in the econometric literature as Granger-causality. The Granger (1969) approach to the question of whether x causes y is to see how much of the current y can be explained by past values of y and then to see whether adding lagged values of x can improve the explanation. y is said to be Granger-caused by x if x helps in the prediction of y, or equivalently if the coefficients on the lagged x's are statistically significant (Audretsch et al., 2005).

heavy engineering sector had upon the growth of other industries in Glasgow for much of the twentieth century.[88] We use it to characterise Scotland and Wales, both of which appear to have a long-standing antipathy to "entrepreneurship", but also North East England (McDonald and Coffield, 1992; Greene et al., 2004).

However, the policy and the region-specific effects interact with one another. This is because, whilst Britain as a whole, in the 1990's, was shifting its policy away from a focus on business start-ups, Scotland explicitly chose the opposite policy. It established a "business birth rate" strategy (Fraser of Allander Institute, 2001) the focus of which was to raise new firm formation in that country. Account therefore has to be taken of these very different policy environments in Britain in 1980's and 1990's and of the differences between Scotland and the rest of Britain in the 1990's.

We investigate the impact of new firms on employment change separately for the 1980s and the 1990s to see whether effects differ between these two decades. We also incorporate slope dummies for Standard Regions to see whether effects for certain regions deviate from the overall effect for Great Britain.

6.5 Variables and Data Sources

The data used is at the spatial aggregation level of NUTS3 regions in Great Britain.[89] This is county level in England and Wales, and local authority region level in Scotland. In this partitioning, Great Britain comprises 60 regions, each disaggregated by six sectors. This facilitates correction for sectoral differences between regions, i.e. to apply the shift-share procedure described earlier. Different regional and sectoral classifications in the original data files meant some linking operations were performed to ensure uniformity for the whole period 1980-98. These linking operations and the exact classification schemes employed are reported in Appendix 6.A2. The agricultural sector is excluded, as this sector is fundamentally different from the rest of the economy, having, during this period, exceptionally low startup and death rates.

---

[88] To our knowledge Lloyd and Mason (1984) were the first to use Checkland's analogy in this context.

[89] To investigate the employment impact of new firms, using data at the firm level would be more convenient as the net job growth in a region could then be decomposed in (gross) job increases and decreases due to entry and exit, and changes in the number of jobs originating from incumbent firms. However, as we do not dispose of micro data, we are forced to use a more indirect approach, using data on number of startups and employment at the regional level.

Variable definitions and their sources are now provided:

- *Sector adjusted (lagged) employment change.* This is the change in regional employment, expressed in percentages (excluding agriculture). For each region, sectoral employment growth rates are weighted by employment per sector for *Great Britain as a whole.* Data on employment are taken from the Census of Employment and the Annual Employment Survey and are supplied by Nomis. Employment figures include both full-time and part-time employees, and exclude self-employed workers and unpaid family workers. Employment is measured in September of each year.

- *Sector adjusted startup rate.* This is the sectoral startup rate, weighted by employment per sector for Great Britain as a whole . Using this weighting implies an identical sector structure for each region. Regional employment, rather than regional workforce, is used as the denominator for the LM approach, because of greater data reliability. Startups in the agricultural sector are again excluded. Startups are measured as VAT registrations and these data are supplied by Small Business Service. The consistency and general availability of this data source make it the most generally useful source of data on firm formation for the UK as a whole (Ashcroft et al., 1991). Startup rates are expressed as the number of startups per thousand workers (LM approach).

- *Population density.* Data on both population and area of the regions are obtained from the Office for National Statistics. The variable is expressed in thousands of inhabitants per square kilometre.

- *Wage growth.* This variable measures changes in regional wage rates. We use data from the New Earnings Survey Panel Data-set (NESPD), which is operated by the Office for National Statistics. The estimates of regional wage rates refer to average hourly earnings excluding overtime payments. The samples from which the mean wages are calculated relate to full time employees whose pay was unaffected by absence during the survey week (which falls in April of each year) and exclude those employed in agriculture, forestry and fishing.

6.6 Research Design and Regression Diagnostics

In this section we describe our research design and several regression diagnostics that we will use in order to test validity of regression results. From Table 6.A2b in Appendix 6.A2 we can see that we cannot utilise employment data for all the years in our sample period 1980-98. We also had to make several harmonizations to correct for changes in regional and sectoral classifications over time. Both these aspects hamper the use of panel data regression techniques. Instead, we estimate each regression cross-sectionally, i.e. using 60 observations (one for each region). Because of missing (employment) data, the region Orkney/Shetland/Western Isles had to be dropped, generating a total of 59 observations. The models are estimated using OLS.

We want to estimate separate models for the 1980s and the 1990s to see whether the relationship between firm births and job creation has changed over time. Given the (limited) availability of employment data and our preference to measure employment change in a period after the period in which we measure startups (to obtain the correct direction of causality), Table 6.A2b demonstrates that the most appropriate periods are 1984-91 and 1991-98 for employment change in the 1980s and 1990s.[90] In this way we make optimal use of the full time length of our data set. We measure startup rates in a period directly preceding the employment change periods. We use four-year averages in order to correct for outlier years. This results in startup rates for the periods 1980-83 and 1987-90. In this way the 1980s and 1990s estimations are completely 'symmetric' (seven year period for employment change; four-year averaged startup rate in the preceding period), which enables comparison of the results for the two periods.

Regarding control variables, population density is measured three years before employment growth. For wage growth and lagged employment growth some small inconsistencies concerning the 'symmetry' of the 1980s and 1990s models cannot be avoided, due to the unavailability of data prior to 1981. We measure wage growth over a period of four years, and we want the wage growth period to precede the employment growth period, if possible. Using a four year length this inevatibly results in the period 1981-85. For the 1990s regression we experimented with the lag which resulted in inclusion of wage growth for the period 1985-89 (based on statistical fit). Regarding the lagged dependent variable we want to use the same length as the dependent variable (seven years). For the 1990s regression this results in the period 1984-91. For the 1980s regression however, the first available year in our data set is 1981 and therefore lagged growth is measured over the period 1981-84.

In all instances, four regression diagnostics are presented. These are first, the Jarque-Bera test on normality of the disturbances; second, the Lagrange Multiplier test on heteroscedasticity; third, the Ramsey RESET test on general misspecification of the model. To facilitate direct evaluation of these tests p-values are shown. For all three tests the null

---

[90] A further advantage of this choice is that the computation of employment change is not hampered by the change in sectoral classification in 1991, see Table 6.A2b.

hypothesis corresponds to "correct estimates", i.e. normality at the Jarque-Bera test, no heteroscedasticity at the Lagrange Multiplier test and no sign of misspecification at the Ramsey RESET test.

Finally, the fact that the data relate to spatial variations raises the potential problem of spatial autocorrelation, an issue "which has been widely ignored in the econometric literature, including most previous work on spatial variations in new firm formation" (Keeble et al., 1993, p. 34). Following Keeble et al., account is taken of this by including Standard Region intercept dummies in the equations.[91] To see whether spatial autocorrelation is actually present in our regressions, we report the Durbin-Watson statistic. We test for positive spatial autocorrelation, implying that the null hypothesis of no spatial autocorrelation is accepted (not rejected) if the DW test statistic is greater than a certain upper bound for critical values, which depends on the number of observations and regressors.[92]

When using the DW statistic we acknowledge this statistic is designed for times series analysis with observations being arranged along a 'time line'. In other words, it is designed for one-dimensional concepts such as time. Space, however, is a multi-dimensional concept. Following Ashcroft and Love (1996), we present the data to the estimation by county within each Standard Region. It follows that many adjacent observations are from contiguous counties. Therefore we argue that the DW statistic should measure the degree of spatial dependence reasonably well. But even so, we recognise there remains some arbitrariness in the ordering of neighbouring regions.[93]

6.7 Results

To test whether startup activity has a different impact on employment growth in different time periods several models are estimated. Recalling that a key objective is to test for short or long-run relationships this section begins by examining the relationship between startups, 1980-83, on employment change 1984-91; then it examines startups in the period 1987-90 on employment change 1991-98. This provides an initial assessment of whether the short-term impact of startups differed between the 1980s and the 1990s. Next, we look at possible region-specific deviations in the effect of startups on employment growth.

---

[91] For this purpose the county Greater London is added to the South East region. This is because there is only one county within the London region in our data set.

[92] We test for *positive* autocorrelation as neighbouring regions may be expected to benefit from each other (spillover effects).

[93] For an alternative approach see the methods covered by Anselin (1988).

In the third subsection we investigate whether estimation results are affected by the periods in which startup rates are measured in terms of recession or boom periods. The fourth subsection investigates long-run effects. We also pay attention to the interpretation of the magnitude of the estimated effects. Finally, we compare our results with other studies.

Startups and Employment Change in the 1980s and the 1990s: Short-Term Effects

Table 6.1 presents the regression results for the 1980s and the 1990s. Startup rates are related to subsequent employment growth, while controlling for population density, wage growth, lagged employment growth, and regional dummies. All control variables are measured prior to the period of the dependent variable.

The final rows show all diagnostic tests are passed (p-values are well above 0.05), except for the RESET test in the 1990s, possibly indicating a missing variable. As regards spatial autocorrelation, the null hypothesis of no autocorrelation is accepted (not rejected) as the DW test statistic exceeds the upper bound critical value (which is about 2, in our case).[94]

The impact of startup activity on subsequent regional employment change is different for the 1980s and the 1990s. In the 1980s startups and employment change are unrelated while in the 1990s startups have a significantly positive impact on employment growth. The bigger employment impact of 1987-90 births compared to 1980-83 births *might* reflect that the importance of new and small firms in the process of innovation and economic growth has increased in the last two decades of the 20th century. In this interpretation Great Britain would have moved from a more "managed" type of economy toward a more "entrepreneurial" type of economy (Audretsch and Thurik, 2001). However, perhaps a more testable explanation is that the increased employment impact reflects "Enterprise Policy" changes, with public policy switching from being quantity-oriented in the 1980s towards being more quality-oriented in the 1990s (Greene, 2002).

As for the control variables, we see a significant negative impact of population density (in the 1980s), and a positive impact of wage growth (in the 1990s) and lagged employment growth. The latter effect points at

---

[94] The Durbin-Watson test should be interpreted with caution in the presence of a lagged dependent variable in the model (Stewart, 1991, p. 168). However, as the DW test statistic is clearly greater than the upper bound critical value, we think it is safe to assume that our estimates do not suffer from first-order spatial autocorrelation. Furthermore, when the Standard Region intercept dummies are removed, the DW test statistic falls to 2.10 for the 1980s regression and to 1.64 for the 1990s regression. The latter value falls within the inconclusive region, indicating that the regional dummies are indeed helpful in correcting for spatial autocorrelation.

positive path dependency. Regions that perform relatively well in a certain period, still perform relatively well in the next period.

Table 6.1. Determinants of regional employment growth (%), short-term equations 1980s and 1990s

	Employment growth 1984-91	Employment growth 1991-98
Constant	5.5	-21.3
	(0.5)	(2.8)
Average startup rate,	-0.25	1.11
1980-83 (left column)	(0.3)	(2.3)
1987-90 (right column)		
Population density,	-4.6	-0.36
1981 (left column)	(3.2)	(0.3)
1988 (right column)		
Wage growth,	0.28	0.53
1981-85 (left column)	(0.8)	(2.6)
1985-89 (right column)		
Lagged empl. growth,	0.46	0.20
1981-84 (left column)	(2.1)	(1.8)
1984-91 (right column)		
Adjusted R^2	0.281	0.696
JB test: [p-value]	[0.517]	[0.820]
LM het. test: [p-value]	[0.630]	[0.264]
RESET test: [p-value]	[0.743]	[0.015]
DW test	2.23	2.18

Note: Intercept dummies for Standard Regions not reported. Employment growth rates and startup rates are sector adjusted. Employment growth is measured exclusive of the non-private sector. Absolute t-values in parentheses.

Regional Specific Effects

In this subsection we investigate whether certain regions deviate in the employment effect of new-firm startups. For this purpose we compute slope dummies (startup rate multiplied by regional dummy) for the (ten) Standard Regions. Given the specifications in Table 6.1 (hence, including all *intercept* dummies), we include, one at a time, a *slope* dummy for each Standard Region. Those slope dummies which are significant at 10% level when included separately, are included in Table

6.2. For the 1980s this is the North East region, and for the 1990s Scotland and Wales. The effects for the other regions are not significantly different from the overall effect. The improved value for the RESET test for the 1990s regression (compared to Table 6.1) implies that the slope dummies for Scotland and Wales contribute to the validity of the model.

For the 1980s, the overall effect of the startup rate is nil on employment in Great Britain. However, for North East England new-firm startups contribute *negatively* to employment growth in that region in the 1980s. For the 1990s the overall startup rate effect is positive (and stronger than in Table 6.1), but for Wales the effect is nil, and for Scotland the effect is *negative*.[95]

Whilst the significant negative sign for North-East England in the 1980s may seem a surprise the plausible explanation comes from a reading of McDonald and Coffield (1992). They paint a picture of unemployed young people in North-east England with very modest human capital being press-ganged by public agendas into starting their own enterprise and ending up more disadvantaged than before they started. The effect is to erode confidence leading to declining economic performance.

Matters change in the 1990s. In the right hand side of Table 6.2 it can be seen that it is Wales and particularly Scotland that exhibit the significantly negative signs. The common thread is that North-east England, Scotland and Wales all have rates of new firm foundation that are well below the GB average. Second, for two regions, the North-east and Scotland, the negative deviation coincides with a policy thrust to raise new firm formation. This raises the question whether such policies are productive in 'unenterprising' areas.

It will be recalled that after October 1993 Scotland implements an active policy to raise business birth rates (BBRS) (Fraser of Allander Institute, 2001). Although the periods studied in the current chapter do not entirely coincide with the period during which the BBRS is active (from 1994 onwards), the negative value for the Scotland dummy indicates that the BBRS actually might have had a negative effect on job creation in Scotland.

The results from Table 6.2 call into question the impact of policies seeking to raise new-firm formation, for two reasons. First, in the 1980's, when UK policy was to stimulate starts, there is no effect on employment in the UK as a whole, and even a negative effect for the North East. Second, in the 1990s there is a significantly positive overall effect after the UK policy changed towards more emphasis on established

---

[95] The slope dummies refer to the deviation from the overall effect. For instance, the significant parameter estimate for Wales means that the effect for Wales deviates significantly from England. It does not mean that it deviates significantly from zero. Indeed, the effect for Wales is –0.3 which is not significant (t-value –0.3). The effect for Scotland is –2.7 which is significantly different from zero at 10% level (t-value –1.8).

businesses with the potential to grow. However, for Scotland, which has a business birth rate strategy in the 1990s, the effect is negative.

Table 6.2. Examining region-specific deviations in employment impact of startups

	Employment growth 1984-91	Employment growth 1991-98
Constant	66.7	-28.9
	(2.2)	(3.9)
Startup rate, *overall effect*	-0.18	1.88
	(0.2)	(3.8)
Startup rate, *slope dummy North East*	-10.5	
	(2.2)	
Startup rate, *slope dummy Wales*		-2.2
		(2.0)
Startup rate, *slope dummy Scotland*		-4.6
		(2.9)
Population density	-5.1	0.39
	(3.6)	(0.3)
Wage growth	0.26	0.55
	(0.8)	(2.9)
Lagged employment growth	0.54	0.25
	(2.5)	(2.5)
Adjusted R^2	0.335	0.747
JB test: [p-value]	[0.493]	[0.030]
LM het. test: [p-value]	[0.843]	[0.534]
RESET test: [p-value]	[0.225]	[0.576]
DW test	2.30	2.22

Note: Intercept dummies for Standard Regions not reported. Employment growth rates and startup rates are sector adjusted. Employment growth is measured exclusive of the non-private sector. Except for startup rate slope dummies, variable specifications are as in Table 6.1. Absolute t-values in parentheses.

Recession Births versus Boom Births

In the previous sections we argued that the different short-term impacts of startups in the early and late 1980s may have been caused by "Enterprise Policy" changes. An alternative explanation is that the 1980-83 startups may be a different *type* of startups, compared with the 1987-90 startups. The obvious difference is that, while 1980-83 were recession years, 1987-90 was a "boom" period. During recessions, a higher proportion of startups may be from individuals with lower human capital, who find employment in the employee labour market more difficult (Cressy, 1996). These startups may be less likely to generate jobs. On the other hand, during a period of economic prosperity, it may be the more "entrepreneurial" type of person who starts a business. This type of startup may be more likely to generate jobs in the short and the long-run. So, while recession births may be the result of "push"-factors being at work (possibly creating fewer jobs), boom births may be more "pull-factor" in nature (possibly creating more jobs).

To test this we examine in Table 6.3 the relationship between firm births in the 1990s recession and short-term employment change. Using the same control variables as those reported in Table 6.2, we estimate a regression in which employment change in the period 1993-98 is explained by the average startup rate over the period 1990-93. To facilitate comparison, the results from the right column of Table 6.2 are reported again in Table 6.3. The results are similar: we find a significant positive impact, implying that the lack of a relationship in the 1980s is not because of the choice of recessionary years.[96] Instead, it seems to be the case that (new) firms in the late 1980s and early 1990s contribute more to employment change than firms started in the early 1980s irrespective of macro-economic conditions.

---

[96] The estimated effect for the recession period is even stronger, although not significantly. As regards the dummy variables, the deviations of Wales and Scotland seem to be smaller compared to Table 6.2 (t-values –1.3). However, the isolated effects are nil for both Wales (effect –0.8; t-value –0.4) and Scotland (effect –0.7; t-value –0.3), while the effect for the English regions is significantly positive. This implies that Wales and Scotland still lag behind in the employment effect of new firms started in the period 1990-93.

Table 6.3. Examining the impact of recession or boom period

	Employment growth 1991-98	Employment growth 1993-98
Constant	-28.9	-26.8
	(3.9)	(4.0)
Startup rate, *overall effect*	1.88	2.39
1987-90 (left column)	(3.8)	(4.1)
1990-93 (right column)		
Startup rate,	-2.2	-3.2
slope dummy Wales	(2.0)	(1.3)
Startup rate,	-4.6	-3.1
slope dummy Scotland	(2.9)	(1.4)
Population density	0.39	-0.06
	(0.3)	(0.06)
Wage growth	0.55	0.52
	(2.9)	(2.5)
Lagged employment growth	0.25	0.15
	(2.5)	(1.4)
Adjusted R^2	0.747	0.737
JB test: [p-value]	[0.030]	[0.473]
LM het. test: [p-value]	[0.534]	[0.289]
RESET test: [p-value]	[0.576]	[0.534]
DW test	2.22	2.51

Note: Intercept dummies for Standard Regions not reported. Employment growth rates and startup rates are sector adjusted. Employment growth is measured exclusive of the non-private sector. Except for startup rate slope dummies, variable specifications are as in Table 6.1. Absolute t-values in parentheses.

A Long-Term Effect?

In this subsection we test for long-run effects. Given our data set we can only test for long-run effects for employment growth in the 1990s, as we have no startup data prior to 1980. The easiest way to test for long-run effects is to run separate regressions which include different lags of the startup rate. Using the same control variables as in Table 6.2, the coefficients of startup rate in separate regressions explaining employment change 1991-98, are 1.88 for for 1987-90 startups, 2.25 for 1984-87 startups, and 2.44 for 1980-83 startups. So, the impact increases with the lag, seemingly indicating that the long-run effect exceeds the short-run effect.

However, we must be cautious in comparing these coefficients. To avoid multicollinearity we estimated the impact of the startup rates from different periods in separate regressions. A disadvantage of this approach is that, because of the strong intertemporal correlation between startup rates (correlations of up to 0.9), the estimated startup rate coefficient may pick up some of the effect of startup activity from other periods. This means comparing coefficients of the long-term and short-term equations is complex.

A better way of establishing the individual impacts of startup rate variables from different periods draws upon the distributed lag literature (Stewart, 1991). By including startup rates from different periods in one regression, but imposing restrictions on the individual parameters, an accurate approximation of the shape of the lag response can be obtained. In the Almon method, parameter restrictions are imposed in such a way that the coefficients of the lagged variables are a polynomial function of the lag length. In this way the startup rate coefficients are reparameterized in a "smooth" way.

We apply the Almon method for a quadratic polynomial function (i.e. a polynomial of second degree). This choice corresponds to imposing one parameter restriction.[97] The results are shown in Table 6.4, with further details presented in Appendix 6.A3.

---

[97] This can be seen as follows. In the unrestricted regression three startup rate variables are included in the model, while in the first unrestricted regression column, only two variables are included (COMBI1 and COMBI2 in Table 6.4). In the second unrestricted regression column, only one startup rate variable is included (COMBI3), and this corresponds to two parameter restrictions. The startup rate coefficients in the restricted regressions are linear combinations of the combinatory variable coefficients. See Equation (6.A3) in Appendix 6.A2.

Table 6.4. Examining the lag structure

	Employment growth 1991-98		
	Unrestricted regression	Restricted regression (one restr.)	Restricted regression (two restr.)
COMBI1 = $X_{-1}+2X_{-2}+3X_{-3}$		1.29 (0.9)	
COMBI2 = $X_{-1}+4X_{-2}+9X_{-3}$		-0.39 (0.6)	
COMBI3 = $-2(X_{-1}+X_{-2})$			-0.53 (3.8)
Startup rate 1987-90 (X_{-1})	1.2 (0.8)	**0.89** **(1.1)**	**1.06** **(3.8)**
Startup rate 1984-87 (X_{-2})	0.48 (0.2)	**1.00** **(2.6)**	**1.06** **(3.8)**
Startup rate 1980-83 (X_{-3})	0.47 (0.3)	**0.32** **(0.2)**	
Adjusted R^2	0.737	0.743	0.748
JB test: [p-value]	[0.062]	[0.087]	[0.069]
LM het. test: [p-value]	[0.554]	[0.578]	[0.581]
RESET test: [p-value]	[0.657]	[0.661]	[0.642]
DW test	2.21	2.21	2.22
Validity Almon restrictions: F-test statistic		0.062	0.053
Critical value (5% level)		4.1	3.2

Note: Except for startup rates, model specifications are as in right column Table 6.2. Intercept dummies for Standard Regions, startup rate slope dummies for Scotland and Wales, and coefficients of population density, wage growth, and lagged employment growth are not reported. Absolute t-values in parentheses. Null hypothesis for JB test, LM het. test, RESET test, and DW test is "correct model specification". Null hypothesis for F-test is "valid restrictions". Critical values for F-tests are according to F(1;41) and F(2;41) distributions. Bold-printed coefficients are *restricted* parameter estimates.

In Table 6.4, regression results using unrestricted regression (i.e. free estimation) and restricted regressions (i.e. using the Almon method) are presented. For the *unrestricted regression* we see that t-values of the separate startup rates are low. This is due to multicollinearity. In the first *restricted regression* column a corrected lag pattern is presented. We see that the impact of the startup rate 1984-87 is strongest. The impact of 1980-83 startups, however, is zero: the t-value is extremely low.[98] This pattern suggests that the lag is approximately 4 to 7 years. The validity of imposing the Almon restriction is formally confirmed by the F-test on parameter restrictions.

However, as t-values for both combinatory variables are low, we suspect that multicollinearity may still influence results in the middle column to some extent. Therefore, we test an additional restriction. As both parameter estimate and t-value of 1980-83 startup rate are low, we impose the effect of 1980-83 startups to be zero. This extra restriction, which can be written as $\beta_3 = 0$, also implies that the employment impacts of 1987-90 startups and 1984-87 startups are equal.[99] In the last column we see that both the unrestricted and the restricted parameter estimates are significant. Also, the F-test on valid restrictions is not rejected. We therefore conclude that the employment impact of 1980-83 startups is zero and that the employment impacts of 1987-90 startups and 1984-87 startups are equal and significantly positive.

Using the estimation results from the last column in Table 6.4, the employment impact of the startup rate can be written as a function of the lag length of the startup rate as $\beta_i = 1.58\left(i^*/3\right) - 0.53\left(i^*/3\right)^2$, where i^* is the lag length in years.[100] The employment impact of startup rates is maximised after 4.5 years and extinguished after 9 years, counting backwards from 1991.[101] So, according to this formula, startups from 1986-87 contribute most to employment growth 1991-98, whereas new-

---

[98] Recall that in the restricted regression columns in Table 6.4, the coefficients of the startup rate variables 1987-90, 1984-87, and 1980-83 are linear combinations of the coefficients of the combinatory variables COMBI1, COMBI2, and COMBI3. In other words, the bold-printed coefficients are *restricted* parameter estimates.

[99] This is clear when the restriction $\beta_3 = 0$ is substituted in Equation (6.A3) in Appendix 6.A2: this results in $\beta_1 = \beta_2 = -2\gamma_2$. Again, we refer to Appendix 6.A2 for further details.

[100] The lag length in years is denoted as i^*. One unit in i corresponds to a period of three years, i.e. $i = i^*/3$. Again, details are in Appendix 6.A2.

[101] Fritsch and Mueller (2004) apply the Almon method for West-German regions in the period 1983-2002. Using a polynomial of third degree, they find an optimal lag of eight years.

firm startups founded in 1983 or earlier do not contribute to employment growth beyond 1991.

The different results for the unrestricted and restricted regression clearly demonstrate the necessity to take account of intertemporal correlations between the different lags of the startup rate.

Magnitude of the Effects

We now examine the magnitude of the effects. The coefficients from "separate regressions" overestimate the employment effect as these coefficients partly reflect the impact of new-firm startups from different periods, as was shown above. To establish the correct average impact of one new-firm startup, we use the coefficients from the last column of Table 6.4. The estimated parameter of the sector adjusted startup rate 1987-90 is 1.06. But this requires interpretation. The dependent variable equals $100\left(Empl_{1998} - Empl_{1991}\right)/Empl_{1991}$, where Empl stands for employment. The independent variable equals $1000\sum_{i=1987}^{1990} NFF \Big/ \left(4\,Empl_{1987}\right)$, where NFF stands for new-firm formation.

Due to data limitations we use four times 1987-employment, instead of the sum of employment over the years 1987-1990. For simplicity we assume that employment in 1987 equals employment in 1991, so the impact of one new-firm startup on absolute employment change is $(1.06\times(1000/4))/100=2.7$. So, ceteris paribus, one new firm started in the period 1987-90 on average created 2.7 net new jobs in the period 1991-98.[102] The employment impact of 1984-87 is also 2.7 jobs per startup. Note that these jobs are additional to the jobs created by the 1987-90 startups.

Comparing These Results with Those from Other Studies

Our findings for Great Britain show similarities to those of Audretsch and Fritsch (2002) for German regions. They also find no short-term effect on employment of startups in the early to mid 1980s, but they do find a short-term employment effect of the early 1990s startups.[103] The common finding, for both Britain and Germany, is that the short-term effect of new-firm startups is higher in the 1990s than in the 1980s.

---

[102] It is important to realize that these 2.7 jobs do not necessarily have to be created in the new firms themselves. It is also possible that (part of) these jobs are created in incumbent firms, but that this is induced by competitive pressure from the new entries. In other words, the 2.7 jobs is the total net effect; we cannot distinguish between direct and indirect employment effects.

[103] Audretsch and Fritsch however do not control for region-specific effects (by means of regional dummies), or wage growth.

Our results for the 1980s, however, differ from those of Ashcroft and Love (1996) for virtually the same British counties. As noted earlier, they find a strong positive effect of new firms started in the period 1980-88 on net employment change in the period 1981-89. They employ a model in which both employment change and new-firm formation are explained with only a one year lag, allowing for interdependencies between these two variables. The employment effect in their study is certainly stronger than our short-term result for the 1980s.

One possible explanation for the differences may again be the different lag structures employed in the two models. In their model Ashcroft and Love relate new-firm formation 1980-88 to net employment change 1981-89, whereas in this chapter the lags are of a minimum of three years (taking the mid year of our startup rate variables as reference year).[104] Given the findings of this chapter that the relationship strengthens over time, we believe our results to be more robust.

6.8 Discussion and Implications

In contrast with the expectations of the policy makers at the time, this chapter finds no evidence that changes in GB new firm formation rates in the 1980-83 period explained changes in employment 1984–91. Indeed for the "unenterprising" and high unemployment area of the North East of England, raising rates of new firm formation is associated with employment reduction. It is only later in the decade that increased rates of new firm formation nationally appear to lead to job creation. Nevertheless the 1980's was a decade in which national policy focussed on raising new firm formation as a key strategy for creating jobs and lowering unemployment.

That policy, however, began to be reviewed in the early 1990's and, by 1993, had been radically switched. Instead of a focus on startups, British policy, with the exception of Scotland, was directed towards, established, rather than new firms, and the job creation impact of new firms in that decade, nationally, was positive and significant.

Scotland, however, adopted the reverse strategy. It sought, explicitly, to raise new firm formation rate as a mechanism to promote job

---

[104] Note that a lag of three years in the present chapter is not comparable with the one year lag used by Ashcroft and Love. In their method, the one year lag is counted backward from the *end* year of the employment change period, whereas we count back from the *start* year of the employment change period. So the lags in this chapter are considerably larger than the difference between 3 and 1 year suggests. In fact, in Ashcroft and Love, the years in which employment change and startup activity are measured display an 80% overlap, possibly resulting in the reversed causality problems described earlier. In the present chapter we deliberately choose non-overlapping periods.

creation. We show that, in GB, new firm formation in the 1987-90 period was significantly positively associated with employment growth in the 1991-8 period. In Scotland however, increases in new firm formation led to falling employment. The results for Scotland therefore provide no support for policies which seek to raise new firm formation as a mechanism for stimulating job creation, particularly in areas deemed to be "lacking in enterprise." Our interpretation is that the ineffectiveness of the Business Birth Rate Strategy in Scotland (Fraser of Allander Institute, 2001) was probably a blessing in disguise since a rise in new firm formation would, on these grounds, have led to falling employment.

Overall, our findings are important for public policy makers for several reasons. First, the considerably bigger short-term (and possibly long-term) employment impact of 1990s births, compared with early 1980s births, is likely to reflect "Enterprise Policy" changes. As Greene (2002) argues, the 1980s in Britain was a decade in which the key objective was to maximise the number of business startups. In contrast, the 1990s saw a shift towards policies to improve the "quality" of the SME sector as a whole. Given that major policy shift it is unsurprising - although reassuring- to observe bigger employment impacts in the 1990s, than in the previous decade.

Nevertheless this chapter makes it clear that increases in birth rates can lead to additional job creation in the short and medium term. Much less clear is whether a public policy-induced increase in birth rates is a consistently cost-effective way of enhancing employment in the medium term. Our interpretation of our findings is that it is not for two reasons. The first is that the only area, in the 1990s, with a clear (public) policy to promote new-firm births was Scotland. Yet it was Scotland, (along with Wales), where the job creation impact of a new startup was significantly lower than elsewhere.[105] The fact that the business birth rate policy is implemented in 1993 – after the 1990-93 period when we measure birth rates – means that the definitive link cannot be made . However, given the evidence presented in the chapter the likelihood that the business birth rate policy was effective in terms of job creation seems very small.

The second key finding is that startups had a much greater impact on job creation in the 1990s than in the 1980s, even though raising the startup rate was the key policy objective in the 1980s. Our interpretation is that "birth rate policies" lead to individuals with limited human capital - who are often unemployed- being encouraged to start in business. Such

---

[105] In 2002 Scottish Enterprise announced the effective abolition of its Business Birth Rate Strategy, replacing it with a greater focus on SMEs with potential for growth. However, in 2001, an Entrepreneurship Action Plan for Wales was announced with a £300 million budget, one key element of which was to raise birth rates of firms in Wales to the UK average by 2006 (National Assembly for Wales, 2001).

individuals are likely to be very transitory business owners and very unlikely to start and develop businesses with employees (Storey and Strange, 1992; Greene et al., 2004). This suggests that, if the objective is to enhance employment, implementing old- fashioned "birth rate" policies is difficult to justify from this research.

Unfortunately current UK policy documents appear to signal a return to such policies. HM Treasury and Small Business Service (2002) refer consistently to an "enterprise gap", and in its Foreward says "...and across the UK, start-up rates in the best performing areas are ten times those of the worst, contributing to an enterprise gap in our inner cities of 88,000 companies, £5 billion in turnover and tens of thousands of jobs... we cannot close that overnight". In 2004 the focus on startups and enterprise culture is apparent in the government's seven pillars of policy (Small Business Service, 2004). The clear implication is that it is current policy to seek to close the gap by raising new firm formation, particularly in "unenterprising" areas. The lessons from this chapter are that public policies to raise new firm formation, particularly in "unenterprising" areas are likely to be unproductive at best and counter-productive at worst.

6.A1 Appendix: Illustration Shift-Share Procedure

In this appendix we illustrate the shift-share procedure, used in this chapter to compute sector-adjusted startup rates, by means of a numerical example. Basically, the shift-share procedure imposes the same sector structure (that of the country as a whole) on each region. Sector structure in this chapter is measured in terms of employment (labour market approach). As an illustration, we show the calculation of both the unadjusted and the sector-adjusted average startup rate 1980-83 for Derbyshire. This county is chosen because of the relatively large difference between the two types of startup rate for this region.

In the second column of Table 6.A1 the startup rate (averaged over the years 1980-83) is reported for each sector of economy (except for agriculture which is excluded from the current study). The startup rate of a region is a weighted average of the sectoral startup rates. The difference between the unadjusted startup rate and the sector-adjusted startup rate of a region is the weighting scheme applied to the sectoral startup rates. For the unadjusted startup rate, the employment shares of the sectors of the region under consideration (in this case Derbyshire) are taken as weights. This results in a value of 6.890. For the sector adjusted startup rate of Derbyshire, we take the sectoral employment shares of Great Britain as a whole as weights. This results in a value of 8.392.

The difference between the sector-adjusted and the unadjusted startup rate is equal to 21.8%, which is quite large.[106] Closer inspection of Table 6.A1 reveals that the differences between the employment shares of Derbyshire and Great Britain as a whole, of especially the sectors production and trade and catering, account for the large difference between the unadjusted and the sector-adjusted startup rates. The relatively large share of production in Derbyshire (a sector with a low startup rate) and the relatively small share of trade and catering (a sector with a high startup rate) account for the lower value for the unadjusted startup rate, compared to the sector-adjusted startup rate.

Table 6.A1. Illustration shift-share procedure; the case of Derbyshire, 1980-83

Sector	Average startup rate 1980-83, by sector [1]	Employment share 1981, Derbyshire	Employment share 1981, Great Britain
Production	1.519	0.470	0.323
Construction	23.294	0.049	0.052
Trade and catering	24.478	0.145	0.196
Transport and communic.	7.559	0.054	0.067
Other services	3.848	0.282	0.363
Average unadjusted startup rate 1980-83, Derbyshire	6.890		
Average sector-adjusted startup rate 1980-83, Derbyshire		8.392	

[1] Number of VAT registrations per 1000 workers.

6.A2 Appendix: Data Sources

The startup rate and employment change variables used are all constructed from a data base which contains four basic variables: startups, closures, number of enterprises, and employment. This database was constructed by EIM. These four variables are available at the sectoral (1-digit) and regional (NUTS3) aggregation level for the period 1980-99. Except for employment, each of these four variables is available on a yearly basis according to uniform regional and sectoral classifications, for the whole period 1980-99. Achieving this uniformity is not straightforward, since the crude data were delivered according to different regional and sectoral classifications. In this appendix the exact regional and sectoral aggregation levels, at which the four variables are available in

---

[106] In our data set the difference between the sector-adjusted and the unadjusted startup rate ranges from –20.9% to +21.8%.

the EIM-data set, are presented. Furthermore, the data sources and some characteristics of the variables are described.

Basic Data

In Tables 6.A2a and 6.A2b, we give an overview of the different classifications (regional and sectoral), according to which the four variables are available in the basic data files. Also, the exact years for which the variables are available (for employment there are some missing years), are tabulated.

Table 6.A2a. Available years and classification schemes in basic data files: startups, closures and number of enterprises [a]

Period	Available years	Regional classification	Sectoral classification
1980-1993	All	pre-LGR [b]	VTC [c]
1994-1999	All	post-LGR	SIC92

[a] The figures of these variables are supplied by Small Business Service.

[b] LGR = local government reorganisation 1995-98.

[c] VTC = VAT Trade Classification. This is effectively SIC68.

Table 6.A2b. Available years and classification schemes in basic data files: employment[a]

Period	Available years	Regional classification	Sectoral classification
1980-1991	1981; '84; '87; '89; '91	pre-LGR [b]	SIC80
1991-1999	1991; '93; '95-'98	pre-LGR	SIC92

[a] The figures of this variable are supplied by Nomis.

[b] LGR = local government reorganisation 1995-98.

Startups, Closures and Number of Enterprises: Source and Description

The figures on startups, closures, and number of enterprises are supplied by Small Business Service. This organisation publishes yearly figures on VAT registrations, VAT deregistrations, and the stock of VAT registered enterprises, based on data from the Inter-Departmental Business Register (IDBR; this register is administered by the Office for National Statistics). See Small Business Service (2000). The VAT-registrations and VAT-deregistrations represent the number of enterprises registering and de-registering for VAT each year. Because there is a turnover threshold for VAT (£52,000 in 2000, for example), the very smallest one person businesses are excluded from the figures. The stock of VAT registered enterprises represents the number of enterprises registered for VAT at the start of the year.

Employment: Source and Description

The figures on employment are taken from the Census of Employment (until 1993) and the Annual Employment Survey (from 1995 onwards) and are supplied by Nomis. The employment figures only relate to employees. Self-employed workers and unpaid family workers are thus excluded from the data. The employment figures include both full-time and part-time employees, and relate to the situation in September of each year.

Regional Aggregation Level and Classification Schemes

The regional aggregation level employed in our data set is the British NUTS3 level. This is county level in England and Wales, and local authority region level in Scotland. We thus have data at the level of the 64 regions which are listed in Table 2 of Ashcroft et al. (1991, p. 397). In the period 1995-98, a local government reorganisation took place in Great Britain. The five tier NUTS level classification was reviewed, and the so-called unitary authorities (UAs) were introduced. As a result, geographical boundaries of some regions have changed. This implies that we have to adjust the data from before and after the reorganisation so that they become comparable (see Table 6.A2a). For the English regions, this is easy, since the data in the basic file are given in terms of both the new and the old regions ("former counties"). But for Wales and Scotland no variables for the period 1994-99 are given in terms of the old classification. Closer inspection of the boundaries of the unitary authorities reveals that the Scottish regions can remain unchanged but that some Welsh regions have to be aggregated into larger regions, due to overlapping "new" and "old" areas. In particular, the "old" counties Gwynedd, Clwyd, and Powys are combined into one region (which might be labeled North/Mid Wales), and the "old" counties Mid Glamorgan, South Glamorgan, and Gwent are also combined (South/East Wales). This implies that the total number of Welsh regions reduces from eight to four (Dyfed and West Glamorgan remain unchanged), and the total number of British regions in our data set from 64 to 60. These 60 regions comprise 46 English counties, 4 Welsh regions, and 10 Scottish local authority regions. In the latter group of regions, the Orkney, Shetland and Western Isles are combined into one region. The 60 regions cover the whole of Great Britain.

Sectoral Aggregation Level and Classification Schemes

At the regional aggregation level described above, the four variables are all available at the sectoral 1-digit level. However, from Tables 6.A2a and 6.A2b, we see that three different sectoral classifications circulate: SIC68, SIC80, and SIC92. These classifications are all different, see Table 6.A3.

Table 6.A3: Three Standard Industrial Classifications: 1-digit level labels

SIC68	SIC80	SIC92
- agriculture, forestry and fishing	**0** agriculture, forestry and fishing	**AB** agriculture; forestry and fishing
- production	**1** energy/water supply industries	**CE** mining and quarrying; electricity, gas and water supply
- construction	**2** extraction/manufacture: minerals/metals	**D** manufacturing
- motor trades	**3** metal goods/vehicle industries, etc	**F** construction
- wholesale	**4** other manufacturing industries	**G** wholesale, retail and repairs
- retail	**5** construction	**H** hotels and restaurants
- catering	**6** distribution, hotels/catering; repairs	**I** transport, storage and communication
- transport and communication	**7** transport and communication	**J** financial intermediation
- finance and professional services	**8** banking, finance, insurance, leasing, etc	**K** real estate, renting and business activities
- business and other personal services	**9** other services	**LO** public administration; other community, social and personal services
		MN education; health and social work

Note: In this table, similarities in covered parts of the economy across columns are coincidental.

As was the case for the regions, some sectors have to be combined to make sectors comparable across different SICs. This results in the six-sector classification in Table 6.A4. In this table, corresponding parts of economic activity across SICs are in the same rows. *By and large*, there are no overlapping sectors in this six-sector classification. As mentioned earlier, we do not use the data for agriculture, forestry and fishing in our analyses.

Table 6.A4. Link between SIC68-SIC80-SIC92 classifications (1-digit level)

SIC68-sectors	SIC80-sectors (codes)	SIC92-sectors (codes)
agriculture, forestry and fishing	0	AB
production	1, 2, 3, 4	CDE
construction	5	F
trade and catering [a]	6	GH
transport and communication	7	I
other services [b]	8, 9	JKLMNO

[a] This is an aggregate of four SIC68 sectors: motor trades; wholesale; retail; catering.

[b] This is an aggregate of two SIC68 sectors: finance and professional services; business and other personal services.

To summarize, the EIM-data set for Great Britain contains the four variables startups, closures, number of enterprises and employment. Apart from some missing years for employment, these variables are available on a yearly basis for the whole period 1980-1999, at relatively disaggregated sectoral and spatial aggregation levels (6 sectors, 60 regions), and according to uniform sectoral and regional classifications.

6.A3 Appendix: The Almon Method [107]

The Almon method is a reparameterization method that corrects for correlation between different time lags of an exogenous variable (distributed lags). Correlation between exogenous variables in a regression model is not desirable as it causes multicollinearity. This problem is often prevalent in the context of distributed lags. When the distributed lag variables are highly correlated, it is difficult to estimate individual response coefficients accurately and regular t-tests on the significance of individual parameter estimates are unreliable. The Almon method assumes that there is some "smoothness" in the lag distribution. By imposing a specific structure in the lag distribution, the multicollinearity problems inherent to free estimation can be solved. In particular, the Almon method suggests approximating the lag structure by a polynomial function. This is explained below.

Suppose we have a model of the form represented by:

$$(6.A1) \quad Y_t = \alpha + \beta_0 X_t + \beta_1 X_{t-1} + ... + \beta_s X_{t-s} + \delta Z + u_t,$$

where the X variables are the distributed lags, with maximum lag length s, and Z is a vector of other exogenous variables (either lagged

---

[107] This appendix is based on Stewart (1991, pp. 180-182).

or unlagged). It is clear that in our model the distributed lag variables correspond to the startup rate variables from the various periods.

Due to high correlation between the X variables with different lags, free estimation of (6.A1) suffers from multicollinearity. In the Almon method a "smooth" lag distribution is obtained by imposing restrictions on the parameter vector β. In particular, the Almon method suggests approximating the graph of β_i against the lag length i by a continuous function of the form

(6.A2) $\quad \beta_i = \gamma_0 + \gamma_1 i + \gamma_2 i^2 + ... + \gamma_r i^r \, ; r \leq s \, ,$

where r is the degree of the polynomial (6.A2) and s is the maximum lag length.

Imposing a structure like (6.A2) on the estimated parameters is implemented by estimating a restricted model. The restricted model is obtained by writing explicit expressions for (6.A2), and rearranging the distributed lag variables, as we will show below for our employment growth model. First, we establish the time periods that correspond to the lags 0, 1, ..., s. A straightforward application of our model suggests that lag 0 corresponds to the period 1991-1998, while the lags 1, 2, and 3 correspond to the periods 1987-1990, 1984-1987, and 1980-1983, respectively. So s equals 3. Taking the mid years of these periods, i.e. 1988, 1985, and 1982, we see that in terms of Equation (6.A2), the values $i = 1$, 2, and 3 correspond to time lags of 3, 6, and 9 years, respectively, measured from 1991 backwards. In other words, one unit of i corresponds to a lag length of three years. Second, we have not included a startup rate with lag 0 in our model, so $\beta_0 = 0$. This restriction reflects our argument that startup rates do not have an immediate (i.e. contemporaneous) effect on growth and inclusion of an unlagged startup rate in the model leads to problems of reversed causality. Third, we choose $r = 2$, i.e. a quadratic polynomial form.[108] Writing out (6.A2) with $r = 2$, $s = 3$, and $\beta_0 = 0$ results in

(6.A3) $\quad \beta_0 = \gamma_0 \equiv 0; \quad \beta_1 = \gamma_1 + \gamma_2; \quad \beta_2 = 2\gamma_1 + 4\gamma_2; \quad \beta_3 = 3\gamma_1 + 9\gamma_2$

Substituting (6.A3) in (6.A1) and rearranging terms results in

(6.A4) $\quad Y_t = \alpha + \gamma_1 \left(X_{t-1} + 2X_{t-2} + 3X_{t-3} \right) + \gamma_2 \left(X_{t-1} + 4X_{t-2} + 9X_{t-3} \right) + \delta Z + u_t$

---

[108] We consider a first degree polynomial (i.e. a straight line) too restrictive.

Equation (6.A4) can be estimated using OLS. The (restricted) parameters of the startup rate variables are obtained by substituting the estimates of γ_1 and γ_2 back into Equation (6.A3). The corresponding standard errors are obtained using the ANALYZ command in TSP 4.5.

To test the validity of the parameter restrictions imposed by the Almon method a standard F-test of the form

$$(6.A5) \quad F = [(S_R - S)/(s - r)]/[S/(n - k)]$$

can be applied, where S_R and S are the restricted and unrestricted residual sum of squares, respectively, r is the degree of the polynomial (6.A2), s is the maximum lag length in Equation (6.A1), n is the number of observations, and k is the number of regressors in the unrestricted model. Under the null hypothesis of valid restrictions, the test statistic under (6.A5) has an F distribution with $s - r$ and $n - k$ degrees of freedom.

In our first application, the number of restrictions $s - r$ equals 3-2=1, while the expression $n - k$ equals 59-18=41. The critical value of the F(1;41) distribution at 5% level is 4.1. From Table 6.4 we see that the value of the test statistic equals 0.062, so the null hypothesis of valid restrictions is not rejected.

In our second application, where we put the employment impact of 1980-83 startups on employment growth 1991-98 equal to zero, the number of restrictions equals two. The extra restriction can be written as $\beta_3 = 0$. Substitution in Equation (6.A3) results in $\gamma_1 = -3\gamma_2; \beta_1 = \beta_2 = -2\gamma_2$. So, the extra restriction also implies that the employment impacts of lags 1 and 2 (startups 1987-90 and 1984-87) are equal. Another implication is that the optimum lag is 1.5 (or 4.5 years). In this case the F-test statistic has an F(2;41) distribution (critical value 3.2). The test statistic equals 0.053. So, the restriction $\beta_3 = 0$ is valid.

Chapter 7

TOTAL ENTREPRENEURIAL ACTIVITY
RATES AND ECONOMIC GROWTH

7.1 Introduction [109]

There are many factors that influence the speed of economic progress. Such factors may include climate, education, property rights, saving propensity, presence of seaports, etc. The empirical growth literature has suggested a large number of economic and non-economic variables that may influence economic growth (Sala-i-Martin, 1997 and Bleaney and Nishiyama, 2002). Entrepreneurship has failed to enter this list of variables (see e.g. Table 1 in Bleaney and Nishiyama, 2002). On the one hand, this is surprising since many economists would claim that entrepreneurial activity is vital to economic progress.[110] They will, for example, refer to the demise of communist economies where entrepreneurial activity was about absent and contributions by Schumpeter (1934) and (neo-)Austrian economists (like Kirzner, 1973).[111] On the other hand, it is less surprising since the measurement of the factor 'entrepreneurship' is far from easy. Most factors contributing to economic progress can be measured using existing secondary sources for a wide variety of countries. However, aside from self-employment measures,

---

[109] This chapter is reprinted from: Van Stel, A.J., M.A. Carree and A.R. Thurik (2005), The Effect of Entrepreneurial Activity on National Economic Growth, *Small Business Economics* 24 (3), pp. 311-321, with kind permission of Springer Science and Business Media, Inc.

[110] The recognition of the importance of entrepreneurial activity has been absent for a while in mainstream (theoretical) economics. Baumol (1968) complained that entrepreneurship, being hard to capture into mathematical equations, disappeared from mainstream (neo-classical) economics. Kirzner (1973) observed that the neo-classical model constrained the decision making of the entrepreneur, in terms of product quality and price, technology, within limits wholly alien to the context in which real world entrepreneurs characteristically operate.

[111] Schumpeter (1950, p. 13): "The function of entrepreneurs is to reform or revolutionize the pattern of production by exploring an invention, or more generally, an untried technological possibility for producing a new commodity or producing an old one in a new way... To undertake such new things is difficult and constitutes a distinct economic function, first because they lie outside of the routine tasks which everybody understands, and secondly, because the environment resists in many ways."

which are questionable measures of entrepreneurial activity, there were no sources up till recently to compare this activity across countries. The *Global Entrepreneurship Monitor* (GEM) has changed this.

There are various ways in which entrepreneurship may affect economic growth. Entrepreneurs may introduce important innovations by entering markets with new products or production processes (Acs and Audretsch, 1990 and 2003). Entrepreneurs often play vital roles in the early evolution of industries, examples of such (successful American) entrepreneurs include Andrew Carnegie, Michael Dell, Thomas Edison, Henry Ford, Bill Gates, Ray Kroc and Sam Walton. Entrepreneurs may increase productivity by increasing competition (Nickel, 1996). They may enhance our knowledge of what is technically viable and what consumers prefer by introducing variations of existing products and services in the market. The resulting learning process speeds up the discovery of the dominant design for product-market combinations. Knowledge spillovers play an important role in this process (Audretsch and Feldman, 1996; Audretsch and Keilbach, 2004). Lastly, they may be inclined to work longer hours and more efficiently as their income is strongly linked to their working effort.

In this chapter, we empirically investigate the effect of entrepreneurial activity on economic growth at the country level. We use recent and new material provided by the Global Entrepreneurship Monitor (GEM). It contains the so-called *Total Entrepreneurial Activity* (TEA) rate measuring the relative amount of nascent entrepreneurs and business owners of young firms for a range of countries. This variable is (consistently) measured across a variety of countries and appears a useful index for measuring the extent of 'entrepreneurship'. An important element in our analysis is to consider whether entrepreneurial activity plays a similar growth-stimulating role in highly developed economies (relatively rich countries) and in less developed economies (relatively poor countries, including both transformation economies and developing countries). Carree and Thurik (1999a), for example, indicate that the presence of small firms in manufacturing industries benefits growth for the richest among EU-countries, but not for EU-countries with somewhat lower GDP per capita, like Portugal and Spain. This is in line with the regime shift introduced by Audretsch and Thurik (2001). They argue that there has been a shift from a model of the 'managed economy' towards that of the 'entrepreneurial economy' in highly developed economies.

Our test of the influence of 'entrepreneurship' is based on a statistical analysis of whether *Total Entrepreneurial Activity* (TEA) influences GDP growth in the 1999-2003 period for a sample of 36 countries. We test whether this influence depends upon the level of economic development measured as GDP per capita. We also distinguish between the extent of influence of 'entrepreneurship' for three groups of countries, viz. highly developed economies, transition economies and developing countries. Although the limited number of observations does not allow for many competing explanatory variables, we include the so-called *Growth Competitiveness Index* (GCI) into our model. This variable captures a range of alternative explanations for achieving sustained economic growth. In addition, we incorporate the initial level of economic development to correct for convergence.

The rest of this chapter is organized as follows. In Section 7.2 the relation between entrepreneurial activity and economic growth and its dependence on the stage of economic development are discussed and the TEA and GCI rates are introduced. In Section 7.3 we present our model and a description of the variables. Section 7.4 is used for results and Section 7.5 concludes.

7.2 Entrepreneurship, Competitiveness and Growth

There have been efforts to empirically investigate the importance of the impact of entrepreneurship on economic performance, especially at the firm, region or industry level (e.g. Audretsch, 1995, Audretsch and Fritsch, 2002 and Caves, 1998).[112] However, contributions at the level of the nation state are limited. Two recent exceptions are studies into the effect of self-employment rates on economic growth figures: Blanchflower (2000) and Carree et al. (2002). Even in these cases it is questionable whether self-employment rates are an adequate measure of entrepreneurial activity. This chapter is a first attempt to investigate whether differences in the start-up activity and presence of young firms across countries has an impact on their economic performance.

The last two decades have witnessed both large (conglomerate) companies to increasingly concentrate on core competences and experiencing mass lay-offs (especially in traditional manufacturing industries) and high-technology innovative small firms having come at the forefront of technological development in many (new) industries. These developments would suggest the key importance for modern economy of a sound entrepreneurial climate to achieve economic progress. In particular, Audretsch and Thurik (2001) have argued that highly developed economies have experienced a shift from a model of the 'managed economy' towards that of the 'entrepreneurial economy'. The model of the 'managed economy' is the political, social and economic response to an economy dictated by the forces of large-scale production, reflecting the predominance of the production factors of capital and (unskilled) labor as

---

[112] See Carree and Thurik (2003) for a survey of studies of the impact of entrepreneurship on growth at various levels of observation.

the sources of competitive advantage. By contrast, the model of the 'entrepreneurial economy' is the political, social and economic response to an economy dictated not just by the dominance of the production factor of knowledge – which Romer (1990, 1994) and Lucas (1988) identified as replacing the more traditional factors as the source of competitive advantage – but also by a very different, but complementary, factor they had overlooked: the presence of entrepreneurial activity to accommodate knowledge spillovers (see Acs and Audretsch, 2003; Audretsch and Keilbach, 2004).

The transition as described by Audretsch and Thurik (2001) can also be described in more 'Schumpeterian' terms.[113] In Schumpeter (1934) the role of the entrepreneur as prime cause of economic development is emphasized. Schumpeter describes how the innovating entrepreneur challenges incumbent firms by introducing new inventions that make current technologies and products obsolete. This process of creative destruction is the main characteristic of what has been called the Schumpeter Mark I regime. In Schumpeter (1950) the focus is on innovative activities by large and established firms. Schumpeter describes how large firms outperform their smaller counterparts in the innovation and appropriation process through a strong positive feedback loop from innovation to increased R&D activities. This process of creative accumulation is the main characteristic of what has been called the Schumpeter Mark II regime. The extent to which either of the two Schumpeterian technological regimes prevails in a certain period and industry varies. It may depend upon the nature of knowledge required to innovate, the opportunities of appropriability, the degree of scale (dis)economies, the institutional environment, the importance of absorptive capacity, demand variety, etc. Industries in a Schumpeter Mark II regime are likely to develop a more concentrated market structure in contrast to industries in a Schumpeter Mark I regime where small firms will proliferate. The distinction between the Schumpeter Mark I versus Mark II regimes is closely related to that of the 'entrepreneurial' versus 'managed' economy.

These discussions suggest that the role and importance of entrepreneurial ventures may differ from one stage of economic development to another. Theoretical support for this idea is given by Lloyd-Ellis and Bernhardt (2000) who describe how an economy goes through various stages of economic development. Therefore, we should be careful in comparing countries in different stages of economic development. For example, high start-up rates in developing countries could be less a sign of economic strength when compared to such rates in

---

[113] Other terms are also possible, like the transition from the fourth to the fifth Kondratiev wave (Freeman and Perez, 1988).

highly developed economies. That is, a far smaller percentage of these start-ups in developing countries when compared to rich countries may develop into high-growth companies generating substantial value added. In particular, average human capital levels of entrepreneurs may differ between countries (shopkeepers versus Schumpeterian entrepreneurs). High start-up rates, reported in individual surveys, may be a sign of a substantial 'informal sector' in developing countries, not being a characteristic of an economy in progress. The main argument of this chapter is that the impact of 'entrepreneurship' on growth is different for countries at different stages of development. For highly developed countries we expect a positive impact of entrepreneurial activity on subsequent economic performance. For relatively poor countries it is more uncertain what high start-up rates stand for, in terms of an industrial organization conducive to innovation and economic growth.

Countries, even in similar stages of economic development, differ strongly in the rates of entrepreneurial activity. The GEM *Global Executive Reports* show large differences between countries like Japan, France, Belgium and Sweden with low entrepreneurial activity and countries like the U.S., Canada, Australia and South Korea with high entrepreneurial activity. Some developing countries like Thailand and India top the list of countries with high entrepreneurial activity. Entrepreneurial activity is correlated with the self-employment rate (see e.g. Table I in Carree et al., 2002 and Table 2.1 in Audretsch et al., 2002b). However, there are exceptions to this rule. Japan, for example, has self-employment rates that are relatively close to those of the U.S. However, the new entry rate is far smaller in Japan, where there are many (inefficient) small establishments in the retail and wholesale sectors. Carree et al. (2002) show that countries may not only have too few self-employed, but may also have too many. Italy is given as an example for the latter situation.

In case entrepreneurial activity would be important for economic progress, we should find countries that are high on the list of countries ranked in terms of this activity to also grow relatively fast. The usual ceteris paribus condition applies here since there are many other factors that may explain economic progress. These include factors like schooling, inflation, investment in fixed assets, climate, institutional quality and property rights. It is important to gain insight in alternative explanations for economic growth *next to* entrepreneurial activity.

In the present section we will discuss our two key variables, the TEA rate capturing elements of 'entrepreneurial energy' and the GCI rate encompassing a range of alternative explanatory variables.

Total Entrepreneurial Activity (TEA)

Data on total entrepreneurial activity are taken from the *Global Entrepreneurship Monitor* (GEM) Adult Population Survey. This database contains various entrepreneurial measures that are constructed on the basis of surveys of -on average- some 3,000 respondents per country (37 countries in 2002). The total entrepreneurial activity rate (TEA) is defined as that percent of adult population (18-64 years old) that is either actively involved in starting a new venture or the owner/manager of a business that is less than 42 months old (Reynolds et al., 2002). In 2002 the TEA rate (per 100 adults) ranges from values above 15 in Chile, Thailand and India, to 10.5 in the United States, to values below four in Russia, Belgium, France, Japan, Croatia and Hong Kong. See Appendix 1. For most countries, TEA rates in 2002 are lower than in 2001 due to a universal decline in economic growth rates in 2002 compared to 2001. The relative rankings between countries remained quite stable though (Reynolds et al., 2002). For the 28 countries that participated in GEM both in 2001 and in 2002, the rank correlation (Spearman's ρ statistic) is 0.8. This indicates that total entrepreneurial activity may be seen as a *structural* characteristic of an economy. This makes the variable suitable for inclusion in models aiming to explain structural growth such as the model that we estimate in this chapter.

Growth Competitiveness Index (GCI)

The Growth Competitiveness framework is employed by the World Economic Forum's *Global Competitiveness Report* (GCR). A central objective of the GCR is to assess the capacity of the world's economies to achieve sustained economic growth. In the GCR this is done by analyzing the extent to which individual national economies have the structures, institutions, and policies in place for economic growth over the medium term (McArthur and Sachs, 2002). These features of national economies are summarized in the Growth Competitiveness Index (GCI). The GCR identifies three inter-related mechanisms involved in economic growth: efficient division of labor, capital accumulation (including human capital), and technological advance. Concerning the last-mentioned mechanism, a distinction is made between the creation of new technologies (*technological innovation*) and the adoption of technologies that have been developed abroad (*technology transfer*). In the GCR framework technological innovation is seen as the most important factor for achieving long-term economic growth. In this connection the GCR distinguishes between *core economies* (countries that are technological innovators) and *non-core economies*.[114] The core economies are typically the richest countries. It is argued that economic growth is achieved in

---

[114] A country is defined to be a core economy if it achieves at least 15 US utility patents per million population. Twenty-four countries met this criterion in 2000.

different ways in these two types of economies. In core economy countries, growth is powered by their capacity to innovate and to win new global markets for their technologically advanced products (technological innovation). High growth rates of non-core economies are often achieved by rapidly absorbing the advanced technologies and capital of the core economies, for example through high levels of foreign direct investment from high-tech multinationals of the core economies (technology transfer). This type of growth process is sometimes also called "catch-up growth".

Besides technology, two other major pillars of growth are identified in the Growth Competitiveness framework: the quality of public institutions and the macro-economic environment. Institutions are crucial for their role in ensuring the protection of property rights, the objective resolution of contract and other legal disputes, and the transparency of government. All these factors are important for achieving an efficient division of labor. Public institutions are also important for establishing societal stability required to achieve economic growth. The macro-economic environment relates to government monetary and fiscal policies and stability of financial institutions. It involves such things as budget balance, modest taxation, high rates of national savings and a realistic level of the exchange rate that preserves the competitiveness of the export sector. Again, these factors are important conditions for achieving capital accumulation and an efficient division of labor which in turn influence economic growth.

In the GCR the growth potential of economies is measured by the *Growth Competitiveness Index* (GCI). This index aims to "measure the capacity of the national economy to achieve sustained economic growth over the medium term, controlling for the current level of economic development" (McArthur and Sachs, 2002). The GCI reflects the three major pillars of economic growth identified in the GCR framework: technology, public institutions, and the macroeconomic environment. It is argued that these factors play different roles at different stages of economic development, and therefore these factors (or sub-indexes) get different relative weights in constructing the overall GCI index for economies at different stages of development. In particular, for the so-called core economies identified in GCR the technology sub-index gets a higher weight compared to the non-core economies. This is because technology is the main source of competitiveness in modern economies. Likewise, within the technology sub-index, innovation gets a higher relative weight compared to technology transfer in the core economies. For the construction of the GCI information from 'hard' data sources (international statistics) and information from the *GCR Executive Opinion Survey* are combined.[115]

The GCI tries to capture factors determining economic growth. In a test regression for 75 countries, McArthur and Sachs (2002) show that the 2001 GCI indeed has a significantly positive influence on economic growth over the period 1992-2000, while controlling for the catch-up effect as measured by initial income level of countries. This supports the view that the GCI indeed captures important factors determining the capacity of national economies to grow. However, a disadvantage of this approach is that the GCI is used to explain past growth instead of future growth, resulting in a clear direction of causality problem. In this chapter, we try to solve this causality problem.

7.3 Model and Data

In this section we discuss our data and present our model. We make use of the *Global Entrepreneurship Monitor* (GEM), the *Global Competitiveness Report* (GCR), and other sources. Data on four basic variables are used in our model: total entrepreneurial activity, growth of GDP, per capita income, and the growth competitiveness index. The sources and definitions of these variables are listed below.

Total Entrepreneurial Activity (TEA). Data on total entrepreneurial activity are taken from the GEM Adult Population Survey for 2002.

Growth of GDP (∆GDP). GDP growth rates are taken from the IMF World Economic Outlook database of the International Monetary Fund, version September 2003.

Per capita income (GNIC). Gross national income per capita 2001 is expressed in (thousands of) purchasing power parities per US$, and these data are taken from the 2002 World Development Indicators database of the World Bank.

Growth Competitiveness Index (GCI). Data on the GCI 2001 are taken from page 32 of The Global Competitiveness Report 2001-2002. The variable was described in Section 7.2.

---

[115] The Executive Opinion Survey is a survey among firms within countries. The goal of the survey is to capture a broad array of intangible factors that cannot be found in official statistics but that nonetheless may influence the growth potential of countries. For details, see Cornelius and McArthur (2002).

In this chapter we investigate whether entrepreneurship may be considered a determinant of economic growth, next to technology, public institutions and the macroeconomic environment (which are captured in a combined way by the GCI). As both entrepreneurship and the factors underlying the GCI are assumed to be structural characteristics of an economy, we do not want to explain *short term* economic growth but rather growth in the *medium term*. Therefore we choose average annual growth over a period of five years (1999-2003) as the dependent variable in this study.

We stay close to the model of McArthur and Sachs (2002) who explain national growth rates over the period 1992-2000 by the GCI, and (the log of) initial income level of countries (catch-up effect). We add two new features to this model. *First*, we include the total entrepreneurial activity rate from the *Global Entrepreneurship Monitor* as an additional determinant. *Second*, we try to solve the causality problem that arises by measuring growth rates in periods preceding the measurement of the GCI. We are not entirely successful in this respect since our dependent variable is measured over the 1999-2003 period and the GCI is measured in 2001. Furthermore, we include a lagged dependent variable (i.e. lagged growth rates) as an explanatory variable to limit the potential impact of reversed causality (see also footnote 87).

As mentioned, we assume that the impact of entrepreneurial activity is dependent upon the stage of economic development. TEA rates may reflect different *types* of entrepreneurs in countries with different development levels. There are two ways in which this hypothesis is tested. The first approach is to include an interaction term of the total entrepreneurial activity rate and per capita income. The model estimated is as follows (i is country index):

(7.1)
$$\Delta GDP_{it} = a + bTEA_{i,t-1} + cTEA_{i,t-1} * GNIC_{i,t-1} + d\log(GNIC_{i,t-1}) + eGCI_{i,t-1} + f\Delta GDP_{i,t-1} + \varepsilon_{it}$$

The hypothesis is then that the value of c is positive. Alternatively, the effect of TEA for different groups of countries (rich versus poor; rich versus transformation versus developing) can be distinguished, this means that the interaction term is substituted for (A and B are groups of countries):

(7.2)
$$\Delta GDP_{it} = a + bTEA_{i,t-1}^{A} + cTEA_{i,t-1}^{B} + d\log(GNIC_{i,t-1}) + eGCI_{i,t-1} + f\Delta GDP_{i,t-1} + \varepsilon_{it}$$

In case A is the group of relatively rich countries (and B the group of relatively poor countries), our hypothesis is that the value of b is larger than that of c.

7.4 Results

Regression results are presented in Table 7.1. The regressions use data for the 37 countries that participated in GEM 2002, minus Croatia.[116] These regressions use TEA 2002 as entrepreneurship measure. The countries participating in GEM 2002 are listed in the Appendix to this chapter. There are five countries that we classify as transition economies, viz. China, Hungary, Poland, Russia and Slovenia. There are seven countries that we classify as developing countries, viz. Argentina, Brazil, Chile, India, Mexico, South Africa and Thailand. Eleven of these twelve countries are classified as (relatively) poor, the exception being Slovenia.[117]

All model specifications in Table 7.1 use initial income and lagged growth as control variables. We present results for a model including the growth competitiveness index only (Model 1), a model including the GCI and a linear TEA term (Model 2), a model including GCI, TEA and the interaction term of TEA and per capita income (Equation (7.1), Model 3), a model including GCI, TEA for the twenty-five (relatively) rich countries and TEA for the eleven (relatively) poor countries (Equation (7.2), Model 4) and a model including GCI, TEA for the twenty-four highly developed countries (the rich countries except Slovenia), TEA for the five transition economies and TEA for the seven developing countries (Model 5).[118]

---

[116] Croatia is excluded because the Growth Competitiveness Index is not available.

[117] The richest of the eleven relatively poor countries is Hungary with a 2001 per capita income of 12,570 US $. The poorest of the twenty-five relatively rich countries is Taiwan with a 2001 per capita income of 16,761 US $. Hence, there is a clear gap in between the two groups of countries in terms of *GNIC*. Slovenia has a 2001 per capita income of 18,160 US $.

[118] Note that our specification in Models 4 and 5 is equivalent to including the variable TEA and slope dummies for rich countries (Model 4) or for transition and highly developed countries (Model 5). We choose to present coefficients and t-values in deviation from zero instead of presenting estimation results in deviation from a reference group. Furthermore, we assume a constant in Equation (7.2) equal for each of the groups of countries. In case the constant is assumed different for rich and poor countries, the difference of the effect of entrepreneurial activity between the rich and poor country groups remains significant. However, in case the constant is assumed different for the three groups of countries (highly developed, transition, developing), the difference of the effect of entrepreneurial activity between the groups fails to be significant. Likelihood ratio tests reveal that Model 2 (which has a log likelihood value of 96.5) is rejected in favour of a

In each of the models we find a negative effect of initial income (logarithm of GNIC), confirming a catch-up effect, and a positive effect of the GCI. The positive effect of the GCI is not significant, though. When we compare Model 2 to Model 1 we find that the addition of only a linear TEA term decreases the adjusted R^2. The effect is also not significant. The addition of a linear term in combination with the interaction term increases the adjusted R^2 considerably, compared to specifications using GCI only. The interaction term has the expected positive effect and this is significant at the 10% significance level.[119] Hence, the impact of entrepreneurial activity increases with per capita income. The impact can be written as $-.428 + .021 GNIC$. This expression has value zero for a per capita income level of about 20,000 US\$. Hence, only beyond this level, increasing levels of entrepreneurial activity benefit economic growth. For comparison, 20 out of the 36 countries in our data set have a 2001 per capita income level that is higher than 20,000 US\$.[120]

---

specification assuming the constant to be identical across the three groups of countries (but having different effects of entrepreneurial activity), but also in favour of a specification assuming identical effects of entrepreneurial activity (but having different constants). However, the log likelihood value of the former specification is higher (106.0 versus 105.3). Hence, we have decided to present these results. The evidence for the three groups of countries should however be interpreted with care.

[119] The correlation between TEA and the interaction term TEA*GNIC is only 0.35 suggesting no problems of multicollinearity.

[120] Spain is closest to the critical value with a 2001 per capita income of 20,150 US\$.

Table 7.1. Estimation results of Equations (7.1) and (7.2) over period 1999-2003 (36 observations)

	Model 1	Model 2	Model 3	Model 4	Model 5
constant	0.011 (0.2)	0.018 (0.4)	0.098 (1.5)	0.105** (2.2)	0.076 (1.5)
TEA		-0.058 (0.5)	-0.428 (1.6)		
TEA*GNIC			0.021* (1.9)		
TEA rich				0.161* (1.8)	
TEA poor				-0.267* (2.0)	
TEA highly dev.					0.188** (2.1)
TEA transition					0.080 (0.5)
TEA developing					-0.183 (1.4)
log (GNIC)	-0.025 (1.5)	-0.028 (1.3)	-0.060** (2.1)	-0.052** (2.5)	-0.041** (2.3)
GCI	0.017 (0.9)	0.018 (0.9)	0.021 (1.2)	0.014 (1.0)	0.013 (0.9)
lagged GDP growth	0.013 (0.0)	0.031 (0.1)	0.006 (0.0)	0.003 (0.0)	-0.059 (0.2)
R^2	0.212	0.224	0.363	0.512	0.543
adj. R^2	0.138	0.124	0.257	0.430	0.448

Note: Absolute heteroskedasticity-consistent t-values are between brackets. TEA is total entrepreneurial activity rate (*Global Entrepreneurship Monitor*), GCI is growth competitiveness index 2001 (*Growth Competitiveness Report*), GNIC is per capita income of 2001. Lagged GDP growth is average annual growth of GDP over the period 1994-1998. ** Significant at 0.05 level. * Significant at 0.10 level.

The two models in which the effect of TEA is allowed to be different for two or three groups of countries perform much better than Model 3 in terms of adjusted R^2. The effect of TEA is found to be significantly positive for the relatively rich countries, while it is found to be significantly negative for the relatively poor countries. Model 5 shows that the latter effect is mainly due to the developing countries and not so much the transition economies. For the highly developed economies the effect of TEA is significant at the 5%-confidence interval. The fact that Models 4 and 5 provide a much better fit than Model 3 suggests that the impact of entrepreneurial activity does not change in a continuous way over the course of economic development, but is different in different stages of development (comprising broad ranges of GDP per capita). However, the results should be interpreted with care given the small number of countries (especially the transition and developing economies). In addition, the analysis has a cross-sectional nature and does not follow countries over the entire range of economic development.

The effect of entrepreneurial activity is significant even after correcting for the GCI. This suggests that the two effects are complementary. The additional positive impact of entrepreneurship in highly developed economies may be caused by various factors. It may indicate that entrepreneurial activity is important in the process of the *commercialization* of new (technological) knowledge. It may also indicate that entrepreneurial activity is important for a healthy development of the business population. Eliasson (1995) shows that the absence of new entrants is expected to have a negative impact on the economic performance of the Swedish economy after about two decades. New firms are important in the introduction of various (non-technological) innovations and they may also serve as a vehicle of increased work effort since the reward for entrepreneurs is likely to be more effort-dependent than for employees. Entrepreneurs may also be more likely than incumbent firms to enter (or even create) new industries. The history of the software- and biotech-industries shows the importance of new firms in the early phases of the industry evolution.

Because our entrepreneurship data are from 2002, and we want to measure the impact on medium term growth, we cannot avoid that the periods for which we measure economic growth and entrepreneurship partly overlap. This makes it difficult to assess the correct direction of causality. Therefore we have estimated various model specifications in which the lengths of the growth periods vary from two to five years. We also varied the most recent year for which we measure growth (2002 or 2003). This is because 2003 is a growth projection instead of a realization. Results of these exercises are presented in an early version of this chapter (Van Stel et al., 2004). The results imply that the longer the growth period, the less strong the business cycle effect (effect of lagged growth) is. For five-year periods the business cycle effect is almost absent and this may indicate that the length of the average business cycle is about five years. Obviously, for shorter periods the effect of the lagged dependent variable is stronger, leaving less room for the other variables to contribute to explained variation in growth rates. However, the general pattern is the same throughout all estimations. There is a positive effect on growth of GCI and an effect of TEA that increases with per capita income. Therefore we feel that our results are quite robust.

7.5 Discussion

Entrepreneurship fails to be a well documented factor in the empirical growth literature because of difficulties defining and measuring entrepreneurship. The investigation of the impact of entrepreneurial activity on economic growth has been one of the main justifications of the *Global Entrepreneurship Monitor* project. In the present chapter we have critically analyzed whether the acclaimed impact of the Total Entrepreneurial Activity (TEA) rate on economic growth stands the test of adding competing variables. There is an impact but not a simple linear one of the TEA rate on GDP-growth. We find that the TEA rate has a negative effect for the relatively poor countries, while it has a positive effect for the relatively rich countries.[121] The results show that entrepreneurship matters. However, the effect of entrepreneurial activity on growth is not straightforward and can possibly be interpreted using the distinction between the Schumpeter Mark I versus Mark II regimes or the 'entrepreneurial' versus 'managed' economy.

---

[121] As will be explained in Chapter 10, the results from the current chapter are consistent with those of Chapter 2 concerning the different impact of entrepreneurship in economies of different stages of economic development. However, there are also some important differences. First, while Chapter 2 uses a model for a set of countries which are followed over time (i.e. a panel is used), this chapter uses a model for a set of countries at one point in time only (i.e. a cross-section is used). Hence, in Chapter 2 low incomes of countries partly refer to low incomes in earlier years, when technology was less advanced. However, given the state of technology at the time, the countries in the data set were among the most developed. To the contrary, low income countries in this chapter refer to countries lagging behind in economic development compared to other countries at the same point in time. In both situations large firms are important for achieving economic growth, but for different reasons. In Chapter 2 low incomes are associated with earlier points in time when large firms were important in creating new technology (Schumpeter Mark II regime or 'managed' economy). In this chapter low incomes refer to countries lagging behind at a recent point in time. In this situation large firms are important for their role in transfering *existing* technology to the poorer countries. Their role in creating *new* technology is less important though. A second difference is that the countries included in the model of this chapter show a higher variation in per capita income levels, compared to Chapter 2. In particular, a number of developing countries is included in the GEM data base, making the difference in estimated effects between low and high income countries more pronounced.

Most of the 20th century can be described as a period of accumulation. From the Second Industrial Revolution till at least the conglomerate merger wave of the late 1960s the large firm share was on the rise in most industries and the economy as a whole. It was the period of "scale and scope" (Chandler, 1990). It was the era of the hierarchical industrial firm growing progressively larger through exploiting economies of scale and scope in areas like production, distribution, marketing and R&D. The period has the characteristics of the Schumpeter Mark II regime. However, by the end of the 20th century things seemed to have changed (Carree et al., 2002). The results of the present study provide some support for such a regime switch. Even so, the small number of observations and the specificity of the time period under investigation do not allow for too strong conclusions.

A striking result of our study is the negative impact of entrepreneurship on GDP growth for developing countries. The result that poorer countries fail to benefit from entrepreneurial activity does not imply that entrepreneurship should be discouraged in these countries. Instead, it may be an indication that there are not enough larger companies present in these countries. Large firms play an important role in the transformation process from a developing economy to a developed economy. Through exploitation of economies of scale and scope they are able to produce medium-tech products. Many local workers may be employed by the large firms and by training on the job these local workers may become more productive compared to when they would run a small store and struggle to survive as an "entrepreneur". Furthermore, in the proximity of large firms, smaller firms may also flourish, as they may act as suppliers for large firms (outsourcing) and may learn a lot of the large companies.

A second possible explanation for the negative effect in poorer countries is that the entrepreneurs have lower human capital levels compared to entrepreneurs in developed countries, as we hypothesized earlier. It is likely that the negative effect reflects the presence of many "marginal" entrepreneurs (shopkeepers) in small crafts who may be more productive as wage-earner in a bigger firm. To the contrary, in developed countries TEA may reflect more innovative entrepreneurs in new sectors (for instance software companies). Of course, the human capital levels of the entrepreneurs cannot be identified from the TEA variable, which hampers interpretation. For poorer countries, even if there are not many large firms and also not many people with high human capital levels, it may still be wise to encourage entrepreneurship if the alternative is unemployment. But perhaps entrepreneurship is not as productive then as in the presence of large firms. Small and large firms often complement each other (Rothwell, 1983; Nooteboom, 1994; Freeman and Perez, 1988). It suggests that developing countries can benefit considerably from foreign direct investment by MNCs since this also increases potential economic contribution of local entrepreneurial activity.

7.A Appendix: Participating Countries in GEM

In this appendix we list the countries that participate in the Global Entrepreneurship Monitor 2002. These are 37 countries. Croatia is excluded from the regressions because the Growth Competitiveness Index is not available for this country. The table also contains the values for the Total Entrepreneurial Activity index for 2002.

Table 7.A: Countries participating in GEM, with values for TEA in 2002

1. United States (US)	0.105	20. Chile (CL)	0.157
2. Russia (RU)	0.025	21. Australia (AU)	0.087
3. South Africa (ZA)	0.065	22. New Zealand (NZ)	0.140
4. The Netherlands (NL)	0.046	23. Singapore (SG)	0.059
5. Belgium (BE)	0.030	24. Thailand (TH)	0.189
6. France (FR)	0.032	25. Japan (JP)	0.018
7. Spain (ES)	0.046	26. Korea (KR)	0.145
8. Hungary (HU)	0.066	27. China (CH)	0.123
9. Italy (IT)	0.059	28. India (IN)	0.179
10. Switzerland (SW)	0.071	29. Canada (CA)	0.088
11. United Kingdom (UK)	0.054	30. Ireland (IE)	0.091
12. Denmark (DK)	0.065	31. Iceland (IS)	0.113
13. Sweden (SE)	0.040	32. Finland (FI)	0.046
14. Norway (NO)	0.087	33. Croatia (HR)	0.036
15. Poland (PL)	0.044	34. Slovenia (SL)	0.046
16. Germany (DE)	0.052	35. Hong Kong (HK)	0.034
17. Mexico (MX)	0.124	36. Taiwan (TW)	0.043
18. Argentina (AR)	0.142	37. Israel (IL)	0.071
19. Brazil (BR)	0.135		

Chapter 8

BUSINESS DYNAMICS AND EMPLOYMENT GROWTH

8.1 Introduction [122]

Several studies argue that in the last 25 years the innovative advantage has moved from large, established enterprises to small and new firms, because new technologies have reduced the importance of scale economies in many sectors (e.g. Meijaard, 2001). Also, an increasing degree of uncertainty in the world economy from the 1970s onwards has created more room for innovative entry (Audretsch and Thurik, 2000). New firms challenge incumbent firms by introducing new inventions that crowd out current technologies and products. In Schumpeter's theory of *creative destruction* not only entries are important but also exits. A high number of exits in an industry might reflect a process of intensive competition, i.e. less-competitive incumbent firms being displaced by new firms. After exiting the market, the human and physical capital that was present in the displaced firms can be allocated more productively elsewhere in the economic process. Hence, both entry and exit are important aspects of business dynamics and both aspects may contribute to the economic performance of an industry.

A commonly used measure of the extent of business dynamics in an industry is turbulence, defined as the sum of entries and exits scaled on some measure of the size of the industry. Several authors study the effect of turbulence on industry performance (e.g. Bosma and Nieuwenhuijsen, 2002). However, a pitfall of these studies is that the *composition* of turbulence is not taken into account: the separate numbers of entries and exits are not distinguished. This is important as the impacts of firm births and firm deaths are fundamentally different. For instance, the direct effect is positive for firm births and negative for firm deaths. The indirect effect (effect on incumbent firms) is also different.

In the current chapter we analyse the effect of business dynamics on employment growth at the country-industry level, allowing for separate effects of both the extent and the composition of business dynamics. The

---

[122] This chapter is based on: Van Stel, A.J. and B.J. Diephuis (2004), Business Dynamics and Employment Growth: A Cross-Country Analysis, Paper 32-2004 on Entrepreneurship, Growth and Public Policy, Jena, Germany: Max Planck Institute of Economics.

extent of business dynamics is an adjusted measure of turbulence, called volatility, while the *composition* is measured as net-entry (entry minus exit). Using both these measures enables to distinguish between situations of high net-entry and low volatility, possibly indicating high survival rates, and situations of low net-entry and high volatility, possibly indicating lower survival rates but more fierce competition (displacement). As these situations may have very different implications for economic growth, it is important to measure the effects of net-entry and volatility separately.

The current chapter claims to make three advances on prior work. First, we make a distinction between the extent and the composition of business dynamics and include measures for both these aspects of business dynamics in a multiple regression model explaining employment growth. Second, we use a unique cross-country data set with harmonized data on numbers of entries and exits for a specific selection of fast-growing and innovative industries. It may be argued that the impact of business dynamics on growth is particularly important for these industries. Third, we test for the existence of an 'optimal' level of business dynamics. Such an optimal level might exist in certain industries if entry and exit levels are too high, possibly indicating that survival probabilities of new firms are too low.

The organization of this chapter is as follows. In Section 8.2 we give an overview of the theory and earlier work. Section 8.3 provides a discussion of the pros and cons of various business dynamics indicators. Next, we present our data and discuss our model. Results are presented in Section 8.5, while the final section is used for discussion.

8.2 Theory and Earlier Empirical Findings [123]

The role of business dynamics (entry and exit of firms) in economic development was first studied by Schumpeter (1934). According to his theory of *creative destruction*, growth, innovation and business dynamics are inherently connected. The economy develops through a process of competition and selection. Firms gain an advantage through innovation and in doing so they achieve excess profits, which encourages imitation and entry. As a result, average profits drop and the firms are stimulated to innovate again. As not all firms have the ability to innovate, selection occurs. From this point of view the entry of new firms is essential because entrants bring with them new ideas, methods and products. Besides, they may force incumbents to perform better because

---

[123] The first paragraph of this section is based on Bosma and Nieuwenhuijsen (2002).

of intensified competition.[124] Hence, the newcomers do not have to be successful themselves in order to contribute to economic development. As far as entry induces improvements on the side of the incumbents, it generates positive effects for the economy even if the new businesses fail and have to exit the market soon after entry (Fritsch and Mueller, 2004). Exiting firms are also important because they create room for new entries. Hence, exiting firms may also contribute to economic growth although their contribution is indirect. In sum Schumpeter states that a high level of business dynamics contributes to economic growth because of its role in selection and innovation.

Several studies have investigated the impact of business dynamics on economic growth. However, the empirical evidence is mixed. This may be caused by the use of different measures for business dynamics as well as for economic growth (Fritsch and Mueller, 2004). Furthermore, the relationship may change over time. Most studies use the regional gross startup rate (number of startups scaled on some measure of the size of the region) as measure of business dynamics. Positive associations between this measure of business dynamics and regional employment change are found for the United States by Reynolds (1999) and Acs and Armington (2004). Ashcroft and Love (1996) find a positive effect for Great Britain in the 1980s. However, Van Stel and Storey (2004), investigating the same relationship for Great Britain, find no such positive effect for the 1980s. Moreover, for one region, the North East of England, they find a negative effect. For the 1990s however, Van Stel and Storey do find a significantly positive effect of the number of startups on regional employment change in Great Britain. Audretsch and Fritsch (2002) find similar results for West-Germany: no effect in the 1980s and a positive effect in the 1990s. The above findings illustrate that there is no consensus in the empirical literature about the exact nature of the relationship.

A further reason for the mixed results between different studies, even when the same countries and the same periods are investigated, may be the different modelling of the time lag involved in the relationship between business dynamics and economic growth. It takes time for new firms to actually contribute to economic growth. According to Caves (1998) turnover from entry and exit makes only a small contribution to economic performance of industries in the short run, but the contribution of entry-exit turnover is far more important in the long run. Two aspects

---

[124] For instance, incumbents imitate innovations made by new firms. The incumbent firms are also stimulated to innovate themselves. Furthermore, to resist the threat of startups, incumbents lower their prices, which, in turn, increases demand for products and services. An overview of the various ways in which incumbents are influenced by startups is provided by Verhoeven (2004). He also presents a scenario analysis of how startups may affect aggregate labor productivity, taking into account both direct and indirect effects (influence on incumbents).

are involved here. First, it may take a new firm a couple of years to expand. Second, it also takes time to become competitive enough to actually challenge the incumbent firms, forcing the latter to perform better.[125] Hence, it may be important to account for a considerable time lag when modelling the relationship. Whereas in most studies the relationship is examined either with no time-lag or with only a short period lag, two recent studies explicitly investigate the time lag of the effect of new firm formation on regional employment change. Van Stel and Storey (2004) report that the effect of new firms is strongest after five years for Great Britain, while Fritsch and Mueller (2004) report an optimal lag of eight years for West-Germany.

Although most studies investigate the relationship between business dynamics and economic growth at the economy-wide level, some studies investigate the relationship also at the sectoral level. For instance, Bosma and Nieuwenhuijsen (2002) investigate the impact of turbulence (sum of entries and exits) on growth of total factor productivity for Dutch regions in the period 1988-1996. They find a positive effect for services and no effect for manufacturing. Acs and Armington (2004) find a similar result for regions in the United States in the period 1991-1996. According to Geroski (1995) entry is not important for employment growth in manufacturing.

Because of these observed differences between services and manufacturing, these sectors will be studied separately in this chapter. For a more extensive overview of the empirical evidence we refer to Carree and Thurik (2003) and Verhoeven (2004).

8.3 Measuring Business Dynamics

Both entries and exits are important aspects of business dynamics. New-firm startups (entries) contribute to economic growth by increasing competition and introducing new innovative products. Exiting firms are also important, as high numbers of exits might reflect a process of intensive competition, i.e. incumbent firms being displaced by new firms entering the market or non-surviving newcomers forcing incumbents to perform better (Fritsch and Mueller, 2004). Three indicators are often used in empirical work relating the extent of business dynamics to the level of economic growth. These indicators are turbulence (entry plus exit), net-entry (entry minus exit) and gross-entry.

Although various studies use turbulence or net-entry as indicator for business dynamics, it should be noted that there are important

---

[125] In the Netherlands, it takes 7 to 8 years before the productivity level of a new-firm startup equals that of an average firm (Verhoeven, 2004).

disadvantages attached to using combinations of entry and exit. This relates to the fact that employment impacts of births and deaths are fundamentally different. The biggest difference in the employment impact of births and deaths is obvious from the *direct* effect. The direct employment effect of births is positive whereas the direct effect of deaths is negative. The different employment impacts of births and deaths make combined indicators like net-entry or turbulence less appropriate, as various authors report. Ashcroft and Love (1996, p. 491) state that "a given change in the stock of firms may have a different impact on employment according to the composition of the stock change. The net employment impact of births and deaths is likely to differ so it is inappropriate to constrain their individual effect to be the same, which is the consequence of defining firm births in net terms". In a study for West-Germany, Fritsch (1996) considers turbulence, net-entry and gross-entry. He states that, due to the often observed high correlation between entries and exits (reflecting processes of displacement and replacement), "the turbulence indicator primarily represents the impact of entries on economic development" (p. 247).

These problems involved in using combinations of entry and exit can be avoided by using the gross startup rate, which is indeed used in most studies investigating the relationship between business dynamics and economic development. However, this measure may still reflect different economic situations. For instance, a relatively high number of startups might reflect that there were too few firms in the market to begin with, i.e. that the 'carrying capacity' of the market was not yet reached (Carree and Thurik, 1999b). Alternatively, it might reflect fierce competition between newcomers and incumbents, battling for market share. In the latter case, the number of exits is expected to be higher than in the former case. The two situations might have very different implications for economic growth and hence, using the gross startup rate is still not ideal.

Ideally, in a regression model explaining some measure of economic growth, a researcher would like to incorporate both a measure of the *extent* of business dynamics (e.g. turbulence) and a measure of the *composition* of business dynamics (*e.g.*, net-entry) in the model, as both aspects are important in their own right. However, in reality, net-entry and turbulence are heavily correlated which makes inclusion of both these measures inappropriate due to multicollinearity (note that the absolute value of net-entry is a lower bound for turbulence).

We will use a measure of turbulence that is corrected for the value of net-entry. This corrected measure is called business volatility and is defined as turbulence (entries plus exits) *minus* the absolute value of net-entry. It is supposed to reflect the degree of turbulence that did not account for the observed changes in the number of firms (Audretsch and Fritsch, 2002). Using this measure enables to include both the *extent* of business dynamics (volatility) and the *composition* of business dynamics (net-entry) in a single regression model.

8.4 Data and Model

International Benchmark Study

      In this section we discuss our data. The various measures of business dynamics are constructed from data on numbers of entries and exits taken from a comparative study of seven countries in the period 1992-1999, conducted by EIM (Verhoeven and Bruins, 2001). In this benchmark study entry and exit data were gathered for a specific set of 15 industries within manufacturing and services, that were considered to be either innovative or fast-growing industries. The industries had to be young, innovative, and/or oriented on competition from abroad (either through import or export), in order to be selected. The 15 industries are listed in Table 8.1. The impact of business dynamics on competitiveness was thought to be especially important for these industries (as they met the above-mentioned criteria). Hence, this selection of industries seems particularly appropriate for the purpose of our study.

      For the selected industries data on numbers of entries and exits were gathered from research institutes in six countries: Belgium, Denmark, Germany, Japan, the Netherlands, and the United States.[126] Data were taken from Chambers of Commerce, VAT-registers and social security records of these countries. As each country uses its own definition of entry and exit, the data had to be harmonized in order to be comparable across countries. For instance, in some countries formations of merger companies or movements of businesses to other regions are counted as new entries, while in other countries these types of changes in business demographics are not counted as new entries.

      EIM harmonized the data and used as definition of entry the start of a new economic activity by a new entrepreneur in a new business (startup) or the start of a new economic activity by an incumbent firm in a new subsidiary company. Furthermore, new firms had to be *active* in order to be counted as entry. Per week, at least one person (owner/manager or employee) has to work in the new business for at least one hour and the business must generate positive turnover. In this way, merger companies, holding companies, corporations that were formed

---

[126] The United Kingdom was also included in the benchmark study of EIM. However, we exclude the U.K. as there were too many missing data for the purpose of our study. In particular, there were no data on business dynamics for the period 1994-1996.

strictly for legal purposes, and the like, were not counted. The definition of exit was chosen consistent with the entry definition.

We use the entry and exit data on the 15 industries reported in Table 8.1 for the six countries from the benchmark study. More details on this data set on entries and exits are in Verhoeven et al. (2001).[127]

---

[127] An alternative cross-country data set on firm demographics is introduced by Bartelsman et al. (2003). They present a harmonized time series data base for ten OECD countries, containing information on entry, exit, survival and employment growth at the firm-level. Their analysis reveals that high technology manufacturing industries and some ICT related industries have higher entry rates than average. In particular, several of the industries listed in Table 8.1 are reported to have higher than average entry rates. This supports our idea that the selection of industries used in the present chapter may be particularly appropriate for studying the relationship between business dynamics and employment growth. An important difference between the data set used in the present chapter and the data set used in Bartelsman et al. is that firms without employees are included in the present study whereas they are excluded in Bartelsman et al. Actually, many of the data sets on startups that are used in the literature exclude firms without employees, such as, for instance, the data set used by Fritsch and Mueller (2004) for Germany, and the data set used by Acs and Armington (2004) for the United States.

Table 8.1. Industries used in this chapter

Nace revision 1.1 code	Industry
	Manufacturing:
2416/17	Manufacture of plastics and synthetic rubber in primary forms
2441/42	Manufacture of basic pharmaceutical products and pharmaceutical preparations
3001/02	Manufacture of office machinery and computers
3110/20	Manufacture of electric motors, generators, and transformers, and electricity distribution and control apparatus
3210/20/30	Manufacture of radio, television and communication equipment and apparatus
3310/20/30/40	Manufacture of medical, precision and optical instruments
3530	Manufacture of aircraft and spacecraft
37	Recycling
15-37, excluding above eight industries	Other manufacturing
	Services:
51.6	Wholesale of machinery, equipment and supplies
64.2	Telecommunications
7210/20/30/40/60	Computer and related activities (excluding maintenance and repair of office machinery)
7310	Research and experimental development on natural sciences and engineering
7420/30	Architectural and engineering activities and related technical consultancy; and technical testing and analysis
72-74, excluding above three industries	Other business services

Source: EIM.

Model

In our multiple regression analysis we will explain the variation in employment growth rates by net-entry and volatility.[128] Furthermore,

---

[128] Data on value added growth or productivity growth were not available. Employment growth may not be the most ideal dependent variable. Although the Schumpeterian process of creative destruction leads to a replacement of less efficient firms with more efficient ones, these efficiencies may manifest themselves in terms of *labour-saving* productivity. Nevertheless, while such a labour-saving effect may occur, it also concurrently results in improved competitiveness as incumbent firms are forced to perform better in order to survive. This, in turn, may lead to rising market shares, for instance by way of a larger

country dummies and lagged employment growth are used as control variables. The dummy variables are included to control for country-specific effects not covered by the model.[129] We also include lagged employment growth as an independent variable to correct for reversed causality, i.e. country/industry combinations with high growth attracting new businesses. Even though we include lagged business dynamics indicators only, the employment impact of net-entry or volatility might be overestimated, due to positive path dependency in the economic performance of country/industry combinations (reflecting business cycle and industry life-cycle effects). We correct for this by including a lagged dependent variable (see also footnote 87).

Although distinguishing between net-entry and volatility gives more insight than just using turbulence, interpretation of regression results is still not straightforward, particularly for net-entry. For instance, if a positive effect of net-entry on employment growth is found, what does that mean? It is conceivable that, in that case, new firms in industries with high net-entry rates are –on average– of a higher quality than new firms in industries with low net-entry rates. In this interpretation a higher net-entry rate would be consistent with a higher proportion of the new-firm startups surviving. This would signal a higher quality of the new firms, which, in turn, would have a positive impact on growth. In addition, the higher number of competing firms, which results from a high net-entry rate, positively affects industry growth. However, we have to be careful with this interpretation, for two reasons. First, a low net-entry rate does not necessarily mean that relatively many new firms did not survive. It may also reflect that incumbent firms were forced out of the market by the increased competition by the new firms. These possibilities cannot be distinguished using our data. Second, a positive effect of net-entry may also reflect an industry life-cycle effect. If demand for products and services produced by a certain industry is growing, then both the number of firms and employment in the industry increase, consistent with a positive coefficient. This would not necessarily imply that the new firms are of an above-average quality. However, the industry life-cycle effect is –at least in part– captured by the lagged dependent variable.

Variables and Sources

The definitions of the variables used in this chapter and their data sources are listed below.

---

supply of different goods through innovation. These *indirect supply-side effects* make that the impact on industry employment can still be positive (Fritsch and Mueller, 2004).

[129] We do not include industry dummies. Structural differences between industries are partly captured by the lagged dependent variable. Also, the model is estimated separately for manufacturing and services.

- Average annual employment growth rates are measured over the period 1997-2000 (dependent variable) and 1994-1997 (lagged dependent variable).

- Turbulence rate: this is the summation of the numbers of entries and exits, scaled on the stock of businesses.

- Net-entry rate: this is the difference between the numbers of entries and exits, scaled on the stock of businesses.

- Volatility rate: this is turbulence minus the absolute value of net-entry, scaled on the stock of businesses.

The three indicators of business dynamics are all measured over the period 1994-1996. We use a three-year average to correct for outlier years, and we measure business dynamics in a period prior to employment growth (i.e. we use a time-lag) in order to obtain the correct direction of causality.

The source of all four above-mentioned variables is the international benchmark study conducted by EIM (Verhoeven and Bruins, 2001).

Descriptive Statistics

As mentioned, we use data for six countries and 15 industries, yielding a maximum number of observations of 90. However, for some country/industry combinations data on business dynamics were missing, especially for Japan. Furthermore, there was one clear outlier, the telecommunications industry in the United States, which has values for turbulence and volatility greater than one.[130] This observation is removed as well. We end up with a data set of 78 observations.

Means and standard deviations of business dynamics indicators for our sample are presented in Table 8.2, both by country and by sector. We see that turbulence, net-entry and volatility are higher for services industries than for manufacturing industries. This reflects the fact that it is easier to start a new business in services than in manufacturing, as —in general— less startup capital is required.

When looking at the data per country, we notice two interesting cases. The United States shows a very high value of volatility and a

---

[130] In their study for ten OECD countries Bartelsman et al. (2003) also find very high entry rates for this industry. They give two explanations for this: first, the privatization of telecoms in a number of countries that has led to the entry of a number of new private operators, and second, the rapid increase in the number of firms operating in the communications area, related to the spread of Internet and e-commerce activities.

below-average value of net-entry.[131] This pattern might reflect a process of intense competition where the strongest firms are selected through the market mechanism. This, in turn, might result in high growth rates. Alternatively, however, it might reflect that survival rates of new firms are (too) low, for instance because entry barriers are too low. This would imply lower growth rates. For the Netherlands we see a reverse pattern: volatility is relatively low while net-entry is relatively high. The high net-entry rate might reflect a higher probability of survival of new firms, possibly indicating a higher quality of the new firms.[132] However, the low volatility might point to a lack of competition, possibly indicating that there is not enough pressure from the market for new and incumbent firms to increase their performance.

In our empirical analysis we try to find out which of the two patterns is more conducive to economic growth. To this end we will include both net-entry and volatility in our regression model.

---

[131] Germany has a relatively high average volatility rate as well. This is caused mainly by two industries with values above 0.6: telecommunications and recycling.

[132] It may also reflect industry life-cycle effects.

Table 8.2. Means and standard deviations of business dynamics indicators by sector and country

	Turbulence rate	Net-entry rate	Volatility rate
Manufacturing (46)	0.160	0.022	0.122
	(0.128)	(0.054)	(0.110)
Services (32)	0.288	0.085	0.202
	(0.184)	(0.080)	(0.143)
TOTAL (78)	0.212	0.048	0.155
	(0.165)	(0.073)	(0.130)
Belgium (15)	0.129	0.027	0.095
	(0.061)	(0.046)	(0.039)
Denmark (14)	0.184	0.023	0.127
	(0.084)	(0.096)	(0.059)
Germany (15)	0.295	0.082	0.213
	(0.261)	(0.074)	(0.194)
Japan (6)	0.121	0.018	0.080
	(0.051)	(0.055)	(0.042)
Netherlands (15)	0.206	0.083	0.123
	(0.123)	(0.074)	(0.065)
United States (13)	0.293	0.033	0.257
	(0.186)	(0.046)	(0.167)
TOTAL (78)	0.212	0.048	0.155
	(0.165)	(0.073)	(0.130)

Source: EIM. Note: Figures between brackets are numbers of observations (first column) or standard deviations (second to fourth column). Statistics for manufacturing and services are based on pooled country/industry data of the respective industries listed in Table 8.1 (unweighted averages).

Correlations between Business Dynamics Indicators

In Section 8.3 it was described that turbulence and net-entry should not be used in one and the same regression model because of problems of multicollinearity. Therefore, we use a corrected measure of turbulence, volatility. As an illustration Table 8.3 presents correlation coefficients between turbulence, net-entry and volatility for our data sample of 78 observations. We see that correlations between net-entry and *turbulence* are indeed strong and highly significant, while the correlation between net-entry and *volatility* is much weaker. This underlines the need to correct the turbulence rate for the impact of net-entry.

Table 8.3. Correlations between business dynamics indicators, by sector

	Manufacturing (46 obs.)			Services (32 observations)		
	Turbul.	Net-entry	Vo-lat.	Turbul.	Net-entry	Vo-lat.
Turbulence	1			1		
Net-entry	0.519 ***	1		0.669 ***	1	
Volatility	0.942 ***	0.274 *	1	0.911 ***	0.304 *	1

*** Significant at 0.01 level. ** Significant at 0.05 level. * Significant at 0.10 level.

8.5 Results

The regression model is estimated separately for manufacturing and services, using OLS. For both sectors we use a pooled estimation sample, containing the respective industries for the six countries listed in Table 8.1. Results are shown in Tables 8.4 and 8.5. Each table contains four model specifications. We start by including net-entry only (Model I). Next, we add volatility (Model II).

Extremely high entry and exit rates in an industry may reflect that survival probabilities are too low, and that the industry attracts too many 'marginal' entrepreneurs, absorbing capital and human energy that could have been allocated more productively elsewhere (Carree et al., 2002). This would imply that volatility can actually be too high (possibly indicating that entry barriers are too low), and that from a certain level of volatility onwards, further increases may have a negative effect on growth. This would be consistent with the existence of an *optimal* level of volatility. To test this we also include a squared volatility term (Model III). If the parameter estimate of the linear volatility term is positive and the estimate of squared volatility is negative and significant, this implies that there is a level of volatility beyond which further increases negatively influence growth.[133]

Although the absolute value of net-entry is corrected for in the volatility rate, the two measures are still correlated, both for manufacturing and services (see Table 8.3). Therefore, we are also interested in the results when including a combined measure such as turbulence. This enables comparison between specifications using measures for both the composition and the extent of business dynamics on the one hand, and specifications using a combined measure on the other hand. The results of the turbulence specification are in the last column of Tables 8.4 and 8.5 (Model IV).

---

[133] This optimal level could then be calculated as $-b/2a$, where a and b are the parameter estimates of volatility squared and volatility, respectively. At this volatility level the effect on growth is maximised.

Manufacturing

Model IV in Table 8.4 shows that turbulence has a significantly positive effect on employment growth for manufacturing industries. From Model II we see that this result reflects positive effects of both net-entry and volatility. The positive effect of net-entry might reflect that high survival probabilities are important for achieving industry growth. However, as described in Section 8.4, we have to be careful in interpreting the effect of net-entry. The positive effect of turbulence (volatility) suggests that a process of 'creative destruction' as described by Schumpeter (1934), may indeed be a requirement in manufacturing industries of modern economies for achieving growth. Innovating new firms challenge incumbent firms by introducing new inventions that render current technologies and products obsolete. The significantly positive effect of volatility underlines the importance of variety and selection through the market in this process. Strong competition between new ideas (either new products or new processes) being exploited by different firms, makes that the best ideas, and hence the best firms, survive in the market.[134] The high quality of the surviving firms, in turn, positively affects economic growth.

From Model III –which includes volatility squared– it is clear that we have not found evidence for the existence of an 'optimal' level of volatility in manufacturing. Inclusion of the squared term does not lead to an increase of adjusted R^2 and t-values for both the linear and the squared term are low. Hence, there are no indications that volatility levels are too high for the manufacturing industries in the countries that we consider.

---

[134] Indeed, the manufacturing sector is known as a very competitive sector in the sense that there is not only domestic competition but also a considerable amount of competition from abroad. Hence, both new firms and incumbents have to be innovative in order to survive.

Table 8.4. Estimation results Manufacturing, dependent variable growth of employment

	Model I	Model II	Model III		Model IV
Constant	-.005	-.055	-.029		-.054
	(0.2)	(1.6)	(0.6)		(1.6)
Net-entry	.48 *	.45 *	.44 *		
	(1.8)	(1.8)	(1.7)		
Volatility		.28 **	.012		
		(2.3)	(0.0)		
Volatility squared			.45		
			(0.7)		
Turbulence					0.28 **
					(2.5)
Lagged growth	.23 **	.12	.094		.16
	(2.0)	(1.0)	(0.8)		(1.3)
Adjusted R^2	.163	.253	.243		.223
Observations	46	46	46		46

Note: Absolute t-values are between brackets. Dependent variable is average annual employment change 1997-2000. Lagged growth is average annual employment change 1994-1997. Turbulence, net-entry, and volatility rates are averages over the period 1994-1996. Country dummies not reported.
*** Significant at 0.01 level. ** Significant at 0.05 level. * Significant at 0.10 level.

Services

Model IV in Table 8.5 shows that there is also a positive effect of turbulence on employment growth for services industries. Again, this reflects positive effects of volatility and, to a smaller extent, net-entry (Model II). The coefficient of net-entry is not significant though. Model III provides no evidence for the existence of an 'optimal' volatility rate in the services industries, as t-values for both the linear and the squared term are low.[135]

---

[135] In part this is caused by the removal of the US telecommunications industry from the sample (see Section 8.4). Estimation results of a test regression for a sample which included this observation, implied that for telecommunications in the United States the volatility rate could be considered suboptimal (i.e. too high).

Table 8.5. Estimation results Services, dependent variable growth of employment

	Model I	Model II	Model III		Model IV
Constant	.045 *	-.003	.026		-.005
	(2.0)	(0.1)	(0.5)		(0.2)
Net-entry	.24 *	.16	.13		
	(2.0)	(1.4)	(1.0)		
Volatility		.14 *	-.060		
		(1.7)	(0.3)		
Volatility squared			.31		
			(0.9)		
Turbulence					.15 ***
					(2.8)
Lagged growth	.21 *	.21 *	.22 *		.21 *
	(1.7)	(1.8)	(1.8)		(1.9)
Adjusted R^2	.339	.394	.388		.420
Observations	32	32	32		32

Note: Absolute t-values are between brackets. Dependent variable is average annual employment change 1997-2000. Lagged growth is average annual employment change 1994-1997. Turbulence, net-entry, and volatility rates are averages over the period 1994-1996. Country dummies not reported.
*** Significant at 0.01 level. ** Significant at 0.05 level. * Significant at 0.10 level.

Comparing Tables 8.4 and 8.5 we notice that the effects of business dynamics on employment growth are stronger for manufacturing than for services. The coefficients for the business dynamics indicators are considerably higher for manufacturing in all four model specifications. Significance levels are also higher (Model II). The weaker effect for services may be related to the different character of innovation in services, compared to manufacturing. In particular, innovations in service industries are often non-technological and they mostly involve small and incremental changes in processes and procedures (De Jong et al., 2003, p. 16). To the contrary, innovations in manufacturing require more R&D and are more radical in nature. In modern economies radical innovation is more conducive to economic growth than incremental innovation. This is because industry life-cycles are shorter and hence, at a given point in time, more (niche) markets are in an early stage of the life cycle where R&D is highly productive and the costs of radical innovation tend to be relatively low (Audretsch and Thurik, 2001). Hence, a lack of business dynamics in manufacturing industries may be particularly damaging to economic performance, as it may imply a lack of incentives to create (radical) innovations.

    We have seen that both net-entry and volatility contribute positively to growth at the country-industry level. Hence, judging from

Table 8.2, countries like Belgium and Japan should improve on both these aspects. We also observe that, although the United States is often considered the world's most dynamic economy (in terms of turbulence this is correct), there is still room for improvement as the US has a below-average value of net-entry (both for manufacturing and for services).[136]

8.6 Discussion

In this chapter the relationship between business dynamics and employment growth has been examined for 15 fast-growing and innovative industries in six developed economies. Harmonized data on numbers of entries and exits are used from an international benchmark study conducted by EIM in 2001. In our multiple regression analysis we allow for separate effects of both the *extent* of business dynamics (volatility of firms) and the *composition* of business dynamics (net-entry of firms). We also test for the existence of an 'optimal' level of business volatility, possibly resulting from too high levels of entry and exit prevailing in certain industries. We find positive employment effects of net-entry rates and volatility rates. These effects are found to be considerably stronger for manufacturing compared to services. We find no evidence for an 'optimal' level of volatility.

Our study has two important research implications. First, in investigating business dynamics, it is important to make a distinction between the extent of business dynamics (volatility of firms) and the composition of business dynamics (net-entry of firms). We have shown that the relative importance of volatility and net-entry may differ across sectors. A second research implication is that the relationship between business dynamics and growth may be industry-specific, even within broader sectors such as manufacturing and services. For instance, the positive effect for manufacturing found in this chapter is in contradiction with earlier studies that did not find an effect of business dynamics on performance for manufacturing (Acs and Armington, 2004; Bosma and Nieuwenhuijsen, 2002). However, these two studies used the manufacturing sector as a whole as unit of analysis, while the present chapter used a specific selection of fast-growing and innovative industries. The industries in our study are young, innovative, and/or oriented on competition from abroad (either through import or export). The difference between the non-result in the earlier studies and the highly significant

---

[136] Bartelsman et al. (2003) report that entry size in the United States is smaller compared to that of most other countries in their data set and conclude that entrant firms in the United States are further away from the minimum efficient scale than entrant firms in most other countries. However, they also report higher post-entry employment growth amongst *surviving* firms in the United States, compared to other countries in their data set.

positive result found in the present study suggests that the process of creative destruction as described by Schumpeter may be particularly prevalent for manufacturing industries with these characteristics (i.e. industries that are fast-growing and/or innovative). More research at sufficiently low sectoral aggregation levels is needed to be able to draw definitive conclusions about this conjecture.

Also some policy implications arise from our study. It is often argued by scholars and policy makers that high levels of business dynamics foster economic growth. This conjecture is confirmed by the results of the present chapter. We find that both net-entry and volatility are important for achieving growth. The positive effect of net-entry suggests that for the (manufacturing) industries used in this chapter, it may be good policy to focus on the quality of new-firm startups in order to increase survival probabilities of the new firms. For instance, a larger initial size of the startups might have a positive impact on the chances of survival, and ultimately on the performance of the industry (see Verhoeven, 2004, for evidence for the Netherlands). The positive effect of volatility implies that a process of competition between new ideas and market selection of the most innovative firms contributes positively to economic growth. To stimulate this process, entry barriers such as high administrative burdens and limited access to finance should be reduced in order to enable as many entrepreneurs as possible to pursue commercialization of their idea in the market. This stimulates the market selection process, which, in turn, positively affects the performance of the industry. A mixture of these different policies is probably the best way to go.

We also find evidence that the importance of business dynamics for achieving growth is higher for manufacturing than for services. The stronger effect for manufacturing may be related to the different character of innovation in manufacturing (more often radical), compared to services (more often incremental). In modern economies radical innovation is more conducive to economic growth than incremental innovation (Audretsch and Thurik, 2001). Hence, a lack of business dynamics in manufacturing industries may be particularly damaging to economic performance, as it may imply a lack of incentives to create radical innovations.

One has to bear in mind that the results found in this chapter apply to a specific set of industries (see Table 8.1). Future research should investigate the relationship between business dynamics and growth for more industries at low sectoral aggregation levels. In this way we can see whether the results found in this chapter may be generalized to the manufacturing and services sectors as a whole.

Chapter 9

COMPENDIA: HARMONIZING BUSINESS OWNERSHIP DATA

9.1 Introduction [137]

In present times there is renewed attention for the role of entrepreneurship in the economy. This is reflected by an increasing amount of research in the field of entrepreneurship. Much of this research is qualitative in nature. Far less entrepreneurship research is quantitative. In particular, there are relatively few studies which use data bases with internationally comparable figures on entrepreneurship.

Operationalizing entrepreneurship for empirical measurement is difficult (Storey, 1991). The degree of difficulty involved increases exponentially when cross-country comparisons are made. Systematic measurement conducive to cross-country comparisons is limited (Audretsch, 2003). Nevertheless, cross-country data bases on entrepreneurship are important in understanding the role of entrepreneurship in economic processes. The measure most often used to operationalize the extent of entrepreneurship in a country is the number of self-employed individuals or business owners, largely because they are measured in most countries, and measured in comprehensive ways facilitating comparisons across countries and over time (Blau, 1987). But even for this measure of entrepreneurship, cross-country comparability is a major problem. The numbers of self-employed reported in *OECD Labour Force Statistics* -one of the most important data sources on the subject- are not comparable across countries as each country supplies figures according to its own self-employment definition. In particular, the extent to which owner/managers of incorporated businesses (OMIBs) are included in the self-employment counts differs across countries. This problem is not very well-known.[138] However, in chapter 5 of *OECD*

---

[137] This chapter is reprinted from: Van Stel, A.J. (2005), COMPENDIA: Harmonizing Business Ownership Data Across Countries and Over Time, *International Entrepreneurship and Management Journal* 1 (1), pp. 105-123, with kind permission of Springer Science and Business Media, Inc.

[138] For instance, during a panel discussion of policy makers at the "First GEM Research Conference" (Berlin, April 2004), participants expressed their surprise because –contrary to what is commonly believed– Germany had relatively more self-employed individuals

Employment Outlook June 2000, attention is being paid to this particular subject, and an overview of self-employment definitions used in various (OECD) countries is provided.

In recent years, EIM has made an attempt to construct an international data base with (macro) self-employment figures for 23 OECD countries that are comparable across countries. The 23 countries are the 15 countries of the (old) European Union plus Iceland, Norway, Switzerland, the United States, Japan, Canada, Australia and New Zealand. The data base is called COMPENDIA (COMParative ENtrepreneurship Data for International Analysis). The data base currently contains figures for the period 1972-2002 (even years only), and is updated every two years.

To arrive at such a uniform data base, we first established the exact definition per country used in OECD Labour Force Statistics. Next, we have chosen a self-employment definition to be used in our uniform data base. In choosing a definition, we acknowledge that business ownership (self-employment) and entrepreneurship are related but not synonymous concepts. Entrepreneurship in a 'Schumpeterian sense' refers to the activity of introducing 'new combinations' of productive means in the market place. Entrepreneurship in a broad economic sense (business ownership or self-employment) means owning and managing a business, or otherwise working on one's own account. Thus, on the one hand Schumpeterian entrepreneurs are a small fraction of the business owners, while on the other hand some entrepreneurs (so-called intrapreneurs) do not work on their own account.[139]

In COMPENDIA we have chosen a strict application of the broad entrepreneurship definition given above. This involves inclusion of owner/managers of both unincorporated and incorporated businesses but exclusion of unpaid family workers. Following statistical convention, our definition also excludes so-called 'side-owners' (self-employment as a secondary activity). Self-employed individuals in the sectors agriculture, hunting, forestry and fishing are also excluded. For countries not following the COMPENDIA definition in OECD Labour Force Statistics, we made a correction to arrive at an estimate for the number of self-employed persons according to the required definition. In the present chapter, we provide explanation on the COMPENDIA data base. We describe in detail what the self-employment figures represent, how the figures were obtained and what corrections were made to the raw data.

---

than the United States, according to OECD statistics. However, this can be explained by the fact that for Germany, OMIBs are included in the OECD self-employment count, whereas for the US, they are excluded. Hence the data are not comparable between the two countries.

[139] For a complete overview about the relation between the concepts entrepreneurship and self-employment/business ownership, see Wennekers and Thurik (1999).

We pay special attention to the United States, as this country alone accounts for about 30% of all self-employed reported in the COMPENDIA data base.

The organization of this chapter is as follows. In Section 9.2, we discuss the self-employment (business ownership) definition used in COMPENDIA. Also, we discuss the data on self-employment published in OECD Labour Force Statistics, which form the main source for our data base. In Section 9.3 we discuss the general method that –in principle– is used for each country to correct the raw LFS data.[140] As an illustration of the many data problems that may arise when constructing a times series on the number of business owners, Section 9.4 discusses in detail the construction of the COMPENDIA times series for the United States. Section 9.5 presents the business ownership rates for the 23 countries and provides some explanation on general trends in business ownership that can be observed across countries. The final section is used for discussion.

9.2 Definitions and Main Data Source

In this section we describe the self-employment (business ownership) definition used in COMPENDIA, i.e. which groups of workers are included in the self-employment count? We also mention the industry groups covered in COMPENDIA and we give a short overview of harmonization problems that have to be solved. Finally, we describe how business ownership data are scaled in COMPENDIA, to arrive at comparable figures across countries. We start this section with a description of self-employment data in OECD Labour Force Statistics.

Self-Employment Data in OECD Labour Force Statistics

OECD Labour Force Statistics forms the basis for our data set on the number of self-employed per country. In this annual publication, in the chapter Country Tables, for every country there is a table called 'Professional status and breakdown by activities'. In this table, total employment is divided in three professional statuses: a) employees, b) employers and persons working on own account, and c) unpaid family workers. In principle, we use the category 'employers and persons working on own account'. At all events, this category includes all *unincorporated* self-employed individuals (sole proprietors and partners). However, as far as *incorporated* self-employed are involved (owner/managers of incorporated businesses), there is a uniformity problem. In some countries they are counted as self-employed and in other

---

[140] In the remainder of this chapter the full name 'OECD Labour Force Statistics' and the abbreviation 'LFS' will be used interchangeably.

countries they are counted as employee. The latter case may prevail because formally, owner/managers of incorporated businesses are employees of their own businesses. The different statistical treatment of incorporated self-employed in different countries forms the main harmonization problem to be dealt with in COMPENDIA, and we will discuss this problem in detail in Section 9.3.

In LFS, professional status applies to the *primary activity* of a person. For example, a person who works as an employee in some business for four days a week, and runs his own business for one day a week (i.e. the person is self-employed as *secondary activity*) is counted in the a)-category rather than in the b)-category mentioned above.[141] In other words, the data in the professional status classification in LFS relate to the main job. In COMPENDIA, we follow this practice and we exclude the so-called side owners (secondary activity) from our self-employment count.

Which Groups of Workers are Included in COMPENDIA?

In constructing a data set on numbers of self-employed, we have to decide which groups of workers are included in the self-employment count, and which are not. In particular, we have to deal with the following two cases: unpaid family workers and owner/managers of incorporated businesses. In some studies, these groups of workers are counted as self-employed, and in other studies they are counted as employees. As regards unpaid family workers, we consider these workers not relevant for measuring the extent of 'entrepreneurship'. These people do not own the business they work for, and thus do not bear responsibility and risk in the same way as 'real' self-employed individuals do. We exclude this group of workers from our self-employment count. As regards owner/managers of incorporated businesses, we do consider this group as highly relevant, because in an 'entrepreneurial' sense, this group is not essentially different from the unincorporated self-employed. We include the incorporated self-employed in our self-employment definition.

Which Industry Groups are Covered in COMPENDIA?

In LFS, the employment status division is applied separately for the agriculture, hunting, forestry and fishing industries on the one hand and the 'non-agricultural activities' on the other hand.[142] The agricultural industries are structurally different from the rest of the economy, in that self-employment is the natural employment status in these industries. We

---

[141] The minimum weekly amount of time that a person has to work in order to be included in the (self-) employment count of LFS is one hour (OECD, 2002, pp. xi-xii).

[142] The 'agricultural industries' are thus defined to include agriculture, hunting, forestry and fishing.

exclude the agricultural industries from our self-employment count and concentrate on the numbers of self-employed in the non-agricultural industries.

Summarizing we use the following self-employment (business ownership) definition in COMPENDIA:

> the total number of unincorporated and incorporated self-employed outside the agriculture, hunting, forestry and fishing industries, who carry out self-employment as their primary employment activity.

We use the terms business owners and self-employed interchangeably, to indicate that we also include owner/managers of incorporated businesses in our self-employment notion.

Harmonizing the OECD Labour Force Statistics Data

In constructing a harmonized data set for the number of business owners across countries and over time, two types of comparability problems can be identified. The first problem involves comparability across countries, i.e. different countries using different self-employment definitions. Having chosen a self-employment definition to be used in our data set COMPENDIA, we have to adjust the raw LFS data for those countries which use a different definition in LFS. The corrections that we apply mainly involve corrections for the numbers of incorporated self-employed in certain countries. We aim at applying the same method for each country to ensure comparability. This general method is described in Section 9.3. The second problem involves comparability over time, i.e. the occurrence of trend breaks in LFS. A trend break may occur if the set-up of the labour force survey in a country changes from a certain year onwards. Also changes in self-employment definitions over time or changes in industrial classifications may introduce trend breaks. These trend breaks are corrected for in COMPENDIA and the corrections are described in Section 9.4 for the United States. For the corrections made for the remaining 22 countries we refer to Van Stel (2003).

Scaling the Business Ownership Data

In order to compare self-employment figures across countries in a meaningful way, some form of scaling must be applied. A common scaling variable is the size of the labour force. In COMPENDIA, the number of self-employed (business owners) in a country as a fraction of total labour force is indicated as the country's business ownership rate. Total labour force consists of employees, self-employed persons (including OMIBs), unpaid family workers, people employed by the Army and unemployed persons. Data on total labour force are also obtained from OECD Labour Force Statistics. For this variable, comparability problems of the raw LFS figures across countries and over time occur less often than for the variable self-employment. However, in some cases, corrections were still needed, and these are described in Van Stel (2003).

9.3 Harmonizing Self-Employment Data in COMPENDIA

In this section we give a general description of the data collection and data construction of the number of business owners for the 23 countries in the data base, for the period 1972-2002. As mentioned, our business ownership definition includes unincorporated self-employed as well as owner/managers of incorporated businesses (OMIBs). We exclude the agricultural industries. In principle, we use the numbers reported in OECD Labour Force Statistics. At all events, this item includes all unincorporated self-employed. However, the extent of inclusion of OMIBs in the reported numbers varies per country, due to different set-up of labor force surveys in different countries. This involves issues as whether classification in employment status categories is done by the interviewer or by the respondent, the degree of guidance that is given by the interviewer on the term 'self-employment', the number of categories which respondents can choose from, etcetera. For details on these labour force surveys, see OECD (2000), Annex 5A.

Estimating the 1994 Level of the Number of OMIBs

The countries thus differ in the extent to which OMIBs are included in the official statistics. In *OECD Employment Outlook June 2000*, p. 158, countries are categorized in five types as regards the inclusion of OMIBs in OECD Labour Force Statistics:

1) excluding (all) OMIBs,
2) classification of OMIBs is unclear,
3) including (all) OMIBs,
4) including most OMIBs,
5) excluding most OMIBs.

Our desired definition is the third one: including (all) OMIBs. For countries not following this definition, i.e. those countries which are categorized as 1), 2), 4), or 5), we make an estimation of the number of OMIBs *in 1994* using the following procedure.

Estimation Procedure for European Countries

We use as the total number of business owners (unincorporated as well as incorporated self-employed) the maximum of

a) the reported number of self-employed in OECD Labour Force Statistics 1981-2001, and

b) the number of 'non-primary private enterprises' with less than 50 employees, from the data base that is constructed in the framework of *The European Observatory for SMEs: Sixth Report* (KPMG/ENSR, 2000).[143] This data base is largely based on the Eurostat publication *Enterprises in Europe*, which contains harmonized information for the 18 European countries in our COMPENDIA data set on (among other variables) the number of enterprises, by industry and size-class.

We use the number of enterprises with less than 50 employees because in larger companies the manager often does not have the control. Formally, this control rests with the shareholders. A second reason for not including *all* firms in the estimated number of business owners is that not all firms are independent. Dependent firms (subsidiary companies) by definition are not linked to self-employed individuals. By using the number of enterprises smaller than 50 employees, we do not take account of the fact that partnerships have more than one self-employed individual, and on the other hand, that individuals can have more than one corporation or that individuals can run a business as a side activity. However, the number of enterprises smaller than 50 employees should approximately equal the number of business owners, *by and large*.

The comparison is made for the year 1994. In case the number of enterprises exceeds the reported number of 'employers and persons working on own account', as reported by OECD Labour Force Statistics, we can derive a raise-factor that corrects for the number of OMIBs. *In principle*, for such countries we apply this raise-factor constantly, for the whole period 1972-2002. For those 1)-, 2)-, 4)-, or 5)-categorized countries for which the reported number of business owners in LFS exceeds the number of enterprises, we choose the number of LFS-reported business owners. Because such a country does not belong to category 3), we know that such an estimate does not include *all* OMIBs. But we also know that the number of enterprises is lower, and therefore we argue that it is likely that the vast majority of the OMIBs *is* included in the reported LFS number.

Estimation Procedure for Non-European Countries

---

[143] The term 'non-primary' is defined to exclude agriculture, hunting, forestry and fishing.

For the five non-European countries in COMPENDIA, we look again at the categorization in OECD Employment Outlook June 2000. The above-mentioned European Observatory for SMEs does not contain data on non-European countries. Therefore in case the categorization is not '3) including (all) OMIBs', we must estimate the number of OMIBs in another way. We use country-specific sources and we refer to Section 9.4 (United States) and Van Stel (2003) (other countries) for a description. In all cases we apply a procedure that resembles the procedure for the European countries as closely as possible.

Expert Knowledge

For all countries in our data set it holds that we deviate from the above procedures in case we dispose of 'expert knowledge', i.e. additional information from other sources. This is the case for the Netherlands, Iceland, Switzerland, and New Zealand. For the estimation of the number of OMIBs of these countries we refer to Van Stel (2003).

Is the Development Over Time of Numbers of OMIBs Measured Independently?

In Table 9.1, the number of business owners including statistically non-identified OMIBs is estimated for 1994. For some countries this results in a raise-factor that corrects (for) the number of OMIBs. In principle, the raise-factor is applied constantly for the whole period 1972-2002. In a small number of countries, the implicit assumption is that the development over time of the number of incorporated self-employed (ISE; or OMIBs) equals that of the number of unincorporated self-employed (USE). This may be an implausible assumption as the development over time of the numbers of these two groups may be quite different over such a long period of time. This is not a desirable characteristic of using such a procedure.[144]

However, for the majority of countries the actual assumption that lies behind our method of estimating the number of OMIBs, is not so strong. For example, when a country is categorized as 'including most OMIBs', the development over time of 'most' OMIBs *is* included in the published numbers of OECD Labour Force Statistics. The actual assumption that we make when applying a point estimate of the raise-factor constantly for the whole period, is that the proportion of *non-identified* OMIBs in the total number of business owners stays constant over time, and this is a less strong and hence more plausible assumption.

---

[144] Note that for countries where the 1994 number of business owners in LFS exceeds the number of enterprises smaller than 50 employees, i.e. countries that use the reported LFS numbers, the development over time of the number of ISE *is* measured independently of the development of the number of USE.

Additionally, for the United States, we use independent information on the number of OMIBs for the whole period 1972-2002. The only assumption we make here is that the quotient (employer firms)/(*self-reported* incorporated self-employed according to Current Population Survey) stays constant over the period 1972-1986 (see Section 9.4). This is not such a strong assumption, and hence the development over time of the number of estimated OMIBs for the US may be considered reliable.

In Table 9.1 we give an overview of the results of applying the (missing) OMIBs estimation procedure described in this section. The number of enterprises is reported only when it is needed in the OMIB estimation procedure of that country. Hence, the number is not reported for countries with categorization 'including all OMIBs', or for countries where 'expert knowledge' is used. The number of enterprises is also not reported for the non-European countries. In principle, the mentioning of a raise-factor for a country in the last column of Table 9.1 implies that the factor is applied constantly for the whole period 1972-2002. However, in three cases (The Netherlands, United States and Japan), the raise-factor is mentioned for illustrational purposes only.

Table 9.1. Estimating the number of business owners including all OMIBs in 1994 for 23 OECD countries (all numbers expressed in thousands) [1]

Country	OMIB-categori-zation in OECD Empl. Outlook June 2000	1. Number of business owners in OECD LFS 1981-2001	2. Number of enterprises smaller than 50 employees	3. Number of business owners (1994) used in COMPEN-DIA 2002.1	Raise-factor OMIBs (=3./1.; only if 3.>1.)
Austria	unclear	230	281	281	1.22
Belgium	**incl. all**	498		498	
Denmark	incl. most	161	164	164	1.02
Finland	incl. most	193	167	194	
France	incl. most	1817 [3]	2293	2293	1.26
Germany	incl. most	2938	3070	3070	1.04
Greece	incl. most	840	555	840	
Ireland	incl. most	145	72	162	
Italy	unclear	4117 [3]	3681	4117	
Luxembourg	unclear	11.8 [4]	13	13	1.10
Netherlands [2]	incl. most	596		699	1.17 [6]
Portugal	unclear	736	600	736	
Spain	**incl. all**	2052		2052	
Sweden	incl. most	340	335	340	
Unit. Kingdom	incl. most	3002 [3]	3136	3170	1.04
Iceland [2]	unclear	18.1		18.1	
Norway	excl. most	116	168	168	1.45
Switzerland [2]	N.A.	N.A.		292	
United States	excl. all	8955		13929	1.56 [6]
Japan	excl. all	6130		6950	1.13 [6]
Canada	**incl. all**	1804 [5]		1804	
Australia	excl. all	984		1493	1.52
New Zealand [2]	unclear	226		226	

[1] Data on number of enterprises taken from *The European Observatory for SMEs: Sixth Report*; estimation of OMIBs for non-European countries based on country-specific sources. Finland and Ireland: 1994 number of business owners in COMPENDIA 2002.1 adjusted for post-1994 trend breaks.

[2] Expert knowledge: estimation of number of OMIBs deviates from usual procedure.

[3] OECD Labour Force Statistics, version 1978-1998. UK: raise-factor for COMPENDIA 2000.1 (1.04) has been applied to revised 1994 figure (3035, from LFS 1981-2001).

[4] Including unpaid family workers.

[5] OECD Employment Outlook June 2000.

[6] Raise-factor not used to construct the data, and only mentioned for purpose of illustration.

9.4 Measuring Business Ownership in the United States

As regards the number of self-employed individuals in the United States, many different sources report different figures. The official self-employment definition as practiced by the Bureau of the Census in its *Current Population Survey* (CPS) excludes the incorporated self-employed. The definition thus only includes the unincorporated self-employed which consist of sole proprietors and partners, see SBA (1997), p. 87.[145] As we also include the incorporated self-employed (ISE) in our COMPENDIA definition, we had to resort to other sources as regards the number of ISE.

The organization of this section is as follows. First, we discuss reported figures on (unincorporated) self-employed in various sources. Our estimation of the number of incorporated self-employed is described in Section 9.4.2. This subsection also includes a discussion on some specific measurement problems concerning ISE. Third, we present our business ownership series for the US, and we provide some explanation for the different developments over time of numbers of unincorporated and incorporated self-employed. Finally, we provide a discussion on the large differences between numbers of self-employed according to labour force surveys and numbers of businesses according to tax return data.

9.4.1 Unincorporated Self-Employed

To illustrate the variety of figures on the self-employed, we consider the number of self-employed in 1994 (in thousands). According to OECD (2002) the number of non-agricultural self-employed is 8955. According to SBA (1997), p. 88, Table 3.1, which is taken from the source *Statistical Abstract of the United States* and which corresponds to Bregger (1996), p. 4, Table 1, the number is 9003. Finally, according to SBA (1997), p. 90, Table 3.3, which is a tabulation by Carolyn Looff and Associates based on unpublished CPS data, the number is 8856 (unincorporated self-employed). See Table 9.2a. In this chapter, the sources Bregger (1996) and Carolyn Looff and Associates (as reported in SBA, 1997) will henceforth be abbreviated as Bregger and Carolyn Looff.

---

[145] People who are self-employed as a secondary activity (side owners) are also not included in the Census definition, see SBA (1997), p. 87.

Table 9.2a. Number of non-agricultural self-employed in 1994, according to different sources [1]

Source	Reported self-employed 1994 (x 1000)
OECD Labour Force Statistics 1981-2001	8955
Carolyn Looff and Associates, as reported in SBA (1997)	8856
Statistical Abstract of the United States, as reported in SBA (1997) / Bregger (1996)	9003

[1] Unincorporated self-employed, primary activity, excluding unpaid family workers.

At first sight, Table 9.2a is confusing. Three sources which claim to report the number of non-agricultural self-employed in 1994, all report (slightly) different figures. If we take a closer look the differences can be explained though. One problem is the industrial classification of the agricultural sector. All three sources claim to report the number of self-employed in the 'non-agricultural' industries. However, OECD Labour Force Statistics (LFS) and Carolyn Looff actually refer to 'agriculture' in broad sense. That is, they do not only exclude the agricultural sector, but also the hunting, forestry and fishing sectors.[146] Bregger, on the other hand, excludes only the agricultural sector proper. Indeed, Bregger and LFS actually use the same source, the Current Population Survey. Both sources report the same number of self-employed (and also the same number of total employed) for all industries, namely. Only the division between the agricultural and non-agricultural sectors differs. So, the difference between 9003 (Bregger) and 8955 (LFS) actually represents the number of self-employed workers in the hunting, forestry and fishing sectors. Because we use the sector definition of LFS, the figure of Bregger is inappropriate for our purposes. In other words, we work with the broad definition of agriculture.

We have now found the explanation for the difference between Bregger and LFS. But why does Carolyn Looff also deviate from LFS? Both work with the same agriculture definition and both work with CPS data. An explanation might be that Carolyn Looff reports data from the month March, while LFS reports year averages. In March, the demand for workers is on average lower than for instance in the holiday months July

---

[146] For LFS, we can deduct that this is indeed the case from the observation that the totals for the whole economy are divided between agriculture, hunting, forestry and fishing on the one hand and 'non-agricultural activities' on the other hand. For Carolyn Looff we can deduct the same thing from a related Carolyn Looff-table with an industrial classification of the 'non-agricultural' sectors which does not include the hunting, forestry and fishing sectors, see SBA (1997), pp. 92-93, Table 3.4.

and August. This might be an explanation for the lower figures of Carolyn Looff (the total employment figure is also lower than that of the LFS). In Table 9.2b, the possible explanations for the different figures are summarized.

Table 9.2b. Explanations for different 1994 self-employment figures in different sources

Source	Non-agricultural self-employed 1994 (x 1000)	Definition 'Agriculture'	Time of survey
OECD LFS 1981-2001	8955	broad (incl. hun, for, fish)	year average
Carolyn Looff	8856	broad	March
Bregger	9003	narrow	year average

9.4.2 Incorporated Self-Employed

In the previous section we saw that there is some confusion about the numbers of unincorporated self-employed persons. The confusion gets even bigger if we want to measure the number of incorporated self-employed, i.e. the number of owner/managers of incorporated businesses. As mentioned earlier, this type of self-employment is excluded from the figures in official statistics. As a result, information on the numbers of owner/managers is hard to find. However, there are two sources which report more or less comparable figures on the subject. These are again Bregger (1996) and Carolyn Looff, as reported in SBA (1997), p. 90. In SBA (1997), p. 91, it is reported that the number of incorporated self-employed (the owner/managers) increased with 40% between 1976 and 1979 and with 33.3% between 1979 and 1983. Bregger, p. 8, reports that the number of self-employed owners of incorporated businesses rose from 1.5 mln in 1976 to 2.1 mln in 1979 and to 2.8 mln in 1982. Note that these figures correspond to the 40% and 33.3% increases as reported in SBA (1997). However, it is clear from the latter source that the 33.3% increase relates to a four-year period and not to a three-year period.[147] So, we have a figure of 2.8 mln for all industries (including the agricultural sectors) in 1982 according to Bregger. In SBA (1987), p. 114, Table 4.3 -which is the same type of tabulation as the one of Carolyn Looff in SBA (1997), p. 90- a number of 2.59 million of incorporated self-employed (ISE) in May 1983 is reported for all *non-agricultural* industries. These figures seem to match quite well. Indeed the ratio 2.59/2.8 (non-agricultural ISE/total ISE)

---

[147] The 33.3% increase actually relates to the period 1978-82 instead of 1979-83, and to *all* industries, see SBA (1987), p. 112, Table 4.2. Because the period analysed in that table is 1979-83, the relative changes were assumed equal for the two periods.

closely resembles the corresponding ratio for 1989 that can be derived from Bregger, p. 8, Table 5.[148] Therefore, in order to construct a series of the number of incorporated self-employed between 1976 and 1994, we use the figures for 1983, 1988 and 1994 as provided by SBA (1987), p. 114, Table 4.3 and SBA (1997), p. 90, Table 3.3 (these two tabulations are consistent) and for 1976 and 1979 we apply the 40% and 33.3% increase figures to the 1983 figure of 2.59 mln. We can even go back until 1967.[149] For 1967, Fain (1980), p. 7, reports a number of 850,000 incorporated self-employed. This figure is consistent with the figures for 1976 and 1979 reported by Bregger (1996). In order to correct for the agricultural owner/managers we again apply the relative growth rate (1.5/0.85 between 1967 and 1976, an increase of 76.4%) in order to arrive at an estimate of the number of non-agricultural incorporated self-employed in 1967. See Table 9.3.

Table 9.3. Incorporated self-employed (non-agricultural), 1967-94, preliminary times series

Year	Number (x 1000)	Source / method
1967	786	increase 76.4% 1967-76, reported by Fain (1980)
1976	1388	increase 40.0% 1976-79, reported by SBA (1987), p. 112
1979	1943	increase 33.3% 1979-83, reported by SBA (1987), p. 112
1983	2590	SBA (1987), p. 114
1988	2984	SBA (1997), p. 90
1994	3955	SBA (1997), p. 90

Source: Own calculations, based on SBA.

Underestimation of Numbers of Owner/Managers

Although with help of data reported in SBA (1987, 1997) we have been able to produce some preliminary figures for the number of owner/managers, it is important to note that these figures actually understate the real number of owner/managers. This is because legally,

---

[148] Actually, the ratio in Bregger is somewhat higher. One possible explanation is that agriculture has become less important between 1982/83 and 1989. Another one is that the non-agricultural industries are more broadly defined in Bregger, as discussed earlier.

[149] From 1967 on, because of a change in the Current Population Survey in that year, it is possible to identify those workers who report themselves as self-employed but have incorporated their business. Before 1967, these workers could not be identified separately from other self-employed individuals. See Bregger (1996), p. 4, and Fain (1980), p. 7.

these workers are employees of their own businesses. Now, in the labour force survey people are asked whether they are employed by a government, a private company or a nonprofit organization (in which cases they are classified as wage and salary workers) or whether they are self-employed. In the latter case, the following question is asked: "Is this business incorporated"? The people who answer 'yes' are still classified as wage and salary workers in the official statistics. It is these figures (the numbers of people who answer 'yes' on the incorporated business question) that are tabulated in SBA (1987, 1997) and which figures we have taken over in Table 9.3. However, not *all* incorporated self-employed are detected by the extra question. Owner/managers who answer that they are wage and salary workers (because legally this is the case) are not identified as self-employed workers because no extra question is asked to people who respond that they are employed by a private company. So the reported numbers of incorporated self-employed only relate to people who responded (erroneously, for the purposes of the labour force survey) that they are self-employed. The figures do not include the owner/managers who (correctly, for those purposes) identify themselves as wage and salary workers. These owners cannot be identified. For more details about these questionnaires, see Bregger, p. 8, SBA (1997), p. 113, and OECD (2000), Annex 5A.

So, the reported figures are actually an understatement of the real number of incorporated self-employed. However, the magnitude of the understatement is unknown, see Fain (1980), p. 7: "Another group which cannot be separated and studied are those incorporated self-employed who report themselves initially as wage and salary employees. There is no way to determine how large this group might be or to know whether it has grown larger or smaller over time". The problem of the unidentified owner/managers who report themselves as wage and salary worker seems to prevail not only in the United States but also in other OECD countries. This is because in general, statistical definitions are based on legal employment statuses, see Hakim (1988), p. 422: "Working proprietors or managers of incorporated businesses are classified as employees in statistical surveys, because that is their status in law and for tax and social insurance purposes. However, these distinctions are not necessarily observed by respondents to the labour force surveys that provide the main source of data on self-employment, and errors cannot always be detected and corrected by statistical offices." So, because the official status of owner/managers is that of employee, labour force surveys do not bother to ask respondents who report themselves as employees whether or not they own an incorporated business. Therefore, their numbers are unknown, as Hakim (1988), p. 423, reports: "And we do not have any idea how many more working proprietors and managers of their own incorporated businesses are invisible in the statistics because they classified themselves –according to the rules– as employees of their own small firm".

While Fain (1980) and Hakim (1988) in principle report on the particular measurement problems in the United States and the United Kingdom, respectively, the problems prevail in many other (if not all) OECD countries as well. See for example OECD (1992), p. 185: "Data on the numbers of owner-managers of incorporated businesses are not widely available. In addition, their propensity to report themselves as self-employed is unknown". This implies that those owner/managers who report themselves as employee are not identified, consistent with Fain (1980) and Hakim (1988). See also OECD (2000), Annex 5A.

Correction Based on Number of Employer Firms

Because we want to obtain a plausible estimate of the number of incorporated self-employed, and we know that the series from Table 9.3 is too low, we make a correction on these series. For this purpose we use the number of employer firms, as yearly published in the *The State of Small Business, A Report of the President*, see for example SBA (1998a), p. 118, Table A9, and SBA (1999), p. 205, Table A5. The number of employer firms is a conventional estimate for the number of OMIBs. See SBA (2000), p. 5: "Incorporated self-employment is generally defined as an employer firm [...]". In *The State of Small Business, A Report of the President*, the number of 'nonfarm' employer firms is published each year, both by size-class and by industry.[150] Because we work with the broad definition of agriculture, we subtract the number of employer firms in the industry 'Agricultural services, Forestry, and Fishing' from the total number of 'nonfarm' employer firms. Next, because we try to use a method for the United States that is as uniform as possible with the method for the European countries, we take only the employer firms that are smaller than 50 employees.[151] This leads to the series in Table 9.4 below.

---

[150] The term 'farm' relates to agriculture in narrow sense here, compare Section 9.4.1.

[151] For this purpose the number of firms with employment size between 19 and 50 is approximated at 75% of the firms with size between 19 and 100.

Table 9.4. Estimated number of incorporated self-employed (non-agricultural) in US, 1988-2000, based on number of employer firms (x 1000)

	1988	1990	1992	1994	1996	1998	2000
Inc. SE	4690	4789	4808	4974	5157	5408	5528

Source: Own calculations, based on SBA (1998a), p. 118, Table A9 (years 1988-94), SBA (2000), p. A-2, Table 1.2 (years 1996-98), and SBA (2001), p. A-3, Table 2 (year 2000).

As we see from Table 9.4, the number of employer firms is measured from 1988 onwards. We have no information on the number of employer firms before that year. Therefore, for the year 1988, we compute the ratio employer firms / incorporated self-employed according to the labour force survey (see Table 9.3) and apply this factor to the series in Table 9.3 (for the years prior to 1988). The ratio equals 4690/2984 = 1.57. The implicit assumption is that about two third of the OMIB-respondents in the labour force survey classify themselves as self-employed while one third classify themselves as wage and salary employees. This may be plausible.[152]

9.4.3 Total Number of Self-Employed

Having constructed a series for the incorporated self-employed, we are now able to construct a series for the total self-employed, according to our definition (all incorporated and unincorporated self-employed but excluding the agricultural sectors, the secondary jobs and the unpaid family workers). For the unincorporated self-employed (USE) we use OECD Labour Force Statistics.[153] For the incorporated self-employed (ISE) we use the series from Table 9.4 for 1988 and later years, and the series from Table 9.3, with the correction factor applied to it, for the years prior to 1988. For the years between 1972 and 1988 that are not reported in Table 9.3, we interpolate. This results in the series presented in Table 9.5.

---

[152] In a description of labour force surveys in different countries, OECD (2000), p. 192, states that "It is assumed that when the procedure is self-assessment alone, OMIBs will mainly classify themselves as self-employed".

[153] We use LFS versions 1981-2001 and 1970-1990. For 1990 and 1992, we have used LFS 1974-1994, in order to take account of two (minor) trend breaks in 1990 and 1994 in LFS 1981-2001.

Table 9.5. Total number of US non-agricultural self-employed, 1972-2000 (x 1000)

	1972	1976	1980	1984	1988	1994	2000
USE (OECD LFS)	5342	5754	6956	7748	8474	8955	8630
ISE, uncorrected [1]	1120	1388	2104	2669			
ISE, corrected [2]	1761	2181	3308	4195	4690	4974	5528
Total self-employed	7103	7935	10264	11943	13164	13929	14158
Labour force (OECD LFS)	88847	97826	108544	115241	123378	132474	143774
Business ownership rate	0.080	0.081	0.095	0.104	0.107	0.105	0.098

Source: Own calculations.

[1] See Table 9.3.

[2] See Table 9.4 for 1988-2000, and apply factor 1.57 for period 1972-86.

Different Trends for Incorporated and Unincorporated Business Owners

From Table 9.5, we see that the number of incorporated self-employed (ISE) has increased faster than the number of unincorporated self-employed (USE). For example, in the period 1980-2000, the number of ISE increased with an average of 2.6% per year. In the same period the average annual growth of the number of USE was 1.1%. Apparently, more self-employed individuals choose for incorporation of their business. Why does this occur? There can be many reasons, as Fain (1980), p. 7, reports: "The move towards incorporation is a function of many complex factors. A worker will usually incorporate his business for traditional benefits of the corporate structure, including limited liability, tax considerations, and the increased opportunity to raise capital through the sale of stocks and bonds". Simply put, when an unincorporated business expands, it becomes more attractive to incorporate the business. So, when small businesses perform well and expand, they will often choose for incorporation. In that case however, the status of the entrepreneur in the official statistics changes from self-employed to employee. See Bregger, p. 8: "What undoubtedly occurs is that, as the small businesses expand and bring on employees, the owners incorporate their businesses, thereby shifting the class-of-worker classification to wage and salary employment. This type of transitional shuffling, while not readily measurable, is very likely an ongoing event [...]".

From the previous paragraph, it is clear that data on USE alone can be misleading. For example, if the number of USE stays constant or decreases, one cannot tell whether this is because business ownership really decreases, or whether many small businesses have incorporated their business and as a result are not considered self-employed any more in official statistics. Formulated otherwise, if the number of USE decreases one cannot tell whether the 'real' degree of business ownership is affected as well. The above example underlines the importance of including the owner/managers of incorporated businesses in the self-employment count.

9.4.4 Inconsistency of Self-Employment Data and Business Stock Data

As has become clear from the previous discussion, there are many difficulties in measuring the number of business owners. Another intriguing statistical problem is linking the number of *business owners* to the number of *businesses*. For the United States, striking differences exist between data on the number of self-employed and data on the number of businesses. Business data are collected by the Internal Revenue Service of the U.S. Department of the Treasury (IRS). In Table 9.6, we report for 1994 the number of businesses per type of business from IRS (number of business tax returns), as reported by SBA (1997), p. 25, and the number of self-employed per type of self-employed from Carolyn Looff and Associates, as reported by SBA (1997), p. 90.

Table 9.6. Comparison of business data (IRS) and self-employment data (Carolyn Looff), 1994

Businesses (IRS)	Number (x 1000)	Self-employed (Carolyn Looff)	Number (x 1000)
Corporations	4667	Incorporated self-empl.	3955
Partnerships	1558	Unincorporated self-empl.	8856
Proprietorships	15831	Self-employed as second job [1]	2539
Total	22056	Total	15350

[1] In the tabulation of Carolyn Looff this group is called Wage-and-Salary Workers with Self-Employment (WSSE).

In SBA (1987), p. 135, two explanations are put forward for the differences between IRS data on the number of businesses and the CPS data on the number of business owners: "First, self-employed persons with more than one business are counted only once in the CPS, but all reporting businesses are included in IRS counts. Second, all movement into self-employment during the year is counted in the IRS survey, while the CPS provides only a snapshot view-the month of May".

Difference Corporations / Incorporated Self-Employed

Regarding the first row of Table 9.6 (corporations versus incorporated self-employed), the gap between the number of corporations and the number of incorporated self-employed individuals might be explained more or less satisfactorily by the explanations already mentioned and some other ones. First, people can indeed have more than one corporation. Second, there are corporations without (incorporated) self-employed individuals, like dependent corporations (subsidiary companies). There are also no self-employed in a firm if the majority of the shares is not owned by one (or sometimes two or three) persons but if the shares are divided in a great number of smaller shares (for instance, companies with an exchange quotation). Note that, on the other hand, there may also be corporations with more than one incorporated self-employed individual. But in that case, businesses are counted more than once in the IRS survey. As is reported by SBA (1998b), p. 2, about the IRS data: "Tax return data include all businesses, but it will overstate the number of businesses when a business files more than one tax return". So, firms having more than one self-employed individual is not a cause for the differences between the CPS and IRS data. A third explanation for the differences between CPS and IRS data is that there are also incorporated self-employed individuals who are not counted in the CPS as self-employed (because they report themselves as employee of their own business) but whose businesses *are* counted in the IRS. This is because every business has to pay taxes, so businesses are always counted. Fourth, there is the stock/flow difference as described in SBA (1987), p. 135. All four explanations point in the direction of more corporations in the IRS count than incorporated self-employed individuals in the CPS count. Given that the difference is not extremely large, the figures in the first row of Table 9.6 seem to be more or less plausible.

Difference Proprietorships / Unincorporated Self-Employed

Looking at the second and third row of Table 9.6, the differences between the business figures and the self-employment figures are much larger. If we assume that people who are self-employed as a second job (side owners) do not own incorporated businesses but instead own unincorporated businesses, we can compare the total number of unincorporated businesses (sole proprietorships and partnerships) according to IRS –which is 17,391,000– with the total number of unincorporated self-employed (primary and secondary jobs) according to Carolyn Looff: 11,395,000. So, there is a huge gap of almost 6 million businesses that is unaccounted for. Looking at the four possible explanations that applied to the difference between the number of corporations and the number of incorporated self-employed individuals, we conclude that only the fourth one also applies to the difference for the unincorporated businesses and self-employed. The other three possible explanations do not apply here, as will now be explained. First, people cannot have more than one unincorporated business since one can bear full liability only once. Second, unincorporated businesses always have at least one self-employed individual. Third, the specific problematic of the hidden incorporated self-employed does not apply to the unincorporated self-employed. So, only the stock/flow argument remains to explain the difference between businesses and self-employment. However, the gap of 6 million is far too large to ascribe to this particular argument.

Conclusion: Differences Cannot be Explained

We conclude that the differences between business statistics and (self-) employment statistics cannot be explained in a satisfactory way, particularly for the unincorporated businesses and self-employed. But what's more, also publications that report on the number of businesses in the U.S. are not always consistent in themselves. For example, in SBA (1998b), p. 2, there are two tables on the number of U.S. businesses: one from the IRS which reports 23,155,000 nonfarm business tax returns in 1996 and one from the Bureau of the Census which reports 17,253,000 businesses in 1992 (all industries). Leaving the reasons for the difference between these two figures out of consideration (two of which are the four year difference and the possibility of double tax returns in the IRS count), it is at least striking that in the text covering these tables (SBA, 1998b, p. 1), we read: "The total number of businesses in the U.S. is not definitely known; however, the figure is believed to be between 13 and 16 million". These last figures are thus not consistent with the figures in the tables themselves, which are higher. They *are* however in line with the self-employment figures from Carolyn Looff, see Table 9.6.

Apparently, considering the quotation just mentioned, the status of the (high) figures from several business statistics is not clear. In COMPENDIA, however, we are interested in business owners and not in businesses. Despite all the problems and limitations that also exist for the statistics on the number of self-employed persons, the figures from this type of statistics seem to be more consistent than business statistics. We consider the series on the number of self-employed individuals (business owners) that we constructed in Table 9.5 a reasonably reliable estimate.

9.5 Business Ownership Rates 1972-2002

In this section we present some data on business ownership from the COMPENDIA data base. The complete data base can be found at www.eim.net. From Table 9.7 we see that in 2002 business ownership rates are high in Mediterranean countries, especially Greece and Italy, while they are relatively low in Scandinavian countries and Luxembourg. We also see that for the 23 OECD countries covered by the data set, there are over 44 million business owners, 46% of whom are in European countries, and 31% of whom are in the United States.

Concerning developments over time, most countries display a U-shaped pattern of initial decline, followed by an increase of the business ownership rate. The decline is not always visible from Table 9.7 because the data start only in 1972. However, in the post World War II period business ownership rates have declined constantly in most Western economies. Large firms exploited economies of scale in the production of new economic and technological knowledge, leaving little room for entrepreneurship and small businesses (Schumpeter, 1950). But from the 1970s onwards times have changed and the trend towards less self-employment has reversed, starting in the United States. There are several reasons for the revival of small business and self-employment in Western economies. Notably, in many sectors, new technologies have reduced the necessity of scale economies to arrive at competitive advantages (Meijaard, 2001). Developments like globalization, the ICT-revolution and the increased role of knowledge in the production process have led to increased dynamics and uncertainty in the world economy from the 1970s onwards. In turn, these developments have created room for (groups of) small firms to act as agents of change (Audretsch and Thurik, 2000). The bigger role in technological development for small and new firms is referred to by Audretsch and Thurik (2004) as a regime switch from the 'managed' to the 'entrepreneurial' economy.[154]

---

[154] There are also other reasons for the revival of entrepreneurship such as an increased consumer demand for variety and the increased employment share of services in modern economies. See Carree et al. (2002) for an overview.

Table 9.7. Business ownership rates in 23 OECD countries, 1972-2002

	1972	1980	1988	1996	2002	Share 2002
Austria	0.093	0.073	0.069	0.074	0.083	0.007
Belgium	0.105	0.098	0.109	0.119	0.113	0.011
Denmark	0.082	0.074	0.056	0.064	0.067	0.004
Finland	0.066	0.064	0.076	0.080	0.079	0.005
France	0.113	0.101	0.099	0.088	0.081	0.049
Germany (West)	0.076	0.066	0.070	0.082	0.086	0.078
Greece	0.161	0.182	0.186	0.197	0.193	0.019
Ireland	0.077	0.086	0.101	0.112	0.112	0.005
Italy	0.143	0.148	0.169	0.183	0.183	0.100
Luxembourg	0.107	0.087	0.075	0.067	0.054	0.000
Netherlands	0.100	0.085	0.082	0.102	0.108	0.020
Portugal	0.113	0.119	0.116	0.156	0.137	0.016
Spain	0.118	0.110	0.123	0.130	0.129	0.053
Sweden	0.074	0.070	0.064	0.081	0.081	0.008
United Kingdom	0.078	0.074	0.101	0.111	0.107	0.072
Iceland	0.111	0.088	0.101	0.130	0.123	0.000
Norway	0.097	0.084	0.084	0.071	0.065	0.003
Switzerland	0.066	0.065	0.071	0.085	0.076	0.007
Europe-18	**0.100**	**0.095**	**0.105**	**0.112**	**0.110**	**0.460**
United States	0.080	0.095	0.107	0.104	0.095	0.312
Japan	0.125	0.131	0.123	0.101	0.092	0.139
Canada	0.079	0.087	0.106	0.128	0.122	0.047
Australia	0.126	0.168	0.164	0.155	0.164	0.037
New Zealand	0.106	0.090	0.114	0.139	0.135	0.006
23 Countries	**0.098**	**0.102**	**0.110**	**0.109**	**0.104**	**1.000**
Total number of business owners (x 1000)	29401	34342	40666	44206	44342	

Source: COMPENDIA 2002.1.
Business ownership rates refer to the number of non-agricultural self-employed (unincorporated as well as incorporated) as a fraction of the labour force.
Germany refers to West-Germany until 1991.

Many Western countries have experienced a shift from the 'managed' to the 'entrepreneurial' economy. However, the extent and timing of this shift has not been identical across countries (Audretsch et al., 2002a). The first country to experience the transition from the 'managed' to the 'entrepreneurial' economy was the United States (Verheul et al., 2002). Indeed, from Table 9.7 it can be seen that the United States has the highest increase in business ownership rate between 1972 and 1980. The different extent and timing of the shift across countries is further illustrated by Figure 9.1, where the development of the business ownership rate is depicted for the United States, the United

Kingdom, France and Germany. As mentioned, the upswing in business ownership was first experienced by the United States in the 1970s. The United Kingdom followed in the 1980s. Still later, Germany follows (see also Audretsch, 2000). France however, has had a constantly decreasing business ownership rate.

Institutions and policies of countries play a role in the different extent and timing of the shift across countries. For instance, the steep increase in business ownership in the United Kingdom in the 1980s was stimulated by government policy aiming at maximising the number of new-firm startups in an attempt to fight unemployment (Van Stel and Storey, 2004). In the 1990s however, UK policy changed towards a focus on incumbent business with 'growth potential', which may explain the leveling off of the business ownership rate in the 1990s.[155] The constant decrease in France may be due to French policy, which for a long time focussed on large businesses, for instance by giving the majority of their orders to large businesses. Also, high tax burdens on SMEs and a discrepancy in social security between wage- and self-employed people create few incentives for entrepreneurship. A negative cultural attitude towards entrepreneurship probably also plays a role (Henriquez et al., 2002).

---

[155] In the United States the leveling off may be due to shake out of industries that are in a more advanced stage than elsewhere in modern OECD countries (Audretsch and Thurik, 2004).

Figure 9.1. Development in business ownership in four OECD countries, 1972-2002

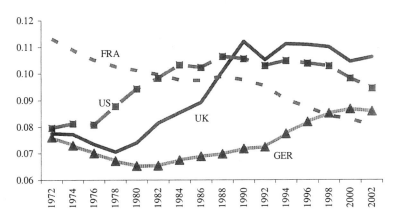

Source: COMPENDIA 2002.1.

Germany refers to West-Germany until 1991.

9.6 Discussion

In this chapter we presented the data set COMPENDIA. The data set contains harmonized information on numbers of business owners and the size of the labour force, for 23 OECD countries over the period 1972-2002. The quotient of these two variables is called the business ownership rate. These harmonized data are helpful for conducting quantitative research on entrepreneurship at the macro level. Our primary data source is OECD Labour Force Statistics and in COMPENDIA we have made an attempt to make business ownership rates comparable across countries and over time. The main problem in harmonizing business ownership data is the different statistical treatment of the incorporated self-employed, as this category of workers is classified as wage-and-salary workers in some countries, and as self-employed workers in other countries. We have chosen our business ownership definition to include the unincorporated *and* the incorporated self-employed, because both categories run their own businesses. Concerning self-employment definitions being in force in different countries, we based ourselves on the definitions reported in OECD Employment Outlook June 2000. Next, for countries not including *all* owner/managers of incorporated businesses in their self-employment count, we made corrections based on numbers of enterprises from The European Observatory for SMEs: Sixth Report, or, for some countries, specific information from national sources.

In making these corrections, we tried to approximate the (unknown) real numbers of business owners as closely as possible. Of course, the quality of the approximations depends on the plausibility of the corrections applied. In this respect, we should mention some limitations of our data set. First, for many countries, we apply a constant correction factor for OMIBs (computed in 1994) to the whole period 1972-2000. This is not ideal as, in reality, the number of OMIBs in proportion to the number of unincorporated self-employed may change over time. In many cases this drawback is however mitigated because our correction only relates to a smaller number of non-identified OMIBs. Second, for many countries, our correction factor for numbers of OMIBs is based on enterprise data, not on employment (i.e. person-based) data. It is well-known that there are many difficulties in relating these two kinds of data sources. Third, for some countries little information on numbers of non-agricultural self-employed was available in OECD Labour Force Statistics, forcing us to use rather crude approximation methods. This holds especially for Switzerland and, prior to 1986, for New Zealand (see Van Stel, 2003, for details). Despite these limitations we think that COMPENDIA provides the most reliable, comparative data set available today, regarding business ownership across industrialized countries and over time.

For harmonizing business ownership data across countries and over time, the ideal situation would be to use actual data on numbers of incorporated self-employed (as for some countries is already done in COMPENDIA 2002.1), but for many countries these numbers cannot be identified from the domestic labour force surveys being in force. For these countries, corrections based on numbers of enterprises are the best approximation possible. Nevertheless, in order to improve cross-country comparability of business ownership data, future research should concentrate on collecting actual data on numbers of incorporated self-employed. If not available from labour force surveys, such data may be obtained from other national sources like tax return data.

Chapter 10

OVERVIEW AND CONCLUSIONS

The present chapter summarizes and concludes. Section 10.1 provides an overview of the separate chapters of this book (excluding the introductory chapter) while Section 10.2 presents conclusions.

10.1 Chapter Overview

In Chapter 2 we address the two-way relationship between business ownership and economic development at the macro level. The chapter focuses upon three issues. First, how is the 'equilibrium' rate of business ownership related to the stage of economic development? Second, what is the speed of convergence towards the equilibrium rate when the rate of business ownership is out-of-equilibrium? Third, to what extent does deviating from the equilibrium rate of business ownership hamper economic growth? Hypotheses concerning all three issues are formulated in the framework of a two-equation model. The first equation deals with the impact of economic development on business ownership, basically estimating a (U-shaped) functional form for the relation between economic development and business ownership. Because this equation is modelled using an error-correction mechanism, and because we find a significant amount of error-correction, the estimated relation may indeed be considered an *equilibrium* relation.[156] The second equation deals with the impact of business ownership on economic development. This equation tests whether differences between the actual and the estimated equilibrium rate of business ownership have a negative impact on subsequent economic growth. In other words, can the 'equilibrium' rate of business ownership also be interpreted as an 'optimal' rate? The model is tested for 23 OECD countries using the COMPENDIA data set mentioned earlier. We find confirmation for the hypothesized economic growth penalty on deviations from the equilibrium rate of business ownership.

---

[156] In Chapters 2 and 3 of this book the term 'equilibrium' is not used in the meaning of markets being in equilibrium. What we actually mean by an 'equilibrium rate of business ownership' is similar to a 'natural rate of business ownership'. As conditions for business ownership tend to change when nations develop economically, countries tend to follow a certain path of business ownership levels when they go through stages of economic development. Hence a 'natural rate' is implied. Accordingly, the error-correction effect may also be interpreted as a regression-to-the-mean effect.

This implies that economies can actually have too few or too many business owners. A shortage of business owners is likely to diminish competition with detrimental effects for static efficiency and competitiveness of the national economy. It will also diminish variety, learning and selection and thereby harm dynamic efficiency (innovation). On the other hand, a glut of self-employment will cause the average scale of operations to remain below optimum. It will result in large numbers of marginal entrepreneurs, absorbing capital and human energy that could have been allocated more productively elsewhere. An important policy implication of the exercises is that low barriers to entry and exit of businesses are necessary conditions for the equilibrium seeking mechanisms that are vital for a sound economic development.

The model analysed in Chapter 2 suffers from an important limitation. It studies the relationship between economic development and business ownership at the economy-wide level without taking into consideration the sectoral structure of the economy. It is well-known that business ownership rates are much higher in the service sector when compared to the manufacturing sector. It is therefore possible that the penalty on deviating from the 'equilibrium' business ownership rate is *not* a problem of having too few or too many self-employed, but a problem of having a too small or a too large share of the service sector. Likewise, Chapter 2 finds that the 'equilibrium' business ownership rates tend to increase with the level of economic development for the highly most developed countries (in terms of GDP per capita). This might be caused by increased interest for the option of self-employment as such across the sectors in the economy, but may also be explained from an employment shift in modern economies away from the manufacturing sector towards the service sector. Chapter 3 focuses on the sectoral component in the two-equation model from Chapter 2 and estimates the model separately for manufacturing and services, using sectoral data for basically the same set of OECD countries. Chapter 3 shows that there is a significant penalty of the business ownership rate deviating from 'equilibrium' for manufacturing. We also find a negative effect for the services sector but it is far smaller than that for manufacturing. This may be related to the greater importance of (radical) innovation in manufacturing. Estimation results also suggest that there is, on average for the countries in our data set, a too low business ownership rate in manufacturing (consistent with a lack of incentives to innovate) and a too high business ownership rate in services (possibly indicating that there are too many marginal entrepreneurs).

Chapter 4 also focuses on a hypothesized growth penalty on deviating from an 'optimal' industry structure. However, in this chapter, industry structure is not measured in terms of business ownership rates but rather in terms of the share of small firms in total value-of-shipments.

Using data for 17 European countries in the early 1990s, it is found that those countries that have shifted their industry structure towards decentralization (i.e. towards a higher share of small firms) in a more rapid fashion have been rewarded by higher growth rates, implying that the majority of the countries in our data set had a below-optimum small-firm share in value-of-shipments in the early 1990s. Although in Chapter 4 we do not distinguish between sectors, it is conceivable that particularly decentralization in manufacturing may have been conducive to economic growth, as this sector is dominated by large enterprises (KPMG/ENSR, 2000). This would be consistent with results from Chapter 3.

Chapter 5 deals with the impact of knowledge spillovers on economic growth at the regional level. As described earlier, knowledge spillovers are an important source of growth in modern, entrepreneurial economies. Using a variant of the model of Glaeser et al. (1992), Chapter 5 investigates which *type* of spillovers is more conducive to economic growth; *intra*-sectoral spillovers (facilitated by a higher degree of specialization in a region) or *inter*-sectoral spillovers (facilitated by a higher degree of diversity). It also investigates the role of local competition in regional economic growth. For our data set of Dutch regions in the period 1987-1995 we find that local competition is important particularly for economic growth in industry sectors (manufacturing and construction), while diversity is important particularly for growth in service sectors. We find no effect for specialization. By and large, this can be interpreted as intensive competition in manufacturing encouraging an 'innovation race', and high degrees of diversity encouraging spillovers from manufacturing towards service sectors.

Chapter 6 deals with the impact of new-firm startups on employment growth at the regional level. It is argued that higher numbers of startups in a region may have positive effects on regional employment, because new firms create jobs, both directly and indirectly (the latter by stimulating the incumbent firms to perform better), and because new firms provide a vehicle for the introduction of new ideas and innovation to the economy. However, the chapter also provides reasons for expecting no relationship or even a negative relationship between startup rates and subsequent employment growth. The case for a negative relationship derives from examining policies to stimulate new firm formation in 'unenterprising' areas (areas with low startup rates and relatively few firms). If entry is subsidised, this may attract individuals with low human capital levels to start a business. The subsidised entrants temporarily have a competitive advantage over incumbents who are forced out of business. However, once the subsidy is removed, the no-longer subsidised entrants may be forced out of business themselves and end up more disadvantaged than before they started. The effect is likely to erode customer confidence leading to lower expenditure and hence lower employment (Greene et al.,

2004). Chapter 6 investigates the impact of startup rates on employment growth for British regions in the period 1980-1998. The key results call into question the impact of policies seeking to raise new firm formation, so as to enhance employment creation, particularly in areas where new firm formation rates are low. Specifically we find that, in the 1980's, when national public policy was focussed on raising new firm formation, there is no evidence that this led to increased employment creation during that decade. Furthermore, although the employment impact is non-significant for the UK as a whole in the 1980's, it is significantly negative for the North East of England, an area with notably low rates of new firm formation. In the 1990's, when UK national policy shifts away from stimulating new firm formation, a positive relationship emerges between new firm formation and employment creation. Crucially, however, in Scotland, which implemented a policy to stimulate new firm births in the 1990's, a significant negative relationship between new firm births and employment creation appears in this decade, although our data do not extend sufficiently in time to imply that Scotland's business birth rate policy led to lower employment. Our interpretation of these results is that implementing 'birth rate' policies (i.e. maximising the number of startups), particularly in 'unenterprising' areas, is likely to be unproductive at best and counter-productive at worst.

In Chapter 7 we return to the country level again. We investigate the impact of the Total Entrepreneurial Activity rate from the Global Entrepreneurship Monitor (GEM) on growth of national GDP for 36 countries. The Total Entrepreneurial Activity rate (TEA) is defined as that percent of adult population that is either actively involved in starting a new venture or the owner/manager of a business that is less than 42 months old (Reynolds et al., 2002). Compared to the data bases that we use in Chapters 2, 3 and 4, the variation in per capita income levels in the GEM data base is much larger. In particular, a number of less developed countries is included in this data base, allowing to test for a possibly different impact of TEA on growth in highly developed economies and in developing countries. We find that entrepreneurial activity affects economic growth, but that the effect increases with per capita income. This suggests that entrepreneurship plays a different role in countries in different stages of economic development. Probably, entrepreneurs in highly developed countries have higher human capital levels compared to entrepreneurs in developing countries, which also leads to a stronger impact on growth in highly developed countries.

Chapter 8 examines the relationship between business dynamics (entry and exit of firms) and employment growth at the country-industry level. We use a cross-country data set with harmonized data on numbers of entries and exits for a selection of fast-growing and innovative industries in six developed economies. In our regression analysis we allow for separate effects of both the *extent* of business dynamics (volatility of firms) and the *composition* of business dynamics (net-entry of firms). Using both these measures enables to distinguish between situations of high net-entry and low volatility, possibly indicating high survival rates, and situations of low net-entry and high volatility, possibly indicating lower survival rates but more fierce competition (displacement). As these situations may have very different implications for economic growth, it is important to measure the effects of net-entry and volatility separately. We also test for the existence of an 'optimal' level of business volatility, possibly indicating that entry and exit levels are too high in certain industries. We find positive employment effects of net-entry rates and volatility rates. These effects are found to be considerably stronger for manufacturing compared to services. We find no evidence for an 'optimal' level of business volatility.

Chapter 9 is devoted to the COMPENDIA data base. This data base, constructed by EIM, contains business ownership rates for 23 OECD countries from 1972 onwards, and is updated regularly. The data base is used for cross-country entrepreneurship research not only in this book (Chapter 2) but also in an increasing number of other studies (e.g. Audretsch et al., 2002b, 2005). Operationalizing entrepreneurship for empirical measurement is difficult for at least two reasons (Storey, 1991). First, there is no straightforward definition of the term entrepreneurship, so how should it be measured? Second, in the case of cross-country analysis, even proxy measures used for entrepreneurship differ across countries. To measure entrepreneurship, economists usually use the number of self-employed. Although the measure of self-employment is accompanied with much critique (Audretsch, 2003), measures of self-employment are widely used to reflect the degree of entrepreneurship, largely because they are measured in most countries, and measured in comprehensive ways facilitating comparisons across countries and over time (Blau, 1987). Nevertheless, in Chapter 9 we argue that the comparability of international self-employment data is a major problem, because each country uses its own self-employment definition. In particular, the extent to which owner/managers of incorporated businesses (OMIBs) are included in the numbers of self-employed as published in *OECD Labour Force Statistics*, differs between countries. The COMPENDIA data base makes an attempt to construct an international data base with self-employment figures for 23 OECD countries that are comparable across countries. The business ownership definition used in COMPENDIA includes owner/managers of both unincorporated and incorporated businesses and excludes unpaid family workers.[157] For

---

[157] In this book we use the terms business ownership and self-employment interchangeably, referring to both the unincorporated and the incorporated self-employed.

countries not following our business ownership definition in OECD Labour Force Statistics, we make corrections. This involves estimating the number of incorporated self-employed as well as removing unpaid family workers from the data. We also correct for trend breaks. Chapter 9 provides a detailed description of the construction of the COMPENDIA data base. Special attention is paid to the United States. This country alone accounts for about 30% of all self-employed reported in the COMPENDIA data set.

10.2 Conclusions

Combining the empirical evidence provided in the various chapters in this book we can formulate some conclusions as regards the effect of entrepreneurship on economic growth. The majority of the empirical evidence presented in this book points to a positive effect. However, we have also found some exceptions to this stylised fact. The evidence suggests that the sign and magnitude of the effect depends on at least three factors: a country's stage of economic development, the sector of economic activity, and the quantity and quality of entrepreneurial supply.

As regards *the stage of economic development*, Chapter 2 shows that deviations from the 'equilibrium' rate of entrepreneurship (here defined as business ownership) negatively affect economic growth. The estimated model implies that the 'equilibrium' number of entrepreneurs is different at different stages of economic development. For instance, in the upward part of the U-shaped equilibrium relationship, a given level of entrepreneurship may be below the optimum for a higher level of economic development while the same level of entrepreneurship is above the optimum for a lower level of economic development. Hence, a further increase in entrepreneurship positively affects economic growth in the higher income country while it negatively affects growth in the lower income country (as the gap between the actual and the equilibrium rate of entrepreneurship becomes bigger). This is consistent with the results from Chapter 7, where increases in entrepreneurship (here defined as the sum of nascent entrepreneurs and young businesses) affect national economic growth positively in high income countries and negatively in low income countries. Hence, entrepreneurship plays a different role in economies in different stages of economic development.

In modern, highly developed economies, growth is powered by their capacity to innovate and to win new global markets for their technologically advanced products (McArthur and Sachs, 2002).

However, in entrepreneurship literature the term self-employment is sometimes understood to include unincorporated self-employed individuals only.

Entrepreneurship is an important aspect of this capacity. Entrepreneurs may introduce important innovations by entering markets with new products or production processes (Acs and Audretsch, 1990, 2003). They may enhance our knowledge of what is technically viable and what consumers prefer by introducing variations of existing products and services in the market. The resulting learning process speeds up the discovery of the dominant design for product-market combinations. In other words, in highly developed economies entrepreneurship contributes to growth by shifting the technology frontier (technological innovation).

Economies at lower stages of economic development may grow through exploitation of economies of scale and scope by large firms and by rapidly absorbing the advanced technologies and capital of the highly developed economies (technology transfer), for example through high levels of foreign direct investment from high-tech multinationals (McArthur and Sachs, 2002). In addition, smaller firms may also flourish as they may act as suppliers for large firms (outsourcing) and may learn a lot from the large companies. However, in these economies small and new firms are not at the front of the innovation process and hence their impact on economic growth is smaller compared to entrepreneurs in modern economies. In fact, in Chapter 7 their impact on economic growth is even estimated to be negative, which may point to a lack of large companies in these countries. High levels of entrepreneurship in poorer countries may reflect hidden unemployment as there may not be enough large companies to employ them as wage-earners.

In terms of the different types of economies –managed versus entrepreneurial– Audretsch and Thurik (2001) distinguish (see also Section 1.1), the role that entrepreneurship plays in lower developed economies is more in line with the managed economy, while the role of entrepreneurship in higher developed economies is more in line with the entrepreneurial economy.

As regards *the sector of economic activity*, results from several studies in this book are consistent with a stronger effect of entrepreneurship on growth for manufacturing compared to services. For instance, Chapter 3 shows that the penalty related to deviating from the 'equilibrium' rate of business ownership is more severe for manufacturing than for services. In Chapter 5, the impact of local competition (the number of firms in the region) on regional economic growth is investigated. We find a significantly positive effect for manufacturing but no effect for services sectors. Finally, in Chapter 8 we examine the effect of business dynamics on employment growth at the country-industry level. Again the impact of business dynamics (net-entry and volatility of firms) on growth is found to be stronger for manufacturing than for services.

The stronger effect in manufacturing may be related to the greater importance of innovation in manufacturing, compared to services. Innovation in service firms has a different character than in manufacturing. In particular, innovations in service industries are often non-technological and they mostly involve small and incremental changes in processes and procedures (De Jong et al., 2003, p. 16). To the contrary, innovations in manufacturing require more R&D and are more radical in nature. In modern entrepreneurial economies radical innovation is more conducive to economic growth than incremental innovation. This is because industry life-cycles are shorter and hence, at a given point in time, more (niche) markets are in an early stage of the life cycle where R&D is highly productive and the costs of radical innovation tend to be relatively low (Audretsch and Thurik, 2001). Hence, a lack of entrepreneurship in manufacturing industries may be particularly damaging to economic performance, as it may imply a lack of incentives to create (radical) innovations.

The conclusion that also *the quantity and quality of entrepreneurial supply* plays a role in the effect on economic performance, is based on Chapter 6 of this book. If government policy is directed towards maximising the number of startups by subsidising entry, this may stimulate individuals to start businesses for the wrong reason, i.e. not because, for instance, they have an idea that they want to try and commercialize, but simply because they can get an amount of money for starting a business. Particularly unemployed individuals may be attracted to start subsidised businesses, as the opportunity cost of not starting a subsidised business is higher for them, compared to wage-earners. As the unemployed often have relatively low human capital levels, the new firms are likely to be unsuccessful once the subsidy is removed. The effect is to erode confidence, both of the customers and of the failed business owners, which leads to declining economic performance of the region. Hence, policies just focusing on the *quantity* of entrepreneurial supply without considering the *quality* of the entrepreneurs may not lead to the intended results. Chapter 6 provides empirical indications that policies of subsidising entry may indeed not be very successful in creating jobs.

In Chapter 2 of this book it is concluded that low barriers to entry and exit of businesses are important for a sound economic development. However, although subsidising entry may be seen as an (extreme) example of lowering entry barriers, the lesson from Chapter 6 is that such policies do not contribute positively to economic development. A policy that could contribute is to lower administrative burdens related to starting a new business (Van Stel and Stunnenberg, 2004). However, enterprise policies that involve creating a financial advantage for some business owners over others (e.g. subsidising entry) should be avoided, as it may attract individuals who are not intrinsically motivated to start a new firm.

In particular, it may attract a substantial number of marginal entrepreneurs, absorbing capital and human energy that could have been allocated more productively elsewhere (see Chapter 2 of this book).

REFERENCES

Acs, Z.J. (1992), Small Business Economics: A Global Perspective, *Challenge* **35**, November/December, 38-44.

Acs, Z.J. (1996), Small Firms and Economic Growth, in: P.H. Admiraal (ed.), *Small Business in the Modern Economy, De Vries Lectures in Economics*, Oxford: Blackwell Publishers, 1-62.

Acs, Z.J. and C. Armington (2004), Employment Growth and Entrepreneurial Activity in Cities, *Regional Studies* **38**, 911-927.

Acs, Z.J. and D.B. Audretsch (1987), Innovation, Market Structure and Firm Size, *Review of Economics and Statistics* **69**, 567-574.

Acs, Z.J. and D.B. Audretsch (1990), *Innovation and Small Firms*, Cambridge, MA: MIT Press.

Acs, Z.J. and D.B. Audretsch (1993), Conclusion, in: Z.J. Acs and D.B. Audretsch (eds.), *Small Firms and Entrepreneurship; an East-West Perspective*, Cambridge, UK: Cambridge University Press, 227-231.

Acs, Z.J. and D.B. Audretsch (2003), Innovation and Technological Change, in: Z.J. Acs and D.B. Audretsch (eds.), *Handbook of Entrepreneurship Research*, Boston, MA: Kluwer Academic Publishers, 55-79.

Acs, Z.J., D.B. Audretsch and D.S. Evans (1994), The Determinants of Variation in the Self-Employment Rates across Countries and over Time, mimeo (fourth draft).

Aghion, P. and P. Howitt (1992), A Model of Growth through Creative Destruction, *Econometrica* **60**, 323-351.

Aghion, P., C. Harris and J. Vickers (1997), Competition and Growth with Step-by-Step Innovation: An Example, *European Economic Review* **41**, 771-782.

Aiginger, K. and G. Tichy (1991), Small Firms and the Merger Mania, *Small Business Economics* **3**, 83-101.

Anselin, L. (1988), *Spatial Econometrics: Methods and Models*, Dordrecht, Netherlands: Kluwer Academic Publishers.

Anselin, L. (2003a), Spatial Externalities, *International Regional Science Review* **26**, 147-152.

Anselin, L. (2003b), Spatial Externalities, Spatial Multipliers and Spatial Econometrics, *International Regional Science Review* **26**, 153-166.

Arrow, K.J. (1962), The Economic Implications of Learning by Doing, *Review of Economic Studies* **29**, 155-173.

Ashcroft, B. and J.H. Love (1996), Firm Births and Employment Change in the British Counties: 1981-89, *Papers in Regional Science* **75**, 483-500.

Ashcroft, B., J.H. Love and E. Malloy (1991), New Firm Formation in the British Counties with Special Reference to Scotland, *Regional Studies* **25**, 395-409.

Audretsch, D.B. (1995), *Innovation and Industry Evolution*, Cambridge, MA: MIT Press.

Audretsch, D.B. (2000), Entrepreneurship in Germany, in: D.L. Sexton and H. Landström (eds.), *The Blackwell Handbook of Entrepreneurship*, Oxford: Blackwell Publishers.

Audretsch, D.B. (2003), Entrepreneurship: A Survey of the Literature, Enterprise Papers No. 14, Brussels: European Commission.

Audretsch, D.B. and M. Feldman (1996), R&D Spillovers and the Geography of Innovation and Production, *American Economic Review* **86**, 630-640.

Audretsch, D.B. and M. Fritsch (1994), On the Measurement of Entry Rates, *Empirica* **21**, 105-113.

Audretsch, D.B. and M. Fritsch (2002), Growth Regimes over Time and Space, *Regional Studies* **36**, 113-124.

Audretsch, D.B., and M. Keilbach (2004), Entrepreneurship Capital and Economic Performance, *Regional Studies* **38**, 949-959.

Audretsch D.B. and A.R. Thurik (1999), Introduction, in: D.B. Audretsch and A.R. Thurik (eds.), *Innovation, Industry Evolution and Employment*, Cambridge, UK: Cambridge University Press, 1-12.

Audretsch D.B. and A.R. Thurik (2000), Capitalism and Democracy in the 21st Century: from the Managed to the Entrepreneurial Economy, *Journal of Evolutionary Economics* **10**, 17-34.

Audretsch D.B. and A.R. Thurik (2001), What is New about the New Economy: Sources of Growth in the Managed and Entrepreneurial Economies, *Industrial and Corporate Change* **10**, 267-315.

Audretsch D.B. and A.R. Thurik (2004), A Model of the Entrepreneurial Economy, *International Journal of Entrepreneurship Education* **2**, 143-166.

Audretsch, D.B., M.A. Carree, A.J. van Stel and A.R. Thurik (2002a), Impeded Industrial Restructuring: The Growth Penalty, *Kyklos* **55**, 81-98.

Audretsch, D.B., M.A. Carree, A.J. van Stel and A.R. Thurik (2005), Does Self-Employment Reduce Unemployment?, Paper 07-2005 on Entrepreneurship, Growth and Public Policy, Jena, Germany: Max Planck Institute of Economics.

Audretsch, D.B., A.R. Thurik, I. Verheul and A.R.M. Wennekers (2002b, eds.), *Entrepreneurship: Determinants and Policy in a European-US Comparison*, Boston/Dordrecht: Kluwer Academic Publishers.

Bartelsman, E., S. Scarpetta and F. Schivardi (2003), Comparative Analysis of Firm Demographics and Survival: Micro-Level Evidence for the OECD Countries, OECD Economics Department Working Papers No. 348, Paris: OECD.

Baumol, W.J. (1968), Entrepreneurship in Economic Theory, *American Economic Review Papers and Proceedings* **58**, 64-71.

Baumol, W.J. (1990), Entrepreneurship: Productive, Unproductive and Destructive, *Journal of Political Economy* **98**, 893-921.

Blair, J.M. (1948), Technology and Size, *American Economic Review* **38**, 121-152.

Blanchflower, D.G. (2000), Self-Employment in OECD Countries, *Labour Economics* **7**, 471-505.

Blau, D. (1987), A Time Series Analysis of Self-Employment, *Journal of Political Economy* **95**, 445-467.

Bleaney, M. and A. Nishiyama (2002), Explaining Growth: A Contest Between Models, *Journal of Economic Growth* **7**, 43-56.

Bosma, N.S. and H.R. Nieuwenhuijsen (2002), Turbulence and Productivity; An Analysis of 40 Dutch Regions in the Period 1988-1996, EIM Scales Paper N200205, Zoetermeer, Netherlands: EIM.

Bregger, J.E. (1996), Measuring Self-Employment in the United States, *Monthly Labor Review* **119** (1), 3-9.

Brock, W.A. and D.S. Evans (1986), *The Economics of Small Businesses: Their Role and Regulation in the U.S. Economy*, New York: Holmes and Meier.

Brock, W.A. and D.S. Evans (1989), Small Business Economics, *Small Business Economics* **1**, 7-20.

Calvo, G.A. and S. Wellisz (1980), Technology, Entrepreneurs and Firm Size, *Quarterly Journal of Economics* **95**, 663-677.

Carlsson, B. (1989), The Evolution of Manufacturing Technology and Its Impact on Industrial Structure: An International Study, *Small Business Economics* **1**, 21-37.

Carlsson, B. (1992), The Rise of Small Business: Causes and Consequences, in: W.J. Adams (ed.), *Singular Europe, Economy and Policy of the European Community after 1992*, Ann Arbor, MI: University of Michigan Press, 145-169.

Carlsson, B. (1996), Differing Patterns of Industrial Dynamics: New Zealand, Ohio and Sweden, 1978-1994, *Small Business Economics* **8**, 219-234.

Carlsson, B. (1999), Small Business, Entrepreneurship, and Industrial Dynamics, in: Z.J. Acs (ed.), *Are Small Firms Important? Their Role and Impact*, Dordrecht, Netherlands: Kluwer Academic Publishers, 99-110.

Carree, M.A. (2002a), Industrial Restructuring and Economic Growth, *Small Business Economics* **18**, 243-255.

Carree, M.A. (2002b), Does Unemployment Affect the Number of Establishments? A Regional Analysis for US States, *Regional Studies* **36**, 389-398.

Carree, M.A. (2003), Technological Progress, Structural Change and Productivity Growth: A Comment, *Structural Change and Economic Dynamics* **14**, 109-115.

Carree, M.A. and L. Klomp (1996), Small Business and Job Creation: A Comment, *Small Business Economics* **8**, 317-322.

Carree, M.A. and A.R. Thurik (1998), Small Firms and Economic Growth in Europe, *Atlantic Economic Journal* **26**, 137-146.

Carree, M.A. and A.R. Thurik (1999a), Industrial Structure and Economic Growth, in: D.B. Audretsch and A.R. Thurik (eds.), *Innovation, Industry Evolution and Employment*, Cambridge, UK: Cambridge University Press, 86-110.

Carree, M.A. and A.R. Thurik (1999b), The Carrying Capacity and Entry and Exit Flows in Retailing, *International Journal of Industrial Organization* **17**, 985-1007.

Carree, M.A. and A.R. Thurik (2003), The Impact of Entrepreneurship on Economic Growth, in: Z.J. Acs and D.B. Audretsch (eds.), *Handbook of Entrepreneurship Research*, Boston, MA: Kluwer Academic Publishers, 437-471.

Carree, M.A, A.J. van Stel, A.R. Thurik and A.R.M. Wennekers (2000), Business Ownership and Economic Growth in 23 OECD Countries, Tinbergen Institute Discussion Paper TI 2000-01/3, Rotterdam: Erasmus University.

Carree, M.A., A.J. van Stel, A.R. Thurik and A.R.M. Wennekers (2002), Economic Development and Business Ownership: An Analysis Using Data of 23 OECD Countries in the Period 1976-1996, *Small Business Economics* **19**, 271-290.

Caves, R.E. (1998), Industrial Organization and New Findings on the Turnover and Mobility of Firms, *Journal of Economic Literature* **36**, 1947-1982.

Chandler, A.D. Jr. (1990), *Scale and Scope: The Dynamics of Industrial Capitalism*, Cambridge, MA: Harvard University.

Checkland, S.G. (1976), *The Upas Tree: Glasgow 1875-1975*, Glasgow: Glasgow University Press.

Cohen, W.M. and S. Klepper (1996), A Reprise of Size and R&D, *Economic Journal* **106**, 925-951.

Cooper, A., C. Woo and W. Dunkelberg (1989), Entrepreneurship and the Initial Size of Firms, *Journal of Business Venturing* **4**, 317-332.

Cornelius, P.K. and J.W. McArthur (2002), The Executive Opinion Survey, in: M.E. Porter, J.D. Sachs, P.K. Cornelius, J.W. McArthur and K. Schwab (eds.), *The Global Competitiveness Report 2001-2002*, New York: Oxford University Press, 166-177.

Cressy, R. (1996), Are Business Start Ups Debt Rationed?, *Economic Journal* **106**, 1253-1270.

Davis, S.J. and M. Henrekson (1999), Explaining National Differences in the Size and Industry Structure of Employment, *Small Business Economics* **12**, 59-83.

Davis, S.J., J. Haltiwanger and S. Schuh (1996), Small Business and Job Creation: Dissecting the Myth and Reassessing the Facts, *Small Business Economics* **8**, 297-315.

De Jong, J.P.J., A. Bruins, W. Dolfsma and J. Meijaard (2003), Innovation in Service Firms Explored: What, How and Why?, EIM Strategic Study B200205, Zoetermeer, Netherlands: EIM.

De Kok, J.M.P. (2002), The Impact of Firm-Provided Training on Production, *International Small Business Journal* **20**, 267-289.

De Wit, G. (1993), Models of Self-Employment in a Competitive Market, *Journal of Economic Surveys* **7**, 367-397.

Dennis, W.J. Jr. (1997), More Than You Think: An Inclusive Estimate of Business Entries, *Journal of Business Venturing* **12**, 175-196.

Disney, R., J. Haskel and Y. Heden (2003), Restructuring and Productivity Growth in UK Manufacturing, *Economic Journal* **113**, 666-694.

Dosi, G. (1988), Sources, Procedures and Microeconomic Effects of Innovations, *Journal of Economic Literature* **26**, 1120-1171.

EIM/ENSR (1993), *The European Observatory for SMEs: First Annual Report*, Zoetermeer, Netherlands: EIM.

EIM/ENSR (1994), *The European Observatory for SMEs: Second Annual Report*, Zoetermeer, Netherlands: EIM.

EIM/ENSR (1995), *The European Observatory for SMEs: Third Annual Report*, Zoetermeer, Netherlands: EIM.

EIM/ENSR (1996), *The European Observatory for SMEs: Fourth Annual Report*, Zoetermeer, Netherlands: EIM.

EIM/ENSR (1997), *The European Observatory for SMEs: Fifth Annual Report*, Zoetermeer, Netherlands: EIM.

Eliasson, G. (1995), Economic Growth through Competitive Selection, Paper Presented at 22nd Annual E.A.R.I.E. Conference, Juan les Pins, 3-6 September 1995.

European Commission (2003), *Green Paper Entrepreneurship in Europe*, Brussels: European Commission.

Eurostat (1994), *Enterprises in Europe, Third Edition*, Luxembourg: Eurostat.

Eurostat (1996), *Industrial Trends Monthly Statistics 1996/6*, Luxembourg: Eurostat.

Evans, D.S. and L.S. Leighton (1989), Some Empirical Aspects of Entrepreneurship, *American Economic Review* **79**, 519-535.

Evans, L., A. Grimes, B. Wilkinson and D. Teece (1996), Economic Reform in New Zealand 1984-95: The Pursuit of Efficiency, *Journal of Economic Literature* **34**, 1856-1902.

Fagerberg, J. (2000), Technological Progress, Structural Change and Productivity Growth: A Comparative Study, *Structural Change and Economic Dynamics* **11**, 393-411.

Fain, T.S. (1980), Self-Employed Americans: Their Number Has Increased, *Monthly Labor Review* **103** (11), 3-8.

Fingleton, B. (2003a), Externalities, Economic Geography and Spatial Econometrics: Conceptual and Modeling Developments, *International Regional Science Review* **26**, 197-207.

Fingleton, B. (2003b), Models and Simulations of GDP per Inhabitant Across Europe's Regions: A Preliminary View, in: B. Fingleton (ed.), *European Regional Growth*, Heidelberg: Springer-Verlag, 11-53.

Folkeringa, M., J. Meijaard and A.J. van Stel (2004), Strategic Renewal and its Effect on Small Firm Performance, EIM Scales Paper N200322, Zoetermeer, Netherlands: EIM.

Fothergill, S. and G. Gudgin (1979), *Unequal Growth*, London: Heineman.

Frank, M.Z. (1988), An Inter-Temporal Model of Industrial Exit, *Quarterly Journal of Economics* **103**, 333-344.

Fraser of Allander Institute (2001), Promoting Business Start-Ups: A New Strategic Formula; Stage 1: Progress Review; Final Report, Glasgow: The Fraser of Allander Institute for Research on the Scottish Economy, University of Strathclyde.

Freeman, C. and C. Perez (1988), Structural Crises of Adjustment: Business Cycles and Investment Behavior, in: G. Dosi, C. Freeman, R. Nelson, G. Silverberg and L. Soete (eds.), *Technical Change and Economic Theory*, London: Pinter Publishers.

Fritsch, M. (1996), Turbulence and Growth in West Germany: A Comparison of Evidence from Regions and Industries, *Review of Industrial Organisation* 11, 231-251.

Fritsch, M., and P. Mueller (2004), The Effects of New Business Formation on Regional Development over Time, *Regional Studies* 38, 961-975.

Galbraith, J.K. (1956), *American Capitalism: The Concept of Countervailing Power*, Boston, MA: Houghton Mifflin.

Garofoli, G. (1994), New Firm Formation and Regional Development: The Case of Italy, *Regional Studies* 28, 381-393.

Geroski, P.A. (1995), What Do We Know about Entry?, *International Journal of Industrial Organization* 13, 421-441.

Glaeser, E.L., H.D. Kallal, J.A. Scheinkman and A. Shleifer (1992), Growth in Cities, *Journal of Political Economy* 100, 1126-1152.

Granger, C.W.J. (1969), Investigating Causal Relations by Econometric Models and Cross-Spectral Methods, *Econometrica* 37, 424-438.

Green, A.E. and I. Turok (2000), Employability, Adaptability and Flexibility: Changing Labour Market Prospects, *Regional Studies* 34, 599-600.

Greene, F.J. (2002), An Investigation into Enterprise Support for Young People, *International Small Business Journal* 20, 315-336.

Greene, F.J., K.F. Mole and D.J. Storey (2004), Does More Mean Worse? Three Decades of Enterprise Policy in the Tees Valley, *Urban Studies* 41, 1207-1228.

Griliches, Z. (1992), The Search for R&D Spillovers, *Scandinavian Journal of Economics* 94, Supplement, 29-47.

Hakim, C. (1988), Self-Employment in Britain: Recent Trends and Current Issues, *Work, Employment and Society* 2, 421-450.

Hébert, R.F. and A.N. Link (1989), In Search of the Meaning of Entrepreneurship, *Small Business Economics* 1, 39-49.

Henderson, J. (1986), Efficiency of Resource Usage and City Size, *Journal of Urban Economics* 19, 47-70.

Henrekson, M. and D. Johansson (1999), Institutional Effects on the Evolution of the Size Distribution of Firms, *Small Business Economics* 12, 11-23.

Henriquez, C., I. Verheul, I. van der Geest and C. Bischoff (2002), Determinants of Entrepreneurship in France, in: D.B. Audretsch, A.R. Thurik, I. Verheul and A.R.M. Wennekers (eds.), *Entrepreneurship: Determinants and Policy in a European-US Comparison*, Boston/Dordrecht: Kluwer Academic Publishers, 83-120.

HM Treasury and Small Business Service (2002), Enterprise Britain: A Modern Approach to Meeting the Enterprise Challenge, London: HM Treasury.

Holmes, T.J. and J.A. Schmitz Jr. (1990), A Theory of Entrepreneurship and its Application to the Study of Business Transfers, *Journal of Political Economy* **98**, 265-294.

Inman, R.P. (1985, ed.), *Managing the Service Economy*, Cambridge, UK: Cambridge University Press.

Iyigun, M.F. and A.L. Owen (1998), Risk, Entrepreneurship, and Human Capital Accumulation, *American Economic Review, Papers and Proceedings* **88**, 454-457.

Jackson, L.F. (1984), Hierarchic Demand and the Engle Curve for Variety, *Review of Economics and Statistics* **66**, 8-15.

Jacobs, J. (1969), *The Economy of Cities*, New York: Vintage.

Jaffe A.B. (1996), Economic Analysis of Research Spillovers: Implications for the Advanced Technology Program, GCR 97-708, Gaithersburg, MD: National Institute of Standards and Technology Program, US Department of Commerce.

Jensen, M.C. (1993), The Modern Industrial Revolution, Exit, and the Failure of Internal Control Systems, *Journal of Finance* **48**, 831-880.

Johnson, P.S. and S. Parker (1996), Spatial Variations in the Determinants and Effects of Firm Births and Deaths, *Regional Studies* **30**, 679-688.

Jovanovic, B. (1982), Selection and Evolution in Industry, *Econometrica* **50**, 649-670.

Jovanovic, B. (1993), The Diversification of Production, *Brookings Papers: Microeconomics*, 197-235.

Keeble, D., S. Walker and M. Robson (1993), New Firm Formation and Small Business Growth in the United Kingdom: Spatial and Temporal Variations and Determinants, Research Series, No. 15, Sheffield, UK: Employment Department.

Kihlstrom, R.E. and J.J. Laffont (1979), A General Equilibrium Entrepreneurial Theory of Firm Formation Based on Risk Aversion, *Journal of Political Economy* **87**, 719-748.

Kirchhoff, B.A. (1996), Self-Employment and Dynamic Capitalism, *Journal of Labor Research* **17**, 627-643.

Kirzner, I.M. (1973), *Competition and Entrepreneurship*, Chicago: University of Chicago Press.

Kirzner, I.M. (1997), Entrepreneurial Discovery and the Competitive Market Process: An Austrian Approach, *Journal of Economic Literature* **35**, 60-85.

Kleijweg, A.J.M. and H.R. Nieuwenhuijsen (1996), Job Creation by Size-Class: Measurement and Empirical Investigation, EIM Research Report 9604/E, Zoetermeer, Netherlands: EIM.

Klepper, S. (1996), Entry, Exit, Growth, and Innovation over the Product Life Cycle, *American Economic Review* **86**, 562-583.

Klodt, H. (1990), Industrial Policy and Repressed Structural Change in West Germany, *Jahrbücher für Nationalökonomie und Statistik* **207**, 25-35.

Klomp, L. and J.J.M. Pronk (1998), *Kennis en Economie 1998* [Knowledge and Economy 1998], in Dutch; Voorburg/Heerlen: Statistics Netherlands.

Knight, F.H. (1921), *Risk, Uncertainty and Profit*, New York: Houghton Mifflin.

KPMG/ENSR (2000), *The European Observatory for SMEs: Sixth Report*, Zoetermeer, Netherlands: EIM.

Krugman, P. (1991), *Geography and Trade*, Cambridge, MA: MIT Press.

Kuznets, S. (1971), *Economic Growth of Nations, Total Output and Production Structure*, Cambridge, MA: Harvard University Press / Belknapp Press.

Lever, M.H.C. and H.R. Nieuwenhuijsen (1999), The Impact of Competition on Productivity in Dutch Manufacturing, in: D.B. Audretsch and A.R. Thurik (eds.), *Innovation, Industry Evolution and Employment*, Cambridge, UK: Cambridge University Press, 111-128.

Lloyd, P.E. and C.M. Mason (1984), Spatial Variations in New Firm Formation in the United Kingdom: Comparative Evidence from Merseyside, Greater Manchester and South Hampshire, *Regional Studies* **18**, 207-220.

Lloyd-Ellis, H. and D. Bernhardt (2000), Enterprise, Inequality and Economic Development, *Review of Economic Studies* **67**, 147-168.

Loveman, G. and W. Sengenberger (1991), The Re-Emergence of Small-Scale Production; an International Comparison, *Small Business Economics* **3**, 1-37.

Lucas, R.E. (1978), On the Size Distribution of Firms, *BELL Journal of Economics* **9**, 508-523.

Lucas, R.E. (1988), On the Mechanics of Economic Development, *Journal of Monetary Economics* **22**, 3-42.

Mackun P. and A.D. Macpherson (1997), Externally-Assisted Product Innovation in the Manufacturing Sector: The Role of Location, In-House R&D and Outside Technical Support, *Regional Studies* **31**, 659-668.

Marshall, A. (1890), *Principles of Economics*, London: Macmillan.

Maslow, A.H. (1970), *Motivation and Personality*, New York: Harper and Row.

McArthur, J.W., and J.D. Sachs (2002), The Growth Competitiveness Index: Measuring Technological Advancement and the Stages of Development, in: M.E. Porter, J.D. Sachs, P.K. Cornelius, J.W. McArthur and K. Schwab (eds.), *The Global Competitiveness Report 2001-2002*, New York: Oxford University Press, 28-51.

McDonald, R. and F. Coffield (1992), *Risky Business*, London: Falmer Press.

McMillan, J. (1998), Managing Economic Change: Lessons from New Zealand, *World Economy* **21**, 827-843.

Meijaard, J. (2001), Making Sense of the New Economy, *E-Commerce Research Forum* **2** (5), Massachusetts Institute of Technology, 27-57.

Meredith, J. (1987), The Strategic Advantages of New Manufacturing Technologies for Small Firms, *Strategic Management Journal* **8**, 249-258.

National Assembly for Wales (2001), National Economic Development Strategy: In Search of Economic Growth, Social Justice and Sustainable and Balanced Development, Cardiff: National Assembly for Wales.

Nickell, S.J. (1996), Competition and Corporate Performance, *Journal of Political Economy* **104**, 724-746.

Nickell, S.J., P. Nicolitsas and N. Dryden (1997), What Makes Firms Perform Well? *European Economic Review* **41**, 783-796.

Nieuwenhuijsen, H.R. and A.J. van Stel (2000), Kennis-Spillovers en Economische Groei [Knowledge Spillovers and Economic Growth], in Dutch; EIM Research Report 0007/N, Zoetermeer, Netherlands: EIM.

Nieuwenhuijsen, H.R., J.S. Bais, N.S. Bosma, J.M.P. de Kok, E.A. van Noort and J.A.C. Vollebregt (1999), Bedrijvendynamiek en Economische Prestaties [Firm Dynamics and Economic Performance], in Dutch; Report commissioned by the Dutch Ministry of Economic Affairs, Zoetermeer, Netherlands: EIM.

Nolan, P. (1995), *China's Rise, Russia's Fall: Politics, Economics and Planning in the Transition from Stalinism*, New York: St Martin's Press.

Nooteboom, B. (1994), Innovation and Diffusion in Small Firms: Theory and Evidence, *Small Business Economics* **6**, 327-347.

OECD (1992), *Employment Outlook July 1992*, Paris: OECD.

OECD (1995), *Competition Policy in OECD Countries 1992-1993*, Paris: OECD.

OECD (1997a), *National Accounts 1983-1995, Volume II*, Paris: OECD.

OECD (1997b), *Labour Force Statistics 1976-1996*, Paris: OECD.

OECD (1998), *Fostering Entrepreneurship*, Paris: OECD.

OECD (2000), *Employment Outlook June 2000*, Paris: OECD.

OECD (2002), *Labour Force Statistics 1981-2001*, Paris: OECD.

Oosterhaven J., G.J. Eding and D. Stelder (2001), Clusters, Linkages and Interregional Spillovers: Methodology and Policy Implications for the Two Dutch Mainports and the Rural North, *Regional Studies* **35**, 809-822.

Oughton, C. and G. Whittam (1997), Competition and Cooperation in the Small Firm Sector, *Scottish Journal of Political Economy* **44**, 1-30.

Peretto, P.F. (1999), Industrial Development, Technological Change and Long-Run Growth, *Journal of Development Economics* **59**, 389-417.

Phillips, B.D. (1985), The Effect of Industry Deregulation on the Small Business Sector, *Business Economics* **20**, 28-37.

Piore, M.J. and C.F. Sabel (1984), *The Second Industrial Divide: Possibilities for Prosperity*, New York: Basic Books.

Porter, M.E. (1990), *The Competitive Advantage of Nations*, New York: Free Press.

Price Waterhouse Coopers (1999), The West Midlands Business Survey, Birmingham, UK: Price Waterhouse Coopers.

Prusa, T.J. and J.A. Schmitz Jr. (1991), Are New Firms an Important Source of Innovation? Evidence from the Software Industry, *Economics Letters* **35**, 339-342.

Rees, H. and A. Shah (1986), An Empirical Analysis of Self-Employment in the UK, *Journal of Applied Econometrics* **1**, 95-108.

Reynolds, P.D. (1999), Creative Destruction: Source or Symptom of Economic Growth?, in Z.J. Acs, B. Carlsson and C. Karlsson (eds.), *Entrepreneurship, Small and Medium-Sized Enterprises and the Macroeconomy*, Cambridge, UK: Cambridge University Press, 97-136.

Reynolds, P.D., D.J. Storey and P. Westhead (1994a), Cross-National Comparisons of the Variation in New Firm Formation Rates: An Editorial Overview, *Regional Studies* **28**, 343-346.

Reynolds, P.D., D.J. Storey and P. Westhead (1994b), Cross-National Comparisons of the Variation in New Firm Formation Rates, *Regional Studies* **28**, 443-456.

Reynolds, P.D., W.D. Bygrave, E. Autio, L.W. Cox and M. Hay (2002), *Global Entrepreneurship Monitor, 2002 Executive Report*, Wellesley, MA: Babson College.

Reynolds, P.D., M. Hay, W.D. Bygrave, S.M. Camp, E. Autio (2000), *Global Entrepreneurship Monitor, 2000 Executive Report*, Kansas City, MO: Kauffman Center for Entrepreneurial Leadership.

Romer, P.M. (1986), Increasing Returns and Long Run Growth, *Journal of Political Economy* **94**, 1002-1037.

Romer, P.M. (1990), Endogenous Technological Change, *Journal of Political Economy* **98**, 71-101.

Romer, P.M. (1994), The Origins of Endogenous Growth, *Journal of Economic Perspectives* **8**, 3-22.

Rothwell, R. (1983), Innovation and Firm Size: A Case for Dynamic Complementarity; Or, Is Small Really So Beautiful? *Journal of General Management* **8**, 5-25.

Rothwell, R. (1984), The Role of Small Firms in the Emergence of New Technologies, *OMEGA* **12**, 19-29.

Sala-i-Martin, X. (1997), I Just Ran Two Million Regressions, *American Economic Review* **87**, 178-183.

Santarelli, E. and A. Sterlacchini (1994), New Firm Formation in Italian Industry: 1985-89, *Small Business Economics* **6**, 95-106.

SBA (=United States Small Business Administration, Office of Advocacy) (1987), *The State of Small Business, A Report of the President 1986*, Washington, DC: US Government Printing Office.

SBA (1997), *The State of Small Business, A Report of the President 1996*, Washington, DC: US Government Printing Office.

SBA (1998a), *The State of Small Business, A Report of the President 1997*, Washington, DC: US Government Printing Office.

SBA (1998b), Small Business Answer Card 1998, Washington, DC: SBA.

SBA (1999), *The State of Small Business, A Report of the President 1998*, Washington, DC: US Government Printing Office.

SBA (2000), Small Business Economic Indicators 1998, Washington, DC: SBA.

SBA (2001), Small Business Economic Indicators 2000, Washington, DC: SBA.

Schaffner, J.A. (1993), Rising Incomes and the Shift from Self-Employment to Firm-Based Production, *Economics Letters* **41**, 435-440.

Scherer, F.M. and D. Ross (1990), *Industrial Market Structure and Economic Performance*, Boston, MA: Houghton Mifflin.

Schiller, B.R. and P.E. Crewson (1997), Entrepreneurial Origins: A Longitudinal Inquiry, *Economic Inquiry* **35**, 523-531.

Schmitz, J.A. Jr. (1989), Imitation, Entrepreneurship, and Long-Run Growth, *Journal of Political Economy* **97**, 721-739.

Schultz, T.P. (1990), Women's Changing Participation in the Labor Force: A World Perspective, *Economic Development and Cultural Change* **38**, 457-488.

Schumpeter, J.A. (1934), *The Theory of Economic Development*, Cambridge, MA: Harvard University Press.

Schumpeter, J.A. (1950), *Capitalism, Socialism and Democracy*, New York: Harper and Row.

Shepherd, W.G. (1982), Causes of Increased Competition in the U.S. Economy, 1939-1980, *Review of Economics and Statistics* **64**, 613-626.

Small Business Service (2000), Business Start-Ups and Closures: VAT Registrations and De-Registrations 1980-99, SBS Statistical Bulletin, Sheffield, UK: Small Business Service.

Small Business Service (2004), A Government Action Plan for Small Business, London: Department of Trade and Industry.

Soete, L.L.G. and B.J. ter Weel (1999), Innovation, Knowledge Creation and Technology Policy: The Case of the Netherlands, *De Economist* **147**, 293-310.

Stewart, J. (1991), *Econometrics*, New York: Philip Allan.

Stopford, J.M. and C.W.F. Baden-Fuller (1994), Creating Corporate Entrepreneurship, *Strategic Management Journal* **15**, 521-536.

Storey, D.J. (1985), Manufacturing Employment Change in Northern England, 1965-78: the Role of Small Businesses, in: D.J. Storey (ed.), *Small Firms in Regional Economic Development*, Cambridge, UK: Cambridge University Press, 6-42.

Storey, D.J. (1991), The Birth of New Enterprises - Does Unemployment Matter? A Review of the Evidence, *Small Business Economics* **3**, 167-178.

Storey, D.J. (1994), *Understanding the Small Business Sector*, London: Routledge.

Storey, D.J. and A. Strange (1992), Entrepreneurship in Cleveland 1979-1989: A Study of the Effects of the Enterprise Culture, Research Series, No. 3, Sheffield, UK: Employment Department.

Storey, D.J. and B.S. Tether (1998), Public Policy Measures to Support New Technology-based Firms in the European Union, *Research Policy* **26**,1037-1057.

Teece, D.J. (1993), The Dynamics of Industrial Capitalism: Perspectives on Alfred Chandler's Scale and Scope, *Journal of Economic Literature* **31**, 199-225.

Thurik, A.R. (1996), Small Firms, Entrepreneurship and Economic Growth, in: P.H. Admiraal (ed.), *Small Business in the Modern Economy, De Vries Lectures in Economics*, Oxford: Blackwell Publishers, 126-152.

Thurik, A.R. (1999), Entrepreneurship, Industrial Transformation and Growth, in: G.D. Libecap (ed.), *The Sources of Entrepreneurial Activity: Vol. 11, Advances in the Study of Entrepreneurship, Innovation, and Economic Growth*, Stamford, CT: JAI Press, 29-65.

Thurik, A.R. and A.R.M. Wennekers (2004), Entrepreneurship, Small Business and Economic Growth, *Journal of Small Business and Enterprise Development* **11**, 140-149.

Thurik, A.R., A.R.M. Wennekers and L.M. Uhlaner (2002), Entrepreneurship and Economic Performance: A Macro Perspective, *International Journal of Entrepreneurship Education* **1**, 157-179.

Van Oort, F.G. (2002), *Agglomeration, Economic Growth and Innovation; Spatial Analysis of Growth- and R&D Externalities in the Netherlands*, Tinbergen Institute Research Series, No. 260, Amsterdam: Thela Thesis.

Van Praag, M. and J. Cramer (2001), The Roots of Entrepreneurship and Labour Demand: Individual Ability and Low Risk Aversion, *Economica* **149**, 45-62.

Van Stel, A.J. (1999), The Determinants of Employment in Europe, the USA and Japan, EIM Research Report 9803/E, Zoetermeer, Netherlands: EIM.

Van Stel, A.J. (2003), COMPENDIA 2000.2: A Harmonized Data Set of Business Ownership Rates in 23 OECD Countries, EIM Research Report 200302, Zoetermeer, Netherlands: EIM.

Van Stel, A.J. and M.A. Carree (2002), Business Ownership and Sectoral Growth, EIM Research Report 200206, Zoetermeer, Netherlands: EIM.

Van Stel, A.J. and D.J. Storey (2002), The Relationship between Firm Births and Job Creation, Tinbergen Institute Discussion Paper TI 2002-052/3, Rotterdam: Erasmus University.

Van Stel, A.J. and D.J. Storey (2004), The Link between Firm Births and Job Creation: Is there a Upas Tree Effect?, *Regional Studies* **38**, 893-909.

Van Stel, A.J. and V. Stunnenberg (2004), Linking Business Ownership and Perceived Administrative Complexity: An Empirical Analysis of 18 OECD Countries, Paper 35-2004 on Entrepreneurship, Growth and Public Policy, Jena, Germany: Max Planck Institute of Economics.

Van Stel, A.J., M.A. Carree and A.R. Thurik (2004), The Effect of Entrepreneurship on National Economic Growth: An Analysis Using the GEM Database, Paper 34-2004 on Entrepreneurship, Growth and Public Policy, Jena, Germany: Max Planck Institute of Economics.

Verheul, I., N.S. Bosma, F. van der Nol and T. Wong (2002), Determinants of Entrepreneurship in the United States of America, in: D.B. Audretsch, A.R. Thurik, I. Verheul and A.R.M. Wennekers (eds.), *Entrepreneurship: Determinants and Policy in a European-US Comparison*, Boston/Dordrecht: Kluwer Academic Publishers, 209-245.

Verhoeven, W.H.J. (2004), Firm Dynamics and Labour Productivity, in: G. Gelauff, L. Klomp, S. Raes and T. Roelandt (eds.), *Fostering Productivity: Patterns, Determinants and Policy Implications*, Amsterdam: Elsevier B.V., 213-241.

Verhoeven, W.H.J., and A. Bruins (2001), Internationale Benchmark Ondernemerschap 2001 [International Benchmark Entrepreneurship 2001], in Dutch; Report commissioned by the Dutch Ministry of Economic Affairs, Zoetermeer, Netherlands: EIM.

Verhoeven, W.H.J., K. Bakker, R. in 't Hout and H.H.M. Peeters (2001), Internationale Benchmark Ondernemerschap 2001; Tabellenboek [International Benchmark Entrepreneurship 2001; Book of Tables], in Dutch; Report commissioned by the Dutch Ministry of Economic Affairs, Zoetermeer, Netherlands: EIM.

Wennekers, A.R.M. and A.R. Thurik (1999), Linking Entrepreneurship and Economic Growth, *Small Business Economics* **13**, 27-55.

Wever E., and E. Stam (1999), Clusters of High Technology SMEs: The Dutch Case, *Regional Studies* **33**, 391-400.

Wintjes, R. and J. Cobbenhagen (2000), Knowledge-Intensive Industrial Clustering around Océ; Embedding a Vertical Disintegrating Codification Process into the Eindhoven-Venlo Region, Maastricht, Netherlands: MERIT Research Memorandum, No. 00-06, University of Maastricht.

Yamada, G. (1996), Urban Informal Employment and Self-Employment in Developing Countries: Theory and Evidence, *Economic Development and Cultural Change* **44**, 289-314.

You, J.I. (1995), Small Firms in Economic Theory, *Cambridge Journal of Economics* **19**, 441-462.

INDEX